# PRENTICE HALL WRITING AND GRAMMAR

## Formal Assessment Blackline Masters

**Grade Eight**

Boston, Massachusetts,
Upper Saddle River, New Jersey

ISBN 0-13-361518-9

1 2 3 4 5 6 7 8 9 10 10 09 08 07

# Contents

## PART 1: WRITING

*For Chapters 4–14, Test 1 is Easy, Test 2 is Average, and Test 3 is Challenging.*


**Chapter 1:** The Writer in You ........ 3
**Chapter 2:** A Walk Through the Writing Process ........ 5
**Chapter 3:** Paragraphs and Compositions ........ 9
**Chapter 4:** Narration: Autobiographical Writing ........ 12
**Test 1** ...... 12 **Test 2** ...... 14 **Test 3** ...... 16
**Chapter 5:** Narration: Short Story ........ 18
**Test 1** ...... 18 **Test 2** ...... 20 **Test 3** ...... 22
**Chapter 6:** Description ........ 25
**Test 1** ...... 25 **Test 2** ...... 27 **Test 3** ...... 30
**Chapter 7:** Persuasion: Persuasive Essay ........ 32
**Test 1** ...... 32 **Test 2** ...... 35 **Test 3** ...... 38
**Chapter 8:** Exposition: Comparison-and-Contrast Essay ........ 41
**Test 1** ...... 41 **Test 2** ...... 44 **Test 3** ...... 47
**Chapter 9:** Exposition: Cause-and-Effect Essay ........ 50
**Test 1** ...... 50 **Test 2** ...... 52 **Test 3** ...... 55
**Chapter 10:** Exposition: How-to Essay ........ 58
**Test 1** ...... 58 **Test 2** ...... 61 **Test 3** ...... 64
**Chapter 11:** Research: Research Report ........ 67
**Test 1** ...... 67 **Test 2** ...... 70 **Test 3** ...... 73
**Chapter 12:** Response to Literature ........ 76
**Test 1** ...... 76 **Test 2** ...... 79 **Test 3** ...... 82
**Chapter 13:** Writing for Assessment ........ 85
**Test 1** ...... 85 **Test 2** ...... 87 **Test 3** ...... 90


## PART 2: GRAMMAR, USAGE, AND MECHANICS


**Grammar, Usage, and Mechanics: Cumulative Diagnostic Test** ........ 95
**Chapter 14:** Nouns and Pronouns ........ 102
**Chapter 15:** Verbs ........ 107
**Chapter 16:** Adjectives and Adverbs ........ 111
**Chapter 17:** Prepositions ........ 115
**Chapter 18:** Conjunctions and Interjections ........ 119
**Chapter 19:** Basic Sentence Parts ........ 124
**Chapter 20:** Phrases and Clauses ........ 128
**Chapter 21:** Effective Sentences ........ 133
**Chapter 22:** Using Verbs ........ 138
**Chapter 23:** Using Pronouns ........ 142
**Chapter 24:** Making Words Agree ........ 145
**Chapter 25:** Using Modifiers ........ 149
**Chapter 26:** Punctuation ........ 153
**Chapter 27:** Capitalization ........ 158
**Grammar, Usage, and Mechanics: Cumulative Mastery Test** ........ 162


## PART 3: ACADEMIC AND WORKPLACE SKILLS


**Chapter 28:** Speaking, Listening, Viewing, and Representing ........ 173
**Chapter 29:** Vocabulary and Spelling ........ 180
**Chapter 30:** Reading Skills ........ 185
**Chapter 31:** Study, Reference, and Test-Taking Skills ........ 191

**ANSWERS** ........ 195

# About the Tests

This Formal Assessment booklet contains one test for each chapter in the *Writing and Grammar* student textbook. To provide you with the greatest flexibility, the tests utilize a number of different formats and may be administered in one or more class periods, depending on your classroom needs and your students' abilities. The complete Formal Assessment program is also available on a Computer Test Bank CD-ROM.

**Tests for Part 1: Writing**

- With the exception of the tests on the Research chapter, the tests on the modes of writing ask students to write a brief paper, applying the skills taught in the chapter. The questions on the tests are designed to lead the students through the writing process. Depending on your students' abilities, you may assign the tests to be done in one class period or as an extended assignment. Three tests (1—easy, 2—average, and 3—challenging) are provided for each mode of writing, the difference in the levels of difficulty being the complexity of the assignment and of some of the tasks students are asked to complete.
- Using multiple-choice and short-answer formats, the tests for Chapters 1, 2, and 3 and for the Research chapter ask students to recognize, respond to, and evaluate the material taught in the chapters.

**Tests for Part 2: Grammar, Usage, and Mechanics**

- Part 2 contains extensive objective tests on all the grammar, usage, and mechanics topics taught in the student textbook. Each test ends with a question bank in one of several standardized-test formats. In the answer key at the back of the booklet, you will find a level designation—easy, average, or challenging—for each question. These designations, together with the ample number of questions provided, give you the flexibility of customizing the tests for individual students or classes.
- In addition to the chapter tests, Part 2 contains a Cumulative Diagnostic Test at the beginning and a Cumulative Mastery Test at the end. These long tests, which may be given in sections, are designed to help you evaluate your students' needs and progress.

**Tests for Part 3: Academic and Workplace Skills**

- The tests for the chapters in Part 3 use multiple-choice and short-answer formats to help you assess your students' mastery of the material.

 

# Part 1: Writing

Name ______________________ Date ____________

# Assessment for Chapter 1: The Writer in You

1. Identify at least four forms that writing can take in everyday life.

2. Why is writing an important form of communication?

3. What advantage can writing have over speaking?

4. Explain how each element below contributes to good writing.
   Organization:

   Word Choice:

   Sentence Fluency:

   Conventions:

5. Why do you think voice can be important in writing?

6. Describe how you would use a writer's notebook or journal to keep track of writing ideas.

7. What things might you include in a research file? How could this help with your writing?

8. Explain the purpose of a writing portfolio. Include a description of what you would include in a portfolio.

9. Which reason below best describes how reading the works of others can help a writer? Circle the letter that corresponds with your choice. Then, explain your answer on the line that follows.
   a. Reading is the only way writers learn grammar.
   b. Writers should never write about the same topics.
   c. The more writers read, the less they have to practice their own skills.
   d. Reading the works of other writers can often stimulate ideas.

Name ______________________________

10. What is a writing environment, and why is it important to the writing process?

11. What three things do you need to consider when organizing your writing environment?

12. Some writers believe in getting their ideas down quickly, then revising; others like to revise as they go. Do you think one approach offers an advantage over the other? Explain.

13. How can trying different approaches help you develop your writing skills?

14. Explain how group brainstorming can contribute to good writing.

15. How can collaborative or cooperative writing contribute to good writing?

16. In what way can peer reviewers contribute to good writing?

17. To which of the following careers is good writing important? Circle the letter that corresponds with your choice. Then, explain your answer on the line that follows.
   a. medicine
   b. journalism
   c. politics
   d. all of the above

18. Think about the writing you have done in the past. Name a project that made you especially proud, and explain why.

19. Name one thing you would most like to improve about your writing.

20. Why might you want to consider publishing something you wrote?

Name ______________________ Date ______________

# Assessment for Chapter 2: A Walk Through the Writing Process

1. The sentences below describe different writing situations. Label each one either *reflexive* or *extensive.*

   a. You write an essay about photosynthesis on your biology test. ______________

   b. You write a letter to your best friend. ______________

   c. You respond to an essay question on a college application. ______________

2. Name two things that writers do during the prewriting stage.

   ______________________________

   ______________________________

3. Explain the difference between the revising stage and the editing and proofreading stage.

   ______________________________

   ______________________________

4. Circle the letter of the definition below that best describes the prewriting stage. Then, explain your answer on the lines that follow.

   a. the time for checking punctuation
   b. the time to write your ideas freely, from beginning to end
   c. the time for brainstorming for ideas
   d. the time for organizing paragraphs

   ______________________________

   ______________________________

5. Narrow the broad topic "entertainment" into three smaller topics that you could cover in short essays.

   Topic 1: ______________

   Topic 2: ______________

   Topic 3: ______________

Name ___

6. Place the broad topic "Entertainment" at the top of the web. Then, insert the smaller topics from Question 5 in the three boxes that extend from the center. Use the remaining boxes to make each topic even more specific.

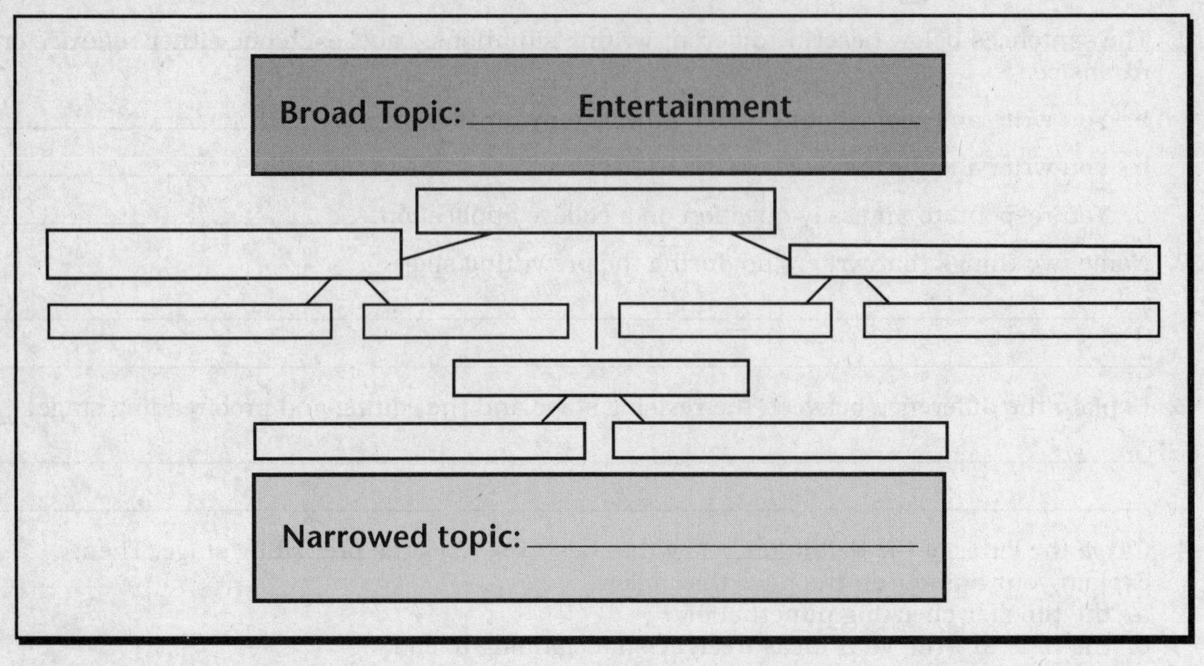


7. Explain how choosing either teenagers or business executives as your audience might affect how you would write an essay on your favorite activity.

___

___

___

8. On the lines that follow, write the letter of the description that corresponds to each purpose for writing.

| | |
|---|---|
| ___ To inform | a. includes reasons and arguments to support a position |
| ___ To reflect | b. summarizes an experience, focusing on what the author learned |
| ___ To persuade | c. includes facts, details, and examples that shed light on a subject |

9. Respond to the questions and prompts below as though you are preparing an essay about your favorite activity.

Purpose: ___

Audience: ___

Essay Title: ___

a. What do my readers already know about my topic? ___

b. What background should I provide for my readers? ___

___

c. What details will interest my readers? ___

___

Name ________________________________________

10. Gather details for an essay on your favorite activity by filling in the Parts of Speech Word Web below.

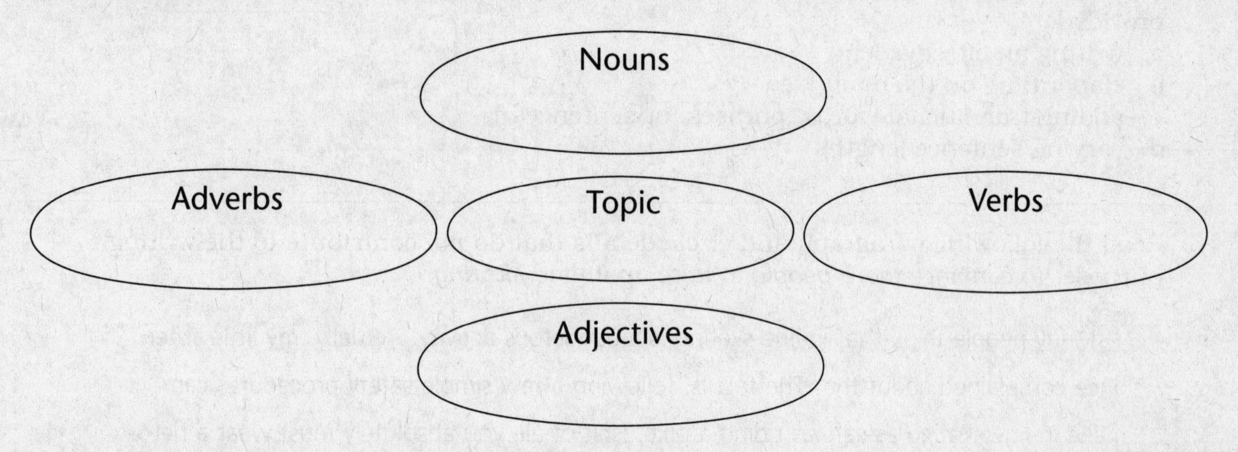


11. Provide more details for an essay about your favorite activity by answering the following questions in the spaces provided.

    a. What is enjoyable about this activity? ________________________

    b. Besides yourself, who enjoys it? ________________________

    c. What are the benefits of this activity? ________________________

    d. What are the drawbacks? ________________________

    e. Where can you participate in this activity? ________________________

    f. What do you need in order to participate? ________________________

12. Name two types of leads that can entice people to read a piece of writing.

________________________________________

________________________________________

13. On the lines that follow, write a strong lead for an essay about your favorite activity. Use at least two active verbs and two adjectives.

________________________________________

________________________________________

14. In the spaces, label the sentences that follow with the correct underlined term from the following group.
<u>Statement</u>—expresses main idea
<u>Extension</u>—expands on main idea
<u>Elaboration</u>—provides more detail

    a. ______________ The first thing you need is a pair of in-line skates that fit properly.

    b. ______________ Then, put on a helmet and pads and get someone to show you the basics.

    c. ______________ Many people think in-line skating is hard, but with a little practice, anyone can do it.

Name ______________________

15. Which method below best helps writing flow smoothly from one paragraph to another? Circle the letter that corresponds with your choice. Then, explain your answer in the space provided.
    a. writing an effective lead
    b. elaborating on the main idea
    c. adding transitional words, phrases, or sentences
    d. varying sentence lengths

______________________

16. Read the following paragraph and circle details that do *not* contribute to the writing purpose: *to convince more people to take up in-line skating.*

    Many people think that in-line skating is a dangerous activity. Actually, my little sister once complained about this. The fact is, following a few simple safety procedures can make in-line skating as safe as riding a bike. First of all, you absolutely must wear a helmet. Even the best skaters can hit an unexpected bump and take a fall. My favorite helmet is neon blue and comes to a point in the back. Knee, wrist, and elbow pads are also important, especially if you are new to the sport.

17. Proofread the following paragraph to find forms of *be* verbs. Draw a line through each of these verbs. Then, above each *be* verb, write a precise action verb.

    Imagine this: The wind is on your back. Birds are in the trees and your best friend is at your side. A helmet protects your head, but your arms and legs are free—free to skate down the sidewalk.

18. Name two specific kinds of errors you should look for when proofreading your writing.

______________________

19. Proofread the following paragraph to find mistakes in punctuation and capitalization. Circle the mistakes and correct them on the lines provided.

    One drawback to in-line skating is this, its often hard to find a good place to skate. Like bikers in-line skaters find city streets too busy to travel on safely. Sidewalks can be too crowded with pedestrians strollers and joggers in-line skaters have joined forces with bikers in working to establish special pathways.

______________________

______________________

______________________

20. What is the purpose of a writing portfolio? How can a writing portfolio be useful to students?

______________________

______________________

 

Name ______________________________ Date ______________

# Assessment for Chapter 3: Paragraphs and Compositions

1. Which definition below best describes a paragraph? Circle the letter that corresponds with your choice. Then, on the lines that follow, explain why the other answers are incorrect.
   a. a description that contains many vivid details
   b. a device used in expository writing
   c. a group of sentences that express a single point or focus
   d. a set of suggestions, directions, or instructions

   ______________________________________________

   ______________________________________________

2. What is a composition? Name three types of writing that might be considered a composition.

   ______________________________________________

3. Complete each of the sentences below with the appropriate term from the following group.

   main idea    stated main idea    implied main idea

   a. The ______________ is the key point expressed in a paragraph.
   b. When a paragraph suggests but does not state a key point, it is called a(n) ______________.
   c. When a key point is expressed directly, it is called a(n) ______________.

4. Underline the topic sentence in the following paragraph. Then, explain the paragraph's main idea in the space provided.

   Julia would anticipate it the minute she turned onto her street: a flash of gold, fur flying, a black-lipped smile, and a wet, pink lick. To Julia, Luna the golden retriever was the most reliable member of the family. Luna woke her in the morning, greeted her every day after school, and came whenever she called.

   ______________________________________________

5. Read the following details. Then, on the line provided, write a topic sentence that expresses the main idea these details imply.

   Jack's wrist ached where the soccer ball had hit him. There were grass stains on his knees. On his wrist bloomed a bruise from a collision with an opposing forward.

   ______________________________________________

6. Match the type of supporting sentence with its definition by writing the correct letter on each line.

   supporting fact: ______________
   supporting statistic: ______________
   illustration: ______________
   detail: ______________

   a. a fact, usually stated with numbers
   b. a specific person, thing, or event that demonstrates a point
   c. a specific part of the whole
   d. something that can be proven

Name ______________________________

7. Write two supporting sentences, using *facts*, for the following topic sentence:

   Living in the city can be very different from living on a farm.

   Fact 1: ______________________________

   Fact 2: ______________________________

8. Write two supporting sentences, using *details*, for the following topic sentence:

   Americans today consume vast quantities of junk food.

   Detail 1: ______________________________

   Detail 2: ______________________________

9. Write a topic sentence for a paragraph about your favorite food.

   ______________________________

   Restate your topic sentence in other words.

   ______________________________

   Support your topic sentence by giving an illustration or an example.

   ______________________________

10. Circle the letter of the answer choice below that best defines a *thesis statement.* Then, explain your answer in the space provided.
    a. the main idea of a composition
    b. a complete work, such as a composition
    c. a paragraph
    d. a supporting detail

    ______________________________

11. Underline the thesis statement in the following paragraph. Circle the sentence that does not contribute to the thesis statement. Then, on the line that follows, explain why this sentence does not fit.

    Performing onstage requires many different types of skills. An actor must speak well, projecting his voice—and his emotions—out to the audience. Watching a play can be fun. An actor must also memorize lines, and often has to sing and dance.

    ______________________________

12. Define the term *coherence.* Name two things a writer must do to establish coherence.

    ______________________________

    ______________________________

13. The list below contains four types of transitional words or phrases. On the lines, provide at least two examples of each type.

    a. shows time ______________________________

    b. shows comparison or contrast ______________________________

    c. shows cause and effect ______________________________

    d. shows location ______________________________

Name ______________________________

14. Explain the purpose of the following elements of a composition.

    a. The purpose of the introduction is to ______________________________.

    b. The purpose of the body paragraphs is to ______________________________.

    c. The purpose of the conclusion is to ______________________________.

15. Write a thesis statement about the importance of computers.

    ______________________________

16. Define the term *topical paragraph.* Then, based on your thesis statement about computers from the previous question, write a brief topical paragraph.

    ______________________________

    ______________________________

    ______________________________

17. On the lines that follow, identify the purpose of the following functional paragraph. Then, name the two other types of functional paragraphs.

    Ellie put her books on the desk and took a deep breath. "I'm not sure I can help you with that, Meg," she said.

    ______________________________

    ______________________________

18. Rewrite the following paragraph on the lines that follow, changing words, sentence length, and sentence structure to add interest and variety.

    Spring is a good season. In spring, the flowers come out. It rains, but then the sun comes out. Birds come back from the South. The temperature becomes warmer. Everyone puts away their winter coats. People wear short sleeves and light jackets. They are in good moods.

    ______________________________

    ______________________________

    ______________________________

    ______________________________

19. In the spaces provided, write an alternate word that conveys a tone of sadness for each word. Then, use the new words in one or two complete sentences that convey a sad tone.

    walked: __________ color: __________ said: __________ expression: __________

    ______________________________

    ______________________________

20. On the lines below, define the terms *formal English* and *informal English.* Name one situation in which each type of writing might be appropriate.

    ______________________________

    ______________________________

    ______________________________

Name ______________________ Date ______________

# Assessment for Chapter 4: Narration: Autobiographical Writing

## Test 1

In this test, you will be asked to draft an autobiographical story of three or four paragraphs. Think of a time when you were surprised by something. Possible examples include a gift, a friend's actions, good or bad news, or an unexpected event. Use "I" to tell your story. Write your topic on the line provided.

______________________________

**Prewriting**

1. Use looping to narrow your topic. After freewriting for a few minutes, circle the idea you find most important, and write it on the lines below.

______________________________

______________________________

______________________________

2. Who is your intended audience? ______________

What do they already know about your topic? ______________.

What do you want them to know or think after reading your essay? In other words, what is your purpose? ______________.

3. Gather details for your topic by describing the following elements.

Time, season, weather: ______________

Location, surroundings: ______________

People: ______________

Events: ______________

______________________________

**Drafting**

4. Organize your story by completing the sentences that follow.

My lead will contain the following elements: ______________

I will write the events in this order: ______________

______________________________

I will describe the surprise by ______________

5. On a separate sheet of paper, use your prewriting and drafting notes to draft your autobiographical essay.

**Revising**

6. Reread one paragraph in your draft. Add or revise a sentence to increase the tension or to better hold the reader's interest. Write the revised sentence on the line and mark the place in your draft where the revision will appear.

______________________________

______________________________

Name ______________________________

7. Find two general or vague nouns in your draft that could be more precise. Circle them and replace them with more precise nouns. List them on the lines below.

   Vague nouns: ______________ ______________

   Precise nouns: ______________ ______________

**Editing and Proofreading**

8. Underline each introductory element below, inserting a comma to separate it from the rest of the sentence. Then, on the line that follows, list an introductory phrase or clause from your autobiographical story. If you don't find any introductory phrases or clauses in your draft, mark a place to insert one and write the phrase below.

   Before I went outside I checked the weather report. Hearing that it might rain I got my umbrella.

   ______________________________

9. Evaluate your draft according to the criteria in the rubric below. List any changes that you may need to make to improve your story.

| | Score 4 | Score 3 | Score 2 | Score 1 |
|---|---|---|---|---|
| Audience and Purpose | Contains an engaging introduction; successfully entertains or presents a theme | Contains a somewhat engaging introduction; entertains or presents a theme | Contains an introduction; attempts to entertain or to present a theme | Begins abruptly or confusingly; leaves purpose unclear |
| Organization | Creates an interesting, clear narrative; told from a consistent point of view | Presents a clear sequence of events; told from a specific point of view | Presents a mostly clear sequence of events; contains inconsistent points of view | Presents events without logical order; lacks a consistent point of view |
| Elaboration | Provides insight into character; develops plot; contains dialogue | Contains details and dialogue that develop character and plot | Contains details that develop plot; contains some dialogue | Contains few or no details to develop characters or plot |
| Use of Language | Uses word choice and tone to reveal story's theme; contains no errors in grammar, punctuation, or spelling | Uses interesting and fresh word choices; contains few errors in grammar, punctuation, and spelling | Uses some clichés and trite expressions; contains some errors in grammar, punctuation, and spelling | Uses uninspired word choices; has many errors in grammar, punctuation, and spelling |

______________________________

______________________________

______________________________

**Publishing and Presenting**

10. Describe two illustrations that could highlight your autobiographical story. Then, tell why these would enhance your writing.

______________________________

______________________________

______________________________

Name ______________________________ Date ______________

# Assessment for Chapter 4: Narration: Autobiographical Writing
## Test 2

In this test, you will draft an autobiographical narrative of three or four paragraphs about an event that triggered a strong emotion. Possible examples of emotions you might wish to write about include joy, confusion, anxiety, sorrow, excitement, pride, or fear. Use "I" to tell your story. Write your topic on the following line.

______________________________

**Prewriting**

1. Complete the following sentences.

   I remember a time when I felt really ______________.

   The time that this event occurred was ______________.

   I felt this way because ______________.

2. Circle the phrase below that best describes the purpose of your autobiographical story. Then, complete the sentence that follows.

   to entertain the reader    to instruct the reader    to capture a character's personality

   I plan to accomplish this purpose by ______________.

3. Identify your topic. Then, gather details for your topic by writing brief notes on the following elements.

   Topic: ______________

   Time: ______________

   Place: ______________

   Events: ______________

   Conflicts: ______________

   People: ______________

   Dialogue: ______________

**Drafting**

4. Define the central conflict of your story by completing the following sentences.
   What does the main character (possibly you, since this is an autobiography) want?

   ______________

   What person, force, or circumstance stands in the way?

   ______________

5. On a separate sheet of paper, use your prewriting and drafting notes to draft your autobiographical essay.

**Revising**

6. Reread your lead and, on the lines provided, revise it to hook the reader more effectively.

   Then, explain why your revision is more effective. ______________

   ______________

   ______________

Name ________________________________________

7. Find two general or vague nouns in your draft that could be more precise. Circle them and replace them with more precise nouns. List them in the spaces provided.

   Vague nouns: ________________ ________________

   Precise nouns: ________________ ________________

**Editing and Proofreading**

8. Underline each introductory element below, inserting a comma to separate it from the rest of the sentence. On the line that follows, write an introductory phrase or clause from your story. If you don't find any in your draft, find a place to insert one, mark the place on your draft, and write the phrase on the line below.

   When I got to the basement the light went out. Digging in my pocket I grabbed a flashlight. The batteries were out. Terrified I dropped the flashlight.

   ________________________________________________________________

9. Evaluate your draft according to the rubric below. List any changes that you need to make to improve your essay.

| | Score 4 | Score 3 | Score 2 | Score 1 |
|---|---|---|---|---|
| Audience and Purpose | Contains an engaging introduction; successfully entertains or presents a theme | Contains a somewhat engaging introduction; entertains or presents a theme | Contains an introduction; attempts to entertain or to present a theme | Begins abruptly or confusingly; leaves purpose unclear |
| Organization | Creates an interesting, clear narrative; told from a consistent point of view | Presents a clear sequence of events; told from a specific point of view | Presents a mostly clear sequence of events; contains inconsistent points of view | Presents events without logical order; lacks a consistent point of view |
| Elaboration | Provides insight into character; develops plot; contains dialogue | Contains details and dialogue that develop character and plot | Contains details that develop plot; contains some dialogue | Contains few or no details to develop characters or plot |
| Use of Language | Uses word choice and tone to reveal story's theme; contains no errors in grammar, punctuation, or spelling | Uses interesting and fresh word choices; contains few errors in grammar, punctuation, and spelling | Uses some clichés and trite expressions; contains some errors in grammar, punctuation, and spelling | Uses uninspired word choices; has many errors in grammar, punctuation, and spelling |

________________________________________________________________

________________________________________________________________

________________________________________________________________

________________________________________________________________

________________________________________________________________

________________________________________________________________

**Publishing and Presenting**

10. Suggest one way in which you might share your autobiographical narrative with your intended audience.

   ________________________________________________________________

   ________________________________________________________________

Name ______________________________ Date ______________

# Assessment for Chapter 4: Narration: Autobiographical Writing

## Test 3

In this test, you will draft an autobiographical sketch of three or more paragraphs about an event that helped you discover something important about yourself. Your sketch should include a conflict, either external or internal. Write your topic on the following line.

______________________________________________________________

**Prewriting**

1. To help gather details, complete the following sentences.

   I remember a time when I discovered ______________________________.

   The time in my life that this event occurred was ______________________________.

   This event helped me learn ______________ because ______________

   ______________________________________________________________.

2. Gather more details for your topic by answering the following questions.

   Details about me *before* the event: ______________________________

   ______________________________________________________________

   Details about the event: ______________________________

   ______________________________________________________________

   Details about me *after* the event: ______________________________

   ______________________________________________________________

**Drafting**

3. Describe the main conflict in your autobiographical narrative and the problems caused by the conflict.

   ______________________________________________________________

   ______________________________________________________________

4. Describe how you plan to create tension in your narrative and why you think your method will be effective.

   ______________________________________________________________

   ______________________________________________________________

5. On a separate sheet of paper, use your prewriting and drafting notes to draft your autobiographical sketch.

**Revising**

6. Identify the climax of your autobiographical narrative. If the climax doesn't represent the point of greatest tension in your sketch, rewrite it on the lines provided. If you think your climax is effective, write it below and explain why it works.

   ______________________________________________________________

   ______________________________________________________________

   ______________________________________________________________

Name ______________________________

7. Check each paragraph for coherence. On the lines below, jot a brief phrase summing up the main idea of each paragraph. Then, review your draft and cross out or rewrite any sentences that do not support the main idea of each paragraph.

### Editing and Proofreading

8. Identify the beginning of each sentence in your autobiographical narrative. If no sentences begin with an introductory phrase or clause, rewrite a sentence on the lines below so that it does begin with an introductory element. Make sure it is punctuated correctly. If your narrative already includes such sentences, write one example on the lines.

9. Evaluate your draft according to the rubric below. List any changes that you need to make in your sketch.

| | Score 4 | Score 3 | Score 2 | Score 1 |
|---|---|---|---|---|
| Audience and Purpose | Contains an engaging introduction; successfully entertains or presents a theme | Contains a somewhat engaging introduction; entertains or presents a theme | Contains an introduction; attempts to entertain or to present a theme | Begins abruptly or confusingly; leaves purpose unclear |
| Organization | Creates an interesting, clear narrative; told from a consistent point of view | Presents a clear sequence of events; told from a specific point of view | Presents a mostly clear sequence of events; contains inconsistent points of view | Presents events without logical order; lacks a consistent point of view |
| Elaboration | Provides insight into character; develops plot; contains dialogue | Contains details and dialogue that develop character and plot | Contains details that develop plot; contains some dialogue | Contains few or no details to develop characters or plot |
| Use of Language | Uses word choice and tone to reveal story's theme; contains no errors in grammar, punctuation, or spelling | Uses interesting and fresh word choices; contains few errors in grammar, punctuation, and spelling | Uses some clichés and trite expressions; contains some errors in grammar, punctuation, and spelling | Uses uninspired word choices; has many errors in grammar, punctuation, and spelling |

### Publishing and Presenting

10. Suggest an outlet, such as a magazine or a classroom presentation, that would be appropriate for publishing your autobiographical sketch. Then, explain why this would be an appropriate place to publish your essay.

Name ______________________ Date ______________

# Assessment for Chapter 5: Narration: Short Story

## Test 1

In this test, you will draft a short story of at least three paragraphs, in which someone faces danger during a hike in the woods. Plan to include some dialogue in your story.

**Prewriting**

1. In the spaces provided, note details that you associate with a hike in the woods. Then, define the conflict in your story by completing the sentence below.

   Hike: ______________________

   Weather: ______________________

   Land features: ______________________

   Equipment: ______________________

   Activities: ______________________

   The element of danger, which constitutes the central conflict in my story, will be

   ______________________.

2. Develop your main character by completing the following sentences.

   My character's name is ____________. This person is ____________ years old.

   My character's family consists of ______________________.

   My character looks like this: ______________________.

   My character has the following interests: ______________________.

3. Describe how your main character will react to the element of danger. Then, describe the personal qualities that lead your character to respond in this way. ______________________

   ______________________

   ______________________

**Drafting**

4. Map out the plot of your story by filling in the plot diagram below.

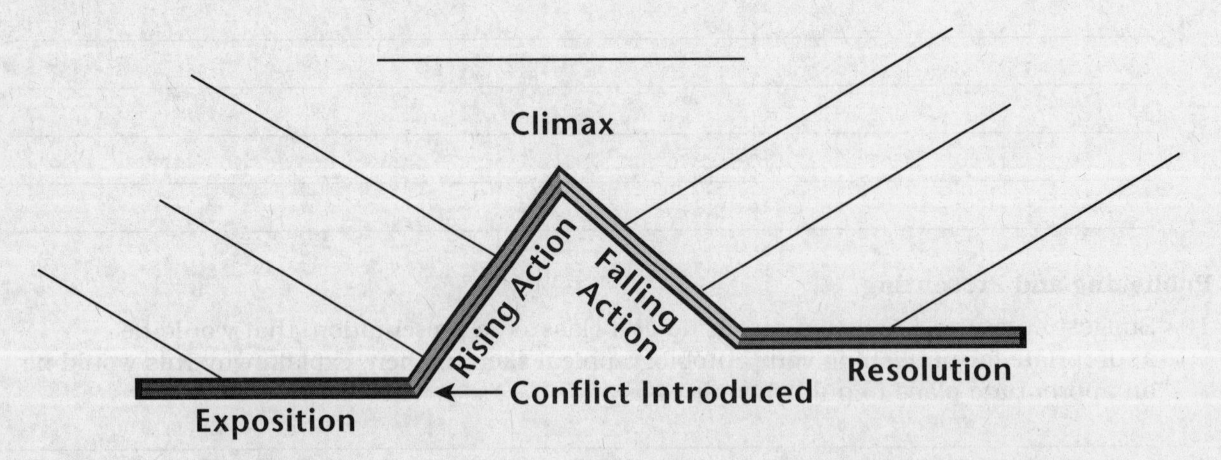


5. On a separate sheet of paper, use your notes and information from the plot diagram to draft your short story. Be sure to *show* rather than *tell* what happens. Do this by including vivid details about the setting, characters, and events.

Name ____________________

**Revising**

6. Find two places in your draft where related sentences are short and choppy. Combine these sentences, using words that tell *when*, *why*, *how*, or *which one*.

____________________

____________________

____________________

7. Find one action verb and one linking verb in your draft that seem colorless or overused. Replace these words with more vivid verbs. List the old and new verbs in the spaces provided.

Colorless verbs: ____________ ____________

Vivid verbs: ____________ ____________

**Editing and Proofreading**

8. Circle each instance of "words announcing speech" in the following paragraph, adding punctuation as needed. Then, review your draft for errors in dialogue punctuation. Write the corrections on the lines below. If your dialogue does not contain errors in punctuation, write *none*.

"I think we're lost" said Gina. She looked around at the landscape. Then she added "I don't recognize anything here"

____________________

____________________

9. Evaluate your draft based on the criteria in the rubric below. List any changes that you may need to make to improve your short story.

| | Score 4 | Score 3 | Score 2 | Score 1 |
|---|---|---|---|---|
| Audience and Purpose | Contains an engaging introduction; successfully entertains or presents a theme | Contains a somewhat engaging introduction; entertains or presents a theme | Contains an introduction; attempts to entertain or to present a theme | Begins abruptly or confusingly; leaves purpose unclear |
| Organization | Creates an interesting, clear narrative; told from a consistent point of view | Presents a clear sequence of events; told from a specific point of view | Presents a mostly clear sequence of events; contains inconsistent points of view | Presents events without logical order; lacks a consistent point of view |
| Elaboration | Provides insight into character; develops plot; contains dialogue | Contains details and dialogue that develop character and plot | Contains details that develop plot; contains some dialogue | Contains few or no details to develop characters or plot |
| Use of Language | Uses word choice and tone to reveal story's theme; contains no errors in grammar, punctuation, or spelling | Uses interesting and fresh word choices; contains few errors in grammar, punctuation, and spelling | Uses some clichés and trite expressions; contains some errors in grammar, punctuation, and spelling | Uses uninspired word choices; has many errors in grammar, punctuation, and spelling |

____________________

____________________

**Publishing And Presenting**

10. Suggest an illustration that could appear on the cover of your short story. Then, explain one thing you learned about writing a short story that might be helpful to someone who is about to write one.

____________________

____________________

____________________

Name ____________________ Date ____________________

# Assessment for Chapter 5: Narration: Short Story

## Test 2

In this test, you will draft an adventure story of at least three paragraphs about something that goes wrong on a class trip. Plan to include some dialogue in your story.

**Prewriting**

1. List details in the spaces provided to help you define the main elements of your story.

   Main character: ____________________

   Class trip: ____________________

   What goes wrong: ____________________

   How the main character reacts to the problem: ____________________

2. Develop your main character by completing the following sentences:

   My character's name is __________. This person is __________ years old.

   My character's family consists of ____________________.

   My character looks like this: ____________________.

   My character has the following interests: ____________________.

3. Define your intended audience and your story's purpose.

   I am writing this story for ____________________.

   My purpose is to ____________________.

**Drafting**

4. Map out the plot of your story by filling in the plot diagram below.

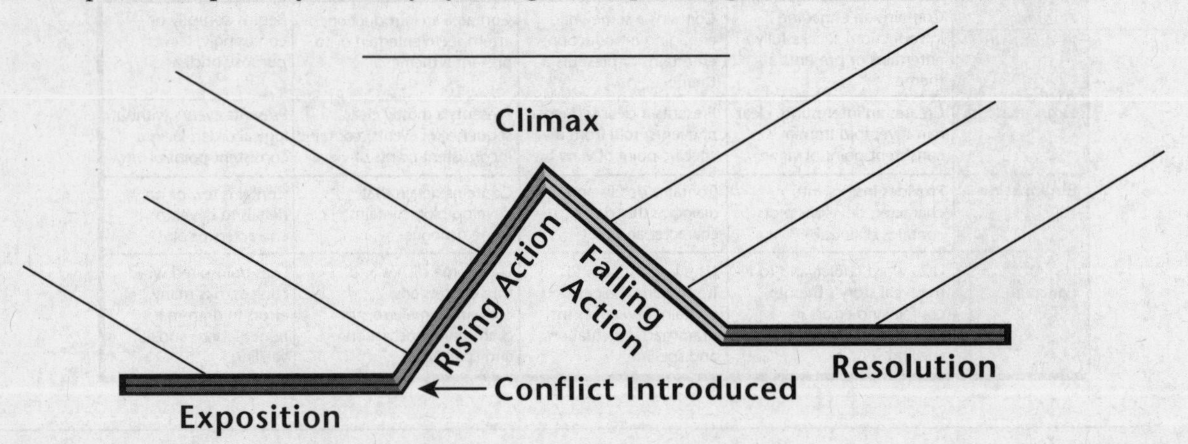


5. On a separate sheet of paper, use your notes and information from the plot diagram to draft your short story. Be sure to *show* rather than *tell* what happens. Do this by including vivid details about the setting, characters, and events.

Name ______________________

**Revising**

6. List two clues from your draft that hint at the climax or resolution. If you can't find any clues, insert two and write them here.

______________________

______________________

7. Find an action verb and a linking verb in your draft that seem colorless or overused. Replace these words with more vivid verbs. List the old and new verbs in the spaces provided.

Colorless verbs: ______________ ______________

Vivid verbs: ______________ ______________

**Editing and Proofreading**

8. Circle each instance of "words announcing speech" in the paragraph below, adding punctuation as needed. Then, review your draft for errors in dialogue punctuation. Write the corrections on the lines below. If your dialogue does not contain errors in punctuation, write *none.*

Then Teri cried "Don't go in there!" Sandy took a deep breath. "I have to" he said "My sister might be inside."

______________________

______________________

9. Evaluate your draft based on the criteria in the rubric below. List any changes that you may need to make to improve your short story.

| | Score 4 | Score 3 | Score 2 | Score 1 |
|---|---|---|---|---|
| Audience and Purpose | Contains an engaging introduction; successfully entertains or presents a theme | Contains a somewhat engaging introduction; entertains or presents a theme | Contains an introduction; attempts to entertain or to present a theme | Begins abruptly or confusingly; leaves purpose unclear |
| Organization | Creates an interesting, clear narrative; told from a consistent point of view | Presents a clear sequence of events; told from a specific point of view | Presents a mostly clear sequence of events; contains inconsistent points of view | Presents events without logical order; lacks a consistent point of view |
| Elaboration | Provides insight into character; develops plot; contains dialogue | Contains details and dialogue that develop character and plot | Contains details that develop plot; contains some dialogue | Contains few or no details to develop characters or plot |
| Use of Language | Uses word choice and tone to reveal story's theme; contains no errors in grammar, punctuation, or spelling | Uses interesting and fresh word choices; contains few errors in grammar, punctuation, and spelling | Uses some clichés and trite expressions; contains some errors in grammar, punctuation, and spelling | Uses uninspired word choices; has many errors in grammar, punctuation, and spelling |

______________________

______________________

______________________

**Publishing and Presenting**

10. List a magazine to which you might submit your short story. Then, in the space provided, list one thing you might do differently the next time you write a short story.

______________________

______________________

______________________

Name ______________________ Date ______________

# Assessment for Chapter 5: Narration: Short Story
## Test 3

In this test, you will draft a short story of three to five paragraphs about a character who experiences an internal conflict. Make sure your story includes a climax and a resolution. Use vivid details and lively dialogue.

**Prewriting**

1. Define the elements of your story by responding to the following prompts.

   Main character: ______________________

   Conflict: ______________________

   Climax: ______________________

   Resolution: ______________________

2. Develop your main character by completing the following sentences.

   My character's name is ____________. This person is ________ years old.

   My character looks like this: ______________________.

   My character's family consists of ______________________.

   My character has the following traits: ______________________.

   What is important to my character is ______________________.

3. Describe the conflict your character faces. How will facing this conflict change your character?

   ______________________

   ______________________

   ______________________

**Drafting**

4. Map out the plot of your story by filling in the plot diagram that follows. Then, on the lines provided, define the terms *setup* and *payoff* and explain how you will create them in your story.

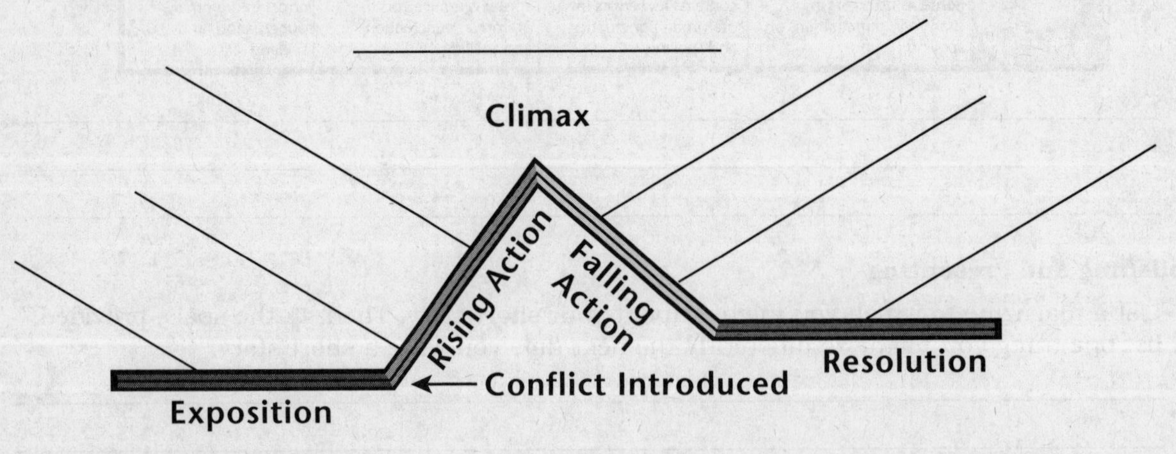


______________________

______________________

Name ______________________________

5. On a separate sheet of paper, use your notes and information from the plot diagram to draft your short story. Be sure to *show* rather than *tell* what happens. Do this by including vivid details about the setting, characters, and events.

**Revising**

6. Circle an event in your draft to which your character has a strong reaction. Write your description of this reaction on the lines that follow, fleshing it out to include more vivid and memorable details.

______________________________

______________________________

______________________________

7. Find two common or colorless linking verbs in your story. Replace them with more vivid action verbs. List the old and new verbs in the spaces provided.

   Colorless verbs: ______________ ______________

   Vivid verbs: ______________ ______________

**Editing and Proofreading**

8. Review the punctuation of dialogue in your draft, and correct any errors or omissions on the lines below. If your dialogue does not contain errors in punctuation, write an example of correctly punctuated dialogue on the lines below.

______________________________

______________________________

Name ______________________________

9. Evaluate your draft based on the criteria in the rubric below. List any changes that you may need to make to improve your short story.

| | Score 4 | Score 3 | Score 2 | Score 1 |
|---|---|---|---|---|
| Audience and Purpose | Contains an engaging introduction; successfully entertains or presents a theme | Contains a somewhat engaging introduction; entertains or presents a theme | Contains an introduction; attempts to entertain or to present a theme | Begins abruptly or confusingly; leaves purpose unclear |
| Organization | Creates an interesting, clear narrative; told from a consistent point of view | Presents a clear sequence of events; told from a specific point of view | Presents a mostly clear sequence of events; contains inconsistent points of view | Presents events without logical order; lacks a consistent point of view |
| Elaboration | Provides insight into character; develops plot; contains dialogue | Contains details and dialogue that develop character and plot | Contains details that develop plot; contains some dialogue | Contains few or no details to develop characters or plot |
| Use of Language | Uses word choice and tone to reveal story's theme; contains no errors in grammar, punctuation, or spelling | Uses interesting and fresh word choices; contains few errors in grammar, punctuation, and spelling | Uses some clichés and trite expressions; contains some errors in grammar, punctuation, and spelling | Uses uninspired word choices; has many errors in grammar, punctuation, and spelling |

______________________________

______________________________

______________________________

**Publishing and Presenting**

10. Write a one- or two-sentence description of your story that you could use when submitting it to a magazine. Then, explain one thing that the experience of writing a short story has taught you about the writing process.

______________________________

______________________________

______________________________

Name ______________________ Date ____________

# Assessment for Chapter 6: Description

## Test 1

In this test, you will draft a three-paragraph description of a place you've visited. Your goal is to show your readers what makes this place unique.

**Prewriting**

1. List three places that are possible topics for your description. Then, list one detail that describes each place. Finally, circle the place that you think will be most interesting to write about.

   Place: ______________ Detail: ______________

   Place: ______________ Detail: ______________

   Place: ______________ Detail: ______________

2. Describe how you will focus your essay.

   I am interested in this topic because ______________.

   My strongest impression of this place is ______________.

3. Select a perspective from which to write by listing in the chart the details about your topic that would most appeal to possible readers. Next, note whether writing from a close-up or big-picture perspective would be most effective for that audience. Then, narrow your topic by completing the sentence that follows.

| Audience | Appealing or Interesting Details | Close-Up or Big-Picture Perspective |
|---|---|---|
| your friends | | |
| small children | | |
| adults | | |

   I will write my description from a ________ perspective, for an audience of ________.

**Drafting**

4. Circle one of the following three methods of organization for your description. Then, note the points you will make.

   Spatial Order Chronological Order Order of Importance

   I will begin with ______________.

   I will follow this with ______________.

   I will conclude with ______________.

5. On a separate sheet of paper, use information from your notes to draft your description.

**Revising**

6. Improve two sentences in your draft by adding additional details. Add one descriptive word to each sentence. Write the revised sentences below and circle the new words.

   ______________

   ______________

Name ____________________

7. Find one vague adjective and one vague adverb in your draft and replace them with more precise modifiers. List the old and new words.

   Vague Modifiers ____________________ Precise Modifiers ____________________

## Editing and Proofreading

8. Circle the places in the following paragraph where two or more adjectives appear before the noun they modify. Correct punctuation errors by adding or deleting commas as needed. On the line that follows, write a sentence from your draft that contains two or more adjectives. Review the punctuation of these adjectives and correct any errors.

   The first things that Julia noticed were the large shiny buildings. Suddenly a whirl of honking screeching sounds assaulted her ears.

   ____________________

9. Evaluate your draft according to the criteria in the rubric below. On the lines, note any changes that you may need to make to improve your description.

| | Score 4 | Score 3 | Score 2 | Score 1 |
|---|---|---|---|---|
| Audience and Purpose | Creates a memorable main impression through effective use of details | Creates a main impression through use of details | Contains details that distract from a main impression | Contains details that are unfocused and create no main impression |
| Organization | Is organized consistently, logically, and effectively | Is organized consistently | Is organized, but not consistently | Is disorganized and confusing |
| Elaboration | Contains rich sensory language that appeals to the five senses | Contains some rich sensory language | Contains some rich sensory language, but it appeals to only one or two of the senses | Contains only flat language |
| Use of Language | Uses vivid and precise adjectives; contains no errors in grammar, punctuation, or spelling | Uses some vivid and precise adjectives; contains few errors in grammar, punctuation, and spelling | Uses few vivid and precise adjectives; contains some errors in grammar, punctuation, and spelling | Uses no vivid adjectives; contains many errors in grammar, punctuation, and spelling |

____________________

## Publishing and Presenting

10. What sort of images—black-and-white sketches, color illustrations, or photographs—do you feel would be most appropriate for your description? Explain your choice.

____________________

Name ______________________ Date ______________

# Assessment for Chapter 6: Description

## Test 2

In this test, you will write a three-paragraph descriptive essay about a favorite outdoor place you've visited more than once. Use specific descriptive details to enable your readers to visualize this special place.

**Prewriting**

1. List three places that are possible subjects for your description. Then, list one detail that describes each place. Finally, circle the place you think will be most interesting to write about.

   Place: ______________ Detail: ______________

   Place: ______________ Detail: ______________

   Place: ______________ Detail: ______________

2. Explore various points of view by noting how each person in the chart might feel about the outdoor place you have chosen to describe. Then, narrow your topic by selecting a perspective and completing the sentence that follows.

| Audience | Reason Place Is Interesting | Most Fascinating or Important Details | Strongest Impression |
|---|---|---|---|
| your friends | | | |
| small children | | | |
| wildlife experts | | | |

I will write my essay for an audience of ______________.

3. Gather details for your description by "cubing" your subject in the chart below.

| STEPS | |
|---|---|
| 1. Describe the place. Explain how it looks, sounds, feels, or smells. | |
| 2. Associate it. List feelings or stories it calls to mind. | |
| 3. Apply it. Show how it can be used or what it does. | |
| 4. Analyze it. Divide it into parts. | |
| 5. Compare or contrast it. Compare or contrast the place with another location. | |

Name ______________________________

**Drafting**

4. Circle one of the following three methods of organization for your description. Then, note the points you will make.

   Spatial Order    Chronological Order    Order of Importance

   I will begin with ______________________________.

   I will follow this with ______________________________.

   I will conclude with ______________________________.

5. On a separate sheet of paper, use information from your notes to draft your description. Be sure to shape your writing by building to a point.

**Revising**

6. Find two consecutive sentences in your draft with details that do not contribute effectively to the overall impression you want to convey. Replace these details with more relevant details, and write the new sentences below.

______________________________

______________________________

______________________________

7. Find one vague adjective and one vague adverb in your draft and replace them with more precise modifiers. List the old and new words.

   Vague Modifiers    More Precise Modifiers

   ______________    ______________

   ______________    ______________

**Editing and Proofreading**

8. Circle the places in the following paragraph where two or more adjectives appear before the noun they modify. Correct punctuation errors by adding or deleting commas as needed. On the lines that follow, write a sentence from your draft that contains two or more adjectives. Review the punctuation of these adjectives, and correct any errors.

   As Jesse stepped into the woods, a loud crackling sound filled her ears. Immediately, she sensed a large dangerous presence. Was it just her imagination, or was a big hungry bear lurking here?

   ______________________________

   ______________________________

Name ______________________________

9. Evaluate your draft according to the criteria in the rubric below. List any changes that you may need to make to improve your description.

| | Score 4 | Score 3 | Score 2 | Score 1 |
|---|---|---|---|---|
| Audience and Purpose | Creates a memorable main impression through effective use of details | Creates a main impression through use of details | Contains details that distract from a main impression | Contains details that are unfocused and create no main impression |
| Organization | Is organized consistently, logically, and effectively | Is organized consistently | Is organized, but not consistently | Is disorganized and confusing |
| Elaboration | Contains rich sensory language that appeals to the five senses | Contains some rich sensory language | Contains some rich sensory language, but it appeals to only one or two of the senses | Contains only flat language |
| Use of Language | Uses vivid and precise adjectives; contains no errors in grammar, punctuation, or spelling | Uses some vivid and precise adjectives; contains few errors in grammar, punctuation, and spelling | Uses few vivid and precise adjectives; contains some errors in grammar, punctuation, and spelling | Uses no vivid adjectives; contains many errors in grammar, punctuation, and spelling |

______________________________

______________________________

______________________________

______________________________

**Publishing and Presenting**

10. Tell how you might look for a place to publish your descriptive essay on-line. Then, note one thing that you learned as you revised your essay.

______________________________

______________________________

______________________________

Name ______________________ Date ____________

# Assessment for Chapter 6: Description

## Test 3

In this test, you will write a descriptive essay of three or four paragraphs. Write a description of a famous or noteworthy person toward whom you feel a strong emotion, such as admiration or irritation. Include specific details that convey the uniqueness of this person and the strength of your feelings.

**Prewriting**

1. In the following chart, list three people who could be subjects for your descriptive essay. For each person, list details that this person brings to mind. Then, complete the sentence that follows the chart.

| People | | | |
|---|---|---|---|
| Details | | | |

I have chosen to write about ______________________.

2. Describe your intended audience and your main purpose for writing a descriptive essay:

I am writing this descriptive essay in order to ______________________.

I am writing for the following readers: ______________________.

My purpose and my intended audience will affect my description in the following ways:

______________________

______________________

______________________.

3. Gather details for your description by "cubing" your subject in the chart that follows.

| STEPS | DETAILS |
|---|---|
| 1. Describe it. | |
| 2. Associate it. | |
| 3. Apply it. | |
| 4. Analyze it. | |
| 5. Compare or contrast it. | |

**Drafting**

4. Circle one of the following three methods of organization for your description. Then, note the points you will make.

Spatial Order Chronological Order Order of Importance

I will begin with ______________________.

I will follow this with ______________________.

I will conclude with ______________________.

5. On a separate sheet of paper, use information from your notes to draft your description.

Name ______________________

## Revising

6. Find two sentences in your draft with details that do not contribute effectively to the overall impression you want to convey. Replace these details in these sentences with more relevant details, and write both versions of the sentences below.

7. Find a functional paragraph in your draft and write it on the lines provided below. If you can't find a functional paragraph, write one. Insert it here and at an appropriate place in your draft.

8. Look through your draft to see if your sentences contain any awkward or faulty parallels. If so, correct them and write the old and new versions of one of them below. If no faulty parallels exist in your description, write *none*.

## Editing and Proofreading

9. Evaluate your draft according to the criteria in the rubric that follows. List any changes that you may need to make to improve your description.

| | Score 4 | Score 3 | Score 2 | Score 1 |
|---|---|---|---|---|
| Audience and Purpose | Creates a memorable main impression through effective use of details | Creates a main impression through use of details | Contains details that distract from a main impression | Contains details that are unfocused and create no main impression |
| Organization | Is organized consistently, logically, and effectively | Is organized consistently | Is organized, but not consistently | Is disorganized and confusing |
| Elaboration | Contains rich sensory language that appeals to the five senses | Contains some rich sensory language | Contains some rich sensory language, but it appeals to only one or two of the senses | Contains only flat language |
| Use of Language | Uses vivid and precise adjectives; contains no errors in grammar, punctuation, or spelling | Uses some vivid and precise adjectives; contains few errors in grammar, punctuation, and spelling | Uses few vivid and precise adjectives; contains some errors in grammar, punctuation, and spelling | Uses no vivid adjectives; contains many errors in grammar, punctuation, and spelling |

## Publishing and Presenting

10. Write a one-sentence blurb that could be printed on a magazine cover to interest readers in your descriptive essay. Then, note any new insights you gained about your subject from writing this descriptive essay.

Name ______________________ Date ____________

# Assessment for Chapter 7: Persuasion: Persuasive Essay

## Test 1

In this test, you will draft a persuasive essay of three or four paragraphs about an environmental issue that affects you. For example, you might address a topic as broad as global warming or as narrow as the need for household recycling.

**Prewriting**

1. Enter at least one specific issue for each of the following environmental topics. Then, indicate your issue topic and position by completing the sentences that follow.

   Pollution: ______________________

   Waste: ______________________

   Wildlife: ______________________

   I have chosen to write about this issue: ______________________.

   My position on this issue is ______________________.

2. Narrow your topic by completing the chart of Reporter's Questions.

| QUESTION | ANSWER |
|---|---|
| Who? | |
| What? | |
| Where? | |
| When? | |
| Why? | |
| How? | |

3. Explore your issue by filling out the T-chart below. Write your topic at the top. On the left side, list three points or arguments in favor of your position; on the right side, list three points that could be used to argue against your position.

   My Topic: ______________________

| Arguments in Favor | Arguments Against |
|---|---|
| | |

Name ____________________

## Drafting

4. Write your thesis statement. Then, circle two types of persuasive techniques from the list below. Finally, use these techniques to write two persuasive sentences that support your thesis statement.

   Thesis statement: ____________________

   ____________________

   Logical arguments  Repetition and parallelism  Appeals to emotions
   Appeals to basic values  Charged words

   Persuasive sentences: ____________________

   ____________________

   ____________________

5. On a separate sheet of paper, draft your persuasive essay using your notes and information from the graphic organizers.

## Revising

6. Find a place in your draft where a main point needs more support. On the lines below, provide support by writing a sentence that presents an additional argument or uses a different persuasive technique. Mark the place in your draft where you would insert the new sentence.

   ____________________

   ____________________

7. Define a complex sentence. Then, find two short, related sentences from your draft that can be combined into one complex sentence. Write the new sentence here.

   ____________________

   ____________________

   ____________________

## Editing and Proofreading

8. Correct the punctuation errors in the following passage by inserting colons, dashes, and capital letters as needed. On the lines that follow, write a sentence from your essay in which you used a colon or a dash. Review your punctuation and correct any errors. If you have not used any colons or dashes in your draft, write *none*.

   On the whale watch, I saw two types humpbacks and finbacks. I also saw this occur a dolphin became trapped in a fishing net.

   ____________________

   ____________________

Name ______________________________

9. Evaluate your draft based on the criteria in the following rubric. List any changes that you may need to make to improve your essay.

| | Score 4 | Score 3 | Score 2 | Score 1 |
|---|---|---|---|---|
| Audience and Purpose | Provides arguments, illustrations, and words that forcefully appeal to the audience and effectively serve the persuasive purpose | Provides arguments, illustrations, and words that appeal to the audience and serve the persuasive purpose | Provides some support that appeals to the audience and serves the persuasive purpose | Shows little attention to the audience or persuasive purpose |
| Organization | Uses a clear, consistent organizational strategy | Uses a clear organizational strategy with occasional inconsistencies | Uses an inconsistent organizational strategy | Shows a lack of organizational strategy; writing is confusing |
| Elaboration | Provides specific, well-elaborated support for the writer's position | Provides some elaborated support for the writer's position | Provides some support, but with little elaboration | Lacks support |
| Use of Language | Uses transitions to connect ideas smoothly; shows few mechanical errors | Uses some transitions; shows few mechanical errors | Uses few transitions; shows some mechanical errors | Shows little connection between ideas; shows many mechanical errors |

______________________________

______________________________

______________________________

## Publishing and Presenting

10. Write brief instructions for an artist who will illustrate your published essay with a black-and-white drawing. Then, reflect on what you now understand about your topic that you were not aware of before you wrote your essay.

______________________________

______________________________

______________________________

______________________________

______________________________

Name ______________________ Date ______________

# Assessment for Chapter 7: Persuasion: Persuasive Essay

## Test 2

In this test, you will draft a persuasive essay of about three or four paragraphs. Your topic will be an issue you care about that affects students at your school. For instance, your issue might relate to after-school activities, language requirements, or the school newspaper.

**Prewriting**

1. Enter at least one specific school issue for each of the following subject areas. Then, indicate your issue topic and position by completing the sentences below.

   Academic classes: ______________________

   After-school activities: ______________________

   Freedom of expression: ______________________

   I have chosen to write about this issue: ______________________.

   My position on this issue is ______________________.

2. Narrow your topic by completing the chart of Reporter's Questions.

| QUESTION | ANSWER |
|---|---|
| Who? | |
| What? | |
| Where? | |
| When? | |
| Why? | |
| How? | |

3. Explore your issue by filling out the T-chart below. Write your topic at the top. On the left side, list three points or arguments in favor of your position; on the right side, list three points that could be used to argue against your position.

   My Topic: ______________________

| Arguments in Favor | Arguments Against |
|---|---|
| | |

Name ______________________________

**Drafting**

4. Write your thesis statement. Then, circle two types of persuasive techniques from the list below. Finally, use these techniques to write two persuasive sentences that support your thesis statement.

   Thesis statement: ______________________________

   Logical arguments — Appeals to basic values — Appeals to emotions
   Repetition and parallelism — Charged words

   Supporting statements or arguments: ______________________________

5. On a separate sheet of paper, use your notes and information from the graphic organizers to draft your persuasive essay.

**Revising**

6. Find a place in your draft where a transition sentence is needed to clarify the connection between two paragraphs. Mark the place in your draft where you would insert the sentence; then, write the sentence on the lines below. If your essay does not need more transitions, choose an effective connecting sentence from your draft and write it here.

7. Define a complex sentence. Then, combine two short, related sentences from your draft into one complex sentence.

**Editing and Proofreading**

8. Correct the punctuation errors in the paragraph below by inserting colons, dashes, and capital letters as needed. On the lines that follow, write a sentence from your persuasive essay in which you used a colon or a dash. Review your punctuation and correct any errors. If you have not used any colons or dashes in your draft, write *none.*

   Two things upset me above all else exclusiveness and snobbery. I also hate when this happens a girl decides to drop her best friend to fit into a clique. What if this happened to you wouldn't you feel hurt?

Name ________________________________

9. Evaluate your draft based on the criteria in the following rubric. List any changes that you may need to make to improve your essay.

| | Score 4 | Score 3 | Score 2 | Score 1 |
|---|---|---|---|---|
| Audience and Purpose | Provides arguments, illustrations, and words that forcefully appeal to the audience and effectively serve the persuasive purpose | Provides arguments, illustrations, and words that appeal to the audience and serve the persuasive purpose | Provides some support that appeals to the audience and serves the persuasive purpose | Shows little attention to the audience or persuasive purpose |
| Organization | Uses a clear, consistent organizational strategy | Uses a clear organizational strategy with occasional inconsistencies | Uses an inconsistent organizational strategy | Shows a lack of organizational strategy; writing is confusing |
| Elaboration | Provides specific, well-elaborated support for the writer's position | Provides some elaborated support for the writer's position | Provides some support, but with little elaboration | Lacks support |
| Use of Language | Uses transitions to connect ideas smoothly; shows few mechanical errors | Uses some transitions; shows few mechanical errors | Uses few transitions; shows some mechanical errors | Shows little connection between ideas; shows many mechanical errors |

________________________________

________________________________

________________________________

________________________________

**Publishing and Presenting**

10. Name two forms of media or types of publications to which you might submit your essay for publication. Then, explain one way you could strengthen your argument if you were to rewrite your essay.

________________________________

________________________________

________________________________

Name ______________________ Date ______________

# Assessment for Chapter 7: Persuasion: Persuasive Essay
## Test 3

In this test, you will draft a persuasive essay of about three or four paragraphs. Your topic will be an issue in the news that you care about. It might be a local issue, a national issue, or an international issue.

**Prewriting**

1. Enter at least one specific political issue for each of the following subject areas. Then, indicate your issue topic and position by completing the sentences below.

   Local issues: ______________________

   National issues: ______________________

   International issues: ______________________

   I have chosen to write about this issue: ______________________.

   My position on this issue is ______________________.

2. Define your audience and purpose by answering these questions:

   I am writing for the following group of readers: ______________________.

   This is what my readers know about the topic: ______________________

   ______________________.

   Their opinions and prejudices will most likely be: ______________________

   ______________________.

   My readers might be most concerned about these aspects of the issue: ______________________

   ______________________.

3. Gather and develop support for your position by writing one relevant argument for each type of support listed below.

   My position: ______________________

| Logical arguments | |
|---|---|
| Statistics (if known) | |
| Expert opinions (if known) | |
| Personal observations | |

Name ______________________________

**Drafting**

4. Write your thesis statement. Then, circle two types of persuasive techniques from the list below. Finally, use these techniques to write two persuasive sentences that support your thesis statement.

   Thesis statement: ______________________________

   Logical arguments — Appeals to basic values — Appeals to emotions
   Repetition and parallelism — Charged words

   Supporting statements or arguments: ______________________________

5. On a separate sheet of paper, draft your persuasive essay using your notes and information from the graphic organizer.

**Revising**

6. Find a main point in your draft that is supported with only logical arguments, statistics, or expert opinions. Add a compelling image or a dramatic anecdote, and write it here.

7. Find a place in your draft where you used parallel sentence structure to convey parallel ideas. Write the sentences here. If you can't find an example, find two parallel ideas and rewrite the sentences using parallel sentence structure.

**Editing and Proofreading**

8. Review your draft for the correct use of colons and dashes. Indicate any needed corrections on the lines that follow. If you have not used any colons or dashes, find places where you could. Consider using them to combine related sentences.

Name ______________________________

9. Evaluate your draft based on the criteria in the following rubric. List any changes that you may need to make to improve your essay.

| | Score 4 | Score 3 | Score 2 | Score 1 |
|---|---|---|---|---|
| Audience and Purpose | Provides arguments, illustrations, and words that forcefully appeal to the audience and effectively serve the persuasive purpose | Provides arguments, illustrations, and words that appeal to the audience and serve the persuasive purpose | Provides some support that appeals to the audience and serves the persuasive purpose | Shows little attention to the audience or persuasive purpose |
| Organization | Uses a clear, consistent organizational strategy | Uses a clear organizational strategy with occasional inconsistencies | Uses an inconsistent organizational strategy | Shows a lack of organizational strategy; writing is confusing |
| Elaboration | Provides specific, well-elaborated support for the writer's position | Provides some elaborated support for the writer's position | Provides some support, but with little elaboration | Lacks support |
| Use of Language | Uses transitions to connect ideas smoothly; shows few mechanical errors | Uses some transitions; shows few mechanical errors | Uses few transitions; shows some mechanical errors | Shows little connection between ideas; shows many mechanical errors |

______________________________

______________________________

______________________________

______________________________

**Publishing and Presenting**

10. Write a cover letter to a local newspaper, summarizing your essay and explaining why you think it should be published on the editorial page. Then, explain one way you could strengthen your argument if you were to rewrite your essay.

______________________________

______________________________

______________________________

Name ______________________ Date ______________

# Assessment for Chapter 8: Exposition: Comparison-and-Contrast Essay

## Test 1

In this test, you will write a three-paragraph comparison-and-contrast essay. Think about different kinds of pets, and consider how they are alike or different.

**Prewriting**

1. In the spaces, enter two types for each of the animal categories specified. The first line has been filled in for you as an example, but you may feel free to change it. Then, choose one of the pairs to compare and contrast, and complete the sentence that follows.

| | | |
|---|---|---|
| Cats: | tabbies | Persians |
| Dogs: | ______ | ______ |
| Snakes and Amphibians: | ______ | ______ |
| Birds: | ______ | ______ |
| Fish: | ______ | ______ |
| Other: | ______ | ______ |

I will write a comparison-and-contrast essay about ______________

and ______________.

2. Gather details about your topic by completing the Venn diagram. Note differences between the two pets in the outside parts of the circles. Note similarities in the overlapping center section.

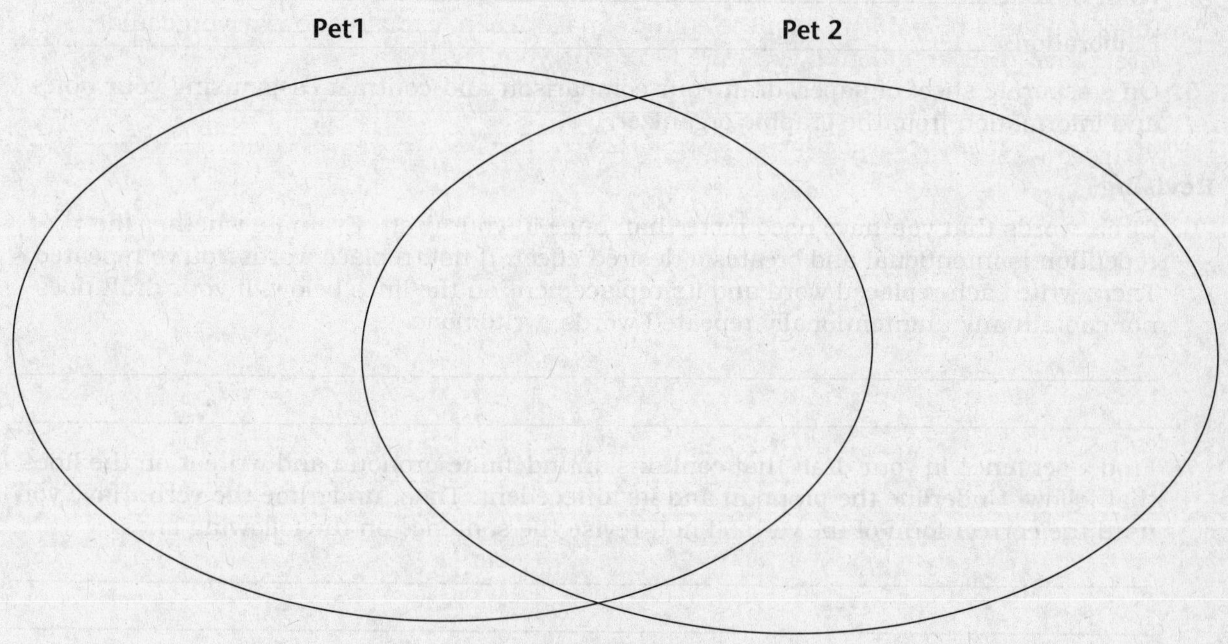

Name ______________________________

**Drafting**

3. Choose how you will organize your essay by circling one of the methods below and completing the accompanying sentences.

   • Block method

   First, I will present all the details about ______________________________.

   Then, I will present all the details about ______________________________.

   • Point-by-Point Method

   First, I will compare and contrast this point about the two pets: ______________________________
   ______________________________.

   Second, I will compare and contrast this point about the two pets: ______________________________
   ______________________________.

   Finally, I will compare and contrast this point about the two pets: ______________________________
   ______________________________.

4. Provide elaboration by identifying the main points you want to make. Then, list some examples, details, or facts that you could use to support your main points.

   Point 1: ______________________________.

   Elaboration: ______________________________.

   Point 2: ______________________________.

   Elaboration: ______________________________.

   Point 3: ______________________________.

   Elaboration: ______________________________.

5. On a separate sheet of paper, draft your comparison-and-contrast essay using your notes and information from the graphic organizer.

**Revising**

6. Circle words that you have used more than once in your draft. Evaluate whether the repetition is intentional and creates a desired effect. If not, replace words you've repeated. Then, write each replaced word and its replacement on the lines below. If your draft does not contain any unintentionally repeated words, write *none.*

   ______________________________

   ______________________________

7. Find a sentence in your draft that contains an indefinite pronoun and write it on the lines that follow. Underline the pronoun and its antecedent. Then, underline the verb. Have you used the correct form of the verb? If not, revise the sentence on the following lines.

   ______________________________

   ______________________________

Name ______________________________

**Editing and Proofreading**

8. Circle each incorrect pronoun in the following sentences, and write the correct pronoun above it. Check your essay for any errors in pronoun-antecedent agreement. On the lines, write any errors you may have made in your draft, and show the correct form. If you have no errors in pronoun-antecedent agreement, write *none.*

   Mothers often say "No" to pets, because she fear the children won't be responsible. A child must prove they is capable of taking care of a pet.

   ______________________________

   ______________________________

9. Evaluate your draft based on the criteria in the following rubric. List any changes you may need to make in your essay.

| | Score 4 | Score 3 | Score 2 | Score 1 |
|---|---|---|---|---|
| Audience and Purpose | Clearly attracts audience interest in the comparison and contrast | Adequately attracts audience interest in the comparison and contrast | Provides a reason for the comparison and contrast | Does not provide a reason for a comparison and contrast |
| Organization | Clearly presents information in a consistent organization best suited to the topic | Presents information using an organization suited to the topic | Chooses an organization not suited to comparison and contrast | Shows a lack of organizational strategy |
| Elaboration | Elaborates ideas with facts, details, or examples; links all information to comparison and contrast | Elaborates most ideas with facts, details, or examples; links most information to comparison and contrast | Does not elaborate all ideas; does not link some details to comparison and contrast | Does not provide facts or examples to support a comparison and contrast |
| Use of Language | Demonstrates excellent sentence and vocabulary variety; includes very few mechanical errors | Demonstrates adequate sentence and vocabulary variety; includes few mechanical errors | Demonstrates repetitive use of sentence structure and vocabulary; includes many mechanical errors | Demonstrates poor use of language; generates confusion; includes many mechanical errors |

______________________________

______________________________

______________________________

______________________________

______________________________

______________________________

**Publishing and Presenting**

10. Name a type of publication that might print a comparison-and-contrast essay about pets. Then, note which writing strategy you found most helpful, and explain why.

______________________________

______________________________

______________________________

Name ______________________ Date ______________

# Assessment for Chapter 8: Exposition: Comparison-and-Contrast Essay
## Test 2

In this test, you will write an essay of at least three paragraphs. Think about a variety of leisure activities and consider how they are alike or different.

**Prewriting**

1. In the spaces, enter two activities for each of the activity types specified. The first line has been filled in for you as an example, but you may feel free to change it. Then, choose any two activities to compare and contrast and complete the sentence that follows. (You may wish to choose activities from different categories, such as one restful and one active.)

| TYPE OF ACTIVITY | | |
|---|---|---|
| Restful | watching TV | reading |
| Active | | |
| Solitary | | |
| Group | | |
| Other | | |

I will compare and contrast ______________ and ______________.

2. Gather details about your topic by completing the Venn diagram. Note differences between your two activity choices in the outside parts of the circles. Note similarities in the overlapping center section.

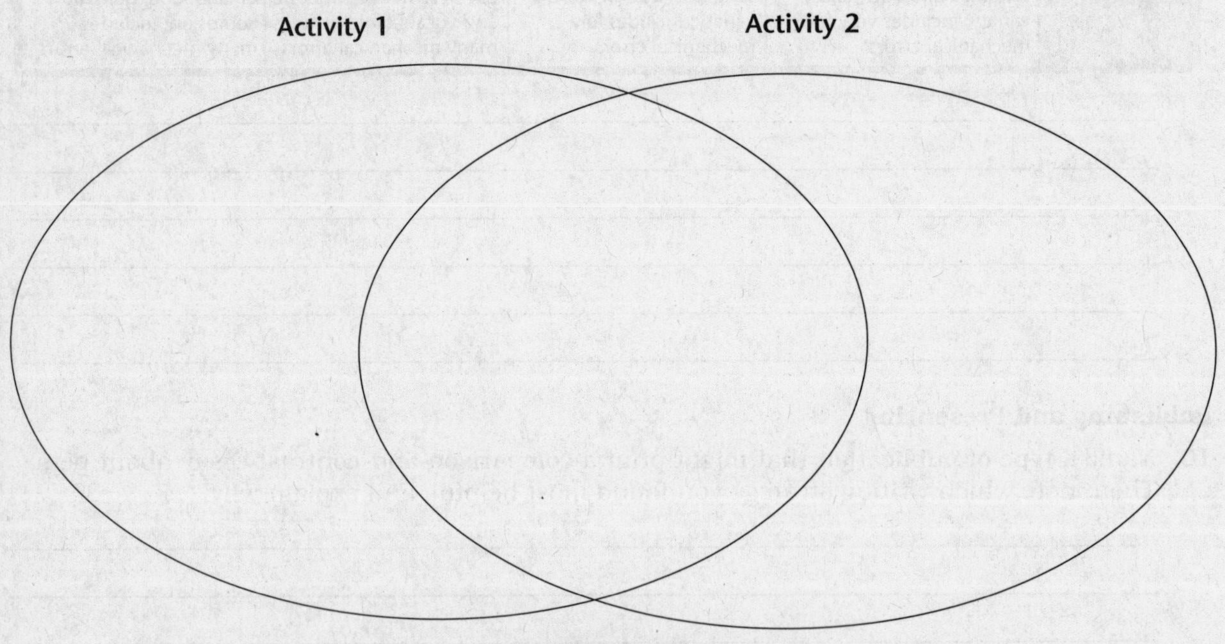


3. Identify the audience and the purpose of your essay, and decide on an appropriate style.

Audience: ______________________

Purpose: ______________________

Style: ______________________

Name ______________________________

**Drafting**

4. Identify the theme of your essay. Then, tell how you will organize your essay by circling one of the methods below and completing the accompanying sentences.

   The theme of my essay is ______________________________.

   - Block Method

   First, I will present all the details about ______________________________.

   Then, I will present all the details about ______________________________.

   - Point-by-Point Method

   First, I will compare and contrast this point about the two activities: ______________________________

   ______________________________.

   Second, I will compare and contrast this point about the two activities: ______________________________

   ______________________________.

   Finally, I will compare and contrast this point about the two activities: ______________________________

   ______________________________.

5. On a separate sheet of paper, draft your comparison-and-contrast essay using your notes and information from the graphic organizer.

**Revising**

6. Find a sentence in your draft that effectively conveys your theme, and write it on the lines below. Then, look in your draft for unfocused details that do not contribute to your theme. Consider deleting details that do not contribute to your theme, or adding details to strengthen your theme. Then, explain on the lines below how you sharpened your theme.

   ______________________________

   ______________________________

   ______________________________

7. Check your paragraphs for the following elements: Topic Sentence, Restatement, Illustration. Then, pick one paragraph, and write a sentence to illustrate each element on the lines below. If you find a paragraph that does not use all three elements, revise it to include these elements, and record your revision on the following lines.

   Topic Sentence—sums up the main idea: ______________________________

   ______________________________.

   Restatement—expanded version of the main idea: ______________________________

   ______________________________.

   Illustration—facts, statistics, or details that support the main idea: ______________________________

   ______________________________.

Name ______________________________

**Editing and Proofreading**

8. Circle each incorrect pronoun in the following paragraph, and write the correct pronoun above it. On the lines that follow, list any errors in pronoun-antecedent agreement you may have made in your essay and show the correct form. If you have no errors in pronoun-antecedent agreement, write *none.*

   People often worry that his or her kids spend too much time on-line. But a parent should realize that their kids learn from computers.

   ______________________________

   ______________________________

9. Evaluate your draft based on the criteria in the following rubric. List any changes that you may need to make in your essay.

| | Score 4 | Score 3 | Score 2 | Score 1 |
|---|---|---|---|---|
| Audience and Purpose | Clearly attracts audience interest in the comparison and contrast | Adequately attracts audience interest in the comparison and contrast | Provides a reason for the comparison and contrast | Does not provide a reason for a comparison and contrast |
| Organization | Clearly presents information in a consistent organization best suited to the topic | Presents information using an organization suited to the topic | Chooses an organization not suited to comparison and contrast | Shows a lack of organizational strategy |
| Elaboration | Elaborates ideas with facts, details, or examples; links all information to comparison and contrast | Elaborates most ideas with facts, details, or examples; links most information to comparison and contrast | Does not elaborate all ideas; does not link some details to comparison and contrast | Does not provide facts or examples to support a comparison and contrast |
| Use of Language | Demonstrates excellent sentence and vocabulary variety; includes very few mechanical errors | Demonstrates adequate sentence and vocabulary variety; includes few mechanical errors | Demonstrates repetitive use of sentence structure and vocabulary; includes many mechanical errors | Demonstrates poor use of language; generates confusion; includes many mechanical errors |

   ______________________________

   ______________________________

   ______________________________

   ______________________________

   ______________________________

   ______________________________

**Publishing And Presenting**

10. Write a title for a class collection of "leisure activity essays." Then, note one new thing you learned about drafting by writing this essay.

   ______________________________

   ______________________________

   ______________________________

 

Name ______________________ Date ______________

# Assessment for Chapter 8: Exposition: Comparison-and-Contrast Essay

## Test 3

In this test, you will write an essay of three or more paragraphs. Think about a variety of careers and consider how they are alike or different.

**Prewriting**

1. In the spaces, enter two careers for each of the career categories specified. The first line has been filled in for you as an example, but you may feel free to change it. Then, choose two careers to compare and contrast and complete the sentence that follows. (You may wish to choose careers from different categories, such as business and technological.)

| TYPE OF CAREER | | |
|---|---|---|
| Athletic | gym teacher | basketball player |
| Artistic | | |
| Technological | | |
| Business | | |
| Other | | |

I will write a comparison-and-contrast essay about __________ and __________.

2. Gather details about your topic by completing the Venn diagram. Note differences between your two career topics in the outside parts of the circles. Note similarities in the overlapping center section. Then, narrow your topic by circling details that highlight what you most want to compare.

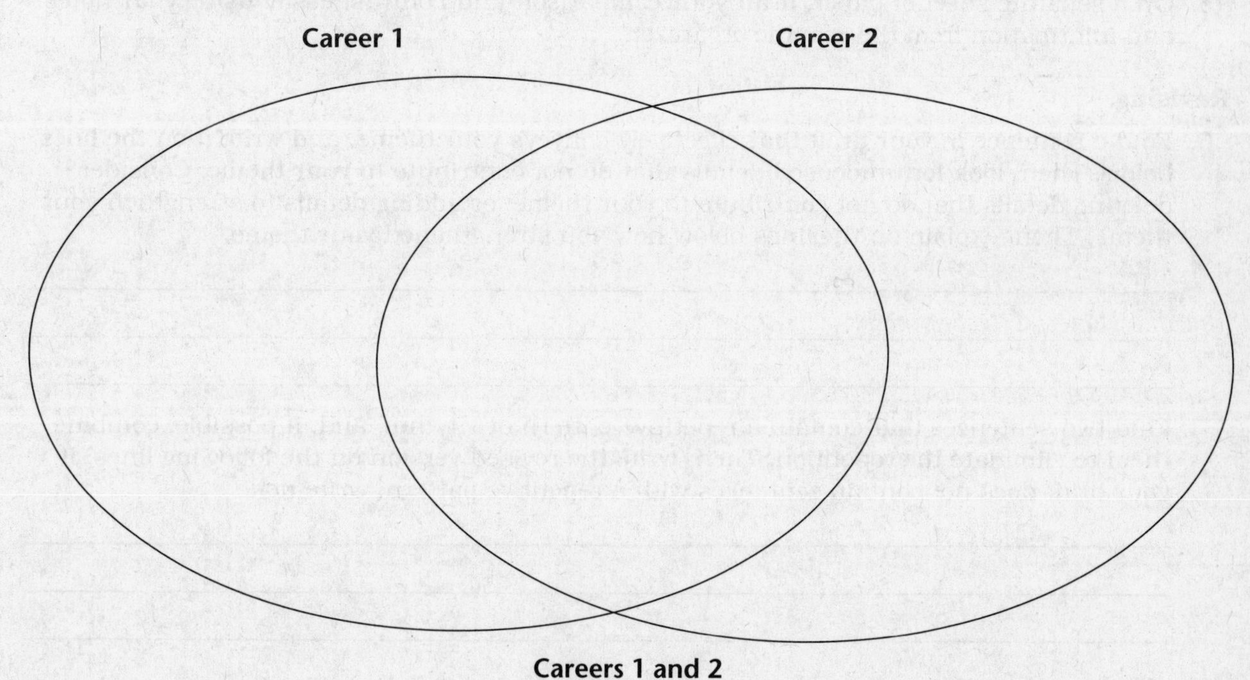

Name ______________________________

**Drafting**

3. Determine a theme for your essay. Then, indicate how you will organize your essay by choosing one of the methods below and completing the accompanying sentences.

   The theme of my essay is ______________________________.

   • Block method

   First, I will present all the details about ______________________________.

   Then, I will present all the details about ______________________________.

   • Point-by-Point Method

   First, I will compare and contrast this point about the two careers: ______________________________.

   Second, I will compare and contrast this point about the two careers: ______________________________.

   Finally, I will compare and contrast this point about the two careers: ______________________________.

4. Use the SEE strategy to elaborate on a paragraph topic by responding to the following steps. Then, use your responses as a guide as you draft your essay.

   State the topic of the paragraph: ______________________________

   Extend the idea by restating it with a different emphasis: ______________________________

   Elaborate on your main idea with examples, explanations, facts, or other details.

   ______________________________

5. On a separate sheet of paper, draft your comparison-and-contrast essay using your notes and information from the graphic organizer.

**Revising**

6. Find a sentence in your draft that effectively conveys your theme, and write it on the lines below. Then, look for unfocused details that do not contribute to your theme. Consider deleting details that do not contribute to your theme, or adding details to strengthen your theme. Then, explain on the lines below how you strengthened your theme.

   ______________________________

   ______________________________

   ______________________________

7. Find two sentences that contain a repetitive pattern or rhythm, and, if possible, combine them to eliminate the repetition. Then, write the revised version on the following lines. If your draft does not contain sentences with a repetitive pattern, write *none*.

   ______________________________

   ______________________________

   ______________________________

   ______________________________

Name ___________________________

**Editing and Proofreading**

8. Find a place in your draft where a pronoun does not agree with its antecedent. Write a revision on the lines provided. If you find no mistakes, write an example from your draft of correct pronoun-antecedent agreement.

_______________________________________________

_______________________________________________

9. Evaluate your draft based on the criteria in the rubric below. List any changes that you may need to make in your essay.

| | Score 4 | Score 3 | Score 2 | Score 1 |
|---|---|---|---|---|
| Audience and Purpose | Clearly attracts audience interest in the comparison and contrast | Adequately attracts audience interest in the comparison and contrast | Provides a reason for the comparison and contrast | Does not provide a reason for a comparison and contrast |
| Organization | Clearly presents information in a consistent organization best suited to the topic | Presents information using an organization suited to the topic | Chooses an organization not suited to comparison and contrast | Shows a lack of organizational strategy |
| Elaboration | Elaborates ideas with facts, details, or examples; links all information to comparison and contrast | Elaborates most ideas with facts, details, or examples; links most information to comparison and contrast | Does not elaborate all ideas; does not link some details to comparison and contrast | Does not provide facts or examples to support a comparison and contrast |
| Use of Language | Demonstrates excellent sentence and vocabulary variety; includes very few mechanical errors | Demonstrates adequate sentence and vocabulary variety; includes few mechanical errors | Demonstrates repetitive use of sentence structure and vocabulary; includes many mechanical errors | Demonstrates poor use of language; generates confusion; includes many mechanical errors |

_______________________________________________

_______________________________________________

_______________________________________________

_______________________________________________

**Publishing and Presenting**

10. Describe where you might publish your essay so that students in your school can read and consider your ideas. Then, note one way in which writing this comparison-and-contrast essay was different from writing other kinds of essays.

_______________________________________________

_______________________________________________

_______________________________________________

Name ______________________________ Date ______________

# Assessment for Chapter 9: Exposition: Cause-and-Effect Essay

## Test 1

In this test, you will draft a cause-and-effect essay of at least three paragraphs. Think about a time when you felt nervous, anxious, or excited, such as before your performance in a school play. Consider the events that led up to that time, including the cause-and-effect relationship between each event.

**Prewriting**

1. Write the topic of your cause-and-effect essay on the following line.

   ______________________________

   Identify the audience for your essay. Based on your answer, what type of language will you use in your essay—formal or informal?

   ______________________________

2. Identify the purpose of your essay. In other words, what do you want your readers to think or do when they finish reading?

   ______________________________

   ______________________________

**Drafting**

3. Choose how you will organize your essay by completing the cause-and-effect graphic organizer that better fits your topic.

| CAUSE → | EFFECT & CAUSE → | EFFECT |
|---|---|---|
| You wake up late for school. | In your hurry to leave, you forget your history book. | In history class, you have trouble following along with the lesson. |

- Chain of Causes and Effects

Cause 1: ______________________________

Effect & Cause: ______________________________

Effect: ______________________________

| CAUSE | | EFFECT |
|---|---|---|
| Sue gets the flu. | → | The drama group has to cancel its performance. |
| Melissa breaks her arm. | | |
| Mandy has to go out of town. | | |

- Many Causes/Single Effect

Cause: ______________________________

Cause: ______________________________

Cause: ______________________________

Effect: ______________________________

Name ______________________________

4. Choose a cause-and-effect relationship that you listed in Question 3. Then, write a sentence that explains the connection between these two events. Use this kind of sentence to elaborate on the connections between causes and effects as you draft your essay.

   ____________________ and ____________________ are connected because __________
   
   ______________________________________________________________________________

5. On a separate sheet of paper, draft your cause-and-effect essay using your notes.

**Revising**

6. Find a topic sentence from a topical paragraph in your draft. Does each sentence in that paragraph support or illustrate this main idea? If not, pick a sentence to revise.

   Topic sentence: ______________________________________________.

   Unrelated sentence: ___________________________________________.

   Revised sentence: _____________________________________________.

7. Find a sentence in your draft in which you have used a perfect tense in combination with other tenses to express a sequence of events. Write the sentence on the line that follows. If the verb tenses do not logically express the sequence of events, revise the sentence.

   ______________________________________________________________________________

**Editing and Proofreading**

8. Underline the prepositional phrase in the following sentence and circle the vivid modifier within it. Then, review your draft for a prepositional phrase that you could strengthen with a vivid modifier. Write the revision on the line provided.

   The small boat rolled dangerously in the churning waves.

   ______________________________________________________________________________

9. Evaluate your draft according to the criteria in the following rubric. List any changes that you may need to make to improve your essay.

| | Score 4 | Score 3 | Score 2 | Score 1 |
|---|---|---|---|---|
| Audience and Purpose | Consistently targets an audience through word choice and details; clearly identifies purpose in introduction | Targets an audience through most word choice and details; identifies purpose in introduction | Misses a target audience by including a wide range of word choice and details; presents no clear purpose | Addresses no specific audience or purpose |
| Organization | Presents a clear, consistent organizational strategy to show cause and effect | Presents a clear organizational strategy with occasional inconsistencies to show cause and effect | Presents an inconsistent organizational strategy; creates illogical presentation of causes and effects | Demonstrates a lack of organizational strategy; creates a confusing presentation |
| Elaboration | Successfully links causes with effects; fully elaborates connections among ideas | Links causes with effects; elaborates connections among most ideas | Links some causes with some effects; elaborates connections among some ideas | Develops and elaborates no links between causes and effects |
| Use of Language | Chooses clear transitions to convey ideas; presents very few mechanical errors | Chooses transitions to convey ideas; presents few mechanical errors | Misses some opportunities for transitions to convey ideas; presents many mechanical errors | Demonstrates poor use of language; presents many mechanical errors |

   ______________________________________________________________________________

   ______________________________________________________________________________

**Publishing and Presenting**

10. Note the biggest challenge you encountered while writing this essay. How did you resolve it?

    ______________________________________________________________________________

    ______________________________________________________________________________

Name ______________________ Date ______________

# Assessment for Chapter 9: Exposition: Cause-and-Effect Essay

## Test 2

In this test, you will draft a cause-and-effect essay of at least three paragraphs. Think about a time when you felt especially happy or received praise for something you did well, such as winning an essay contest. Consider the events that led up to that time, including the cause-and-effect relationship between each event.

**Prewriting**

1. Write the topic of your cause-and-effect essay on the line below.

   ______________________

   Identify the audience for your essay. Based on your answer, what type of language will you use in your essay—formal or informal?

   ______________________

   ______________________

2. Identify the purpose of your essay by answering the following questions. In other words, what do you want your readers to think or do when they finish reading?

   ______________________

   ______________________

**Drafting**

3. Choose how you will organize your essay by completing the cause-and-effect graphic organizer that better fits your topic.

| CAUSE → | EFFECT & CAUSE → | EFFECT |
|---|---|---|
| You wake up late for school. | In your hurry to leave, you forget your history book. | In history class, you have trouble following along with the lesson. |

• Chain of Causes and Effects

Cause 1: ______________________

Effect & Cause: ______________________

Effect: ______________________

| CAUSE | | EFFECT |
|---|---|---|
| Sue gets the flu. | → | The drama group has to cancel its performance. |
| Melissa breaks her arm. | | |
| Mandy has to go out of town. | | |

• Many Causes/Single Effect

Cause: ______________________

Cause: ______________________

Cause: ______________________

Effect: ______________________

Name ___________________________________________

4. Choose a cause-and-effect relationship that you listed in Question 3. Then, write a sentence that explains the connection between these two events. Use this kind of sentence to elaborate on the connections between causes and effects as you draft your essay.

   ______________ and ______________ are connected because: ______________

   ______________________________________________________________________.

5. On a separate sheet of paper, draft a cause-and-effect essay using your notes and information from the graphic organizer.

**Revising**

6. Find a topic sentence from a topical paragraph in your draft. Then, make sure each sentence in that paragraph supports or illustrates this main idea. Revise any sentence that does not support the main idea.

   Topic sentence: ______________________________________________________

   ______________________________________________________________________.

   Revised supporting sentence: __________________________________________

   ______________________________________________________________________.

7. Find a sentence in your draft in which you have used the perfect tense in combination with other tenses to express a sequence of events. Write the sentence on the lines that follow. If the verb tenses do not logically express the sequence of events, revise the sentence.

   ______________________________________________________________________

   ______________________________________________________________________

   ______________________________________________________________________

   ______________________________________________________________________

**Editing and Proofreading**

8. Underline the prepositional phrase in the following sentence and circle the vivid modifier. Then, review your draft for a prepositional phrase that you could strengthen with a vivid modifier. Write the revision on the lines that follow.

   The sunset sent fiery streaks across the shimmering lake.

   ______________________________________________________________________

   ______________________________________________________________________

   ______________________________________________________________________

   ______________________________________________________________________

Name ______________________________

9. Evaluate your draft according to the criteria in the following rubric. List any changes that you may need to make to improve your essay.

| | Score 4 | Score 3 | Score 2 | Score 1 |
|---|---|---|---|---|
| Audience and Purpose | Consistently targets an audience through word choice and details; clearly identifies purpose in introduction | Targets an audience through most word choice and details; identifies purpose in introduction | Misses a target audience by including a wide range of word choice and details; presents no clear purpose | Addresses no specific audience or purpose |
| Organization | Presents a clear, consistent organizational strategy to show cause and effect | Presents a clear organizational strategy with occasional inconsistencies to show cause and effect | Presents an inconsistent organizational strategy; creates illogical presentation of causes and effects | Demonstrates a lack of organizational strategy; creates a confusing presentation |
| Elaboration | Successfully links causes with effects; fully elaborates connections among ideas | Links causes with effects; elaborates connections among most ideas | Links some causes with some effects; elaborates connections among some ideas | Develops and elaborates no links between causes and effects |
| Use of Language | Chooses clear transitions to convey ideas; presents very few mechanical errors | Chooses transitions to convey ideas; presents few mechanical errors | Misses some opportunities for transitions to convey ideas; presents many mechanical errors | Demonstrates poor use of language; presents many mechanical errors |

______________________________

______________________________

______________________________

______________________________

______________________________

**Publishing and Presenting**

10. Explain how publishing your essay on-line might help you reach your intended audience. On what type of Web site might you publish it?

______________________________

______________________________

______________________________

Then, describe the most helpful thing you learned about writing a cause-and-effect essay.

______________________________

______________________________

Name ______________________________ Date ______________

# Assessment for Chapter 9: Exposition: Cause-and-Effect Essay

## Test 3

In this test, you will draft a cause-and-effect essay of at least three paragraphs. Think about a time that represented a turning point in your life. Consider the events that led up to that time, including the cause-and-effect relationship between each event.

**Prewriting**

1. Write your topic on the following line. Then, narrow your topic by answering the Classical Invention questions below. Finally, write a statement that summarizes the causes and effects related to your topic.

   Topic: ______________________________

   a) In what group or category does your topic belong?

   ______________________________

   b) What causes are involved with this topic?

   ______________________________

   c) What effects are involved with this topic?

   ______________________________

   d) What came before this event?

   ______________________________

   e) What might come (or came) after this event?

   ______________________________

   STATEMENT: ______________________________

   ______________________________

   ______________________________.

2. Identify your audience and describe the kind of language and details that will appeal to them.

   ______________________________

   ______________________________

   ______________________________

   ______________________________

   ______________________________

Name ______________________________

**Drafting**

3. Choose an organization for your essay by completing the cause-and-effect graphic organizer that better fits your topic.

CAUSE → EFFECT & CAUSE → EFFECT

You wake up late for school. | In your hurry to leave, you forget your history book. | In history class, you have trouble following along with the lesson.

• Chain of Causes and Effects

Cause 1: ______________________________

Effect & Cause: ______________________________

Effect: ______________________________

Sue gets the flu.
CAUSE

Melissa breaks her arm.
CAUSE

Mandy has to go out of town.
CAUSE

→ The drama group has to cancel its performance.
EFFECT

• Many Causes/Single Effect

Cause: ______________________________

Cause: ______________________________

Cause: ______________________________

Effect: ______________________________

4. Choose a cause-and-effect relationship that you listed in Question 3. Then, write a sentence that explains the connection between these two events. As you draft your essay, use this kind of sentence to elaborate on the connections between causes and effects.

______________ and ______________ are connected because ______________
______________________________.

5. On a separate sheet of paper, draft your cause-and-effect essay using your notes and information from the graphic organizer.

**Revising**

6. Find a topic sentence from a topical paragraph in your draft. Then, make sure each sentence in that paragraph supports or illustrates this main idea. Revise any sentence that does not support the main idea.

a) Topic sentence: ______________________________
______________________________.

b) Unrelated sentence: ______________________________
______________________________.

c) Revised sentence: ______________________________
______________________________.

Name ____________________

7. Find a sentence in your draft in which you have used the perfect tense in combination with other tenses to express a sequence of events. Write the sentence on the lines that follow. If the verb tenses do not logically express the sequence of events, revise the sentence.

____________________

____________________

**Editing and Proofreading**

8. Underline the prepositional phrase in the following sentence and circle the vivid modifier within it. Then, review your draft for prepositional phrases and choose one that you could strengthen by adding a vivid modifier. Write the revision on the lines provided.

   The film crew caused excitement in the sleepy village.

____________________

____________________

9. Evaluate your draft according to the criteria in the following rubric. List any changes that you may need to make to improve your essay.

| | Score 4 | Score 3 | Score 2 | Score 1 |
|---|---|---|---|---|
| Audience and Purpose | Consistently targets an audience through word choice and details; clearly identifies purpose in introduction | Targets an audience through most word choice and details; identifies purpose in introduction | Misses a target audience by including a wide range of word choice and details; presents no clear purpose | Addresses no specific audience or purpose |
| Organization | Presents a clear, consistent organizational strategy to show cause and effect | Presents a clear organizational strategy with occasional inconsistencies to show cause and effect | Presents an inconsistent organizational strategy; creates illogical presentation of causes and effects | Demonstrates a lack of organizational strategy; creates a confusing presentation |
| Elaboration | Successfully links causes with effects; fully elaborates connections among ideas | Links causes with effects; elaborates connections among most ideas | Links some causes with some effects; elaborates connections among some ideas | Develops and elaborates no links between causes and effects |
| Use of Language | Chooses clear transitions to convey ideas; presents very few mechanical errors | Chooses transitions to convey ideas; presents few mechanical errors | Misses some opportunities for transitions to convey ideas; presents many mechanical errors | Demonstrates poor use of language; presents many mechanical errors |

____________________

____________________

____________________

**Publishing and Presenting**

10. Write a summary of an anthology that might contain your essay and others with a similar theme. Then, note one thing you learned about conveying relationships between events by writing this essay.

____________________

____________________

____________________

Name ______________________ Date ____________

# Assessment for Chapter 10: Exposition: How-to Essay

## Test 1

In this test, you will write a how-to essay about a food you know how to prepare.

**Prewriting**

1. Brainstorm about your topic by writing one or two details for each category in the web below. Then, complete the sentence that follows.

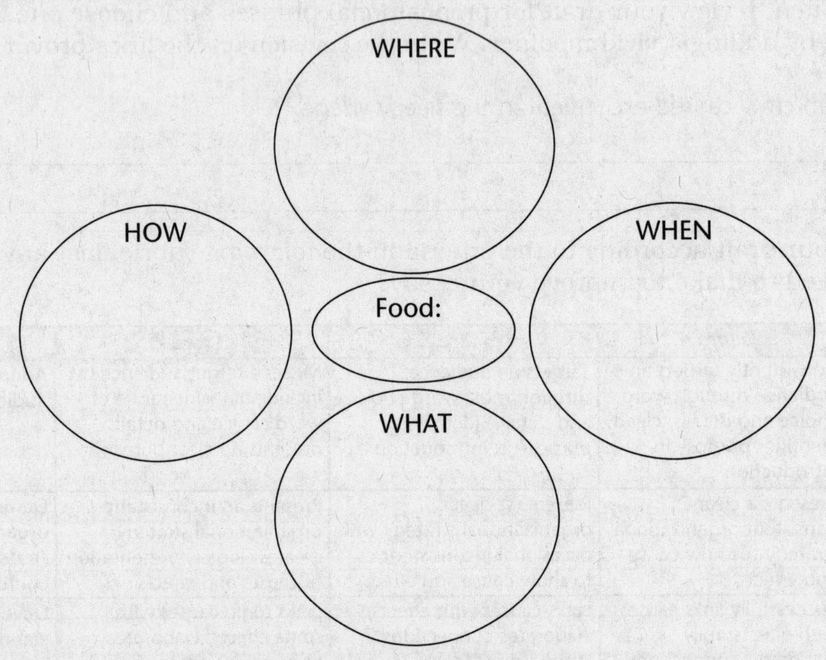


I have chosen to write a how-to essay about preparing ______________________.

2. Prepare to address the needs of your audience by completing the following audience profile questions.

What is the age of my audience? ______________________

How much does my audience know about my topic? ______________________

______________________

What skills do my readers have that relate to my topic? ______________________

______________________

3. Describe a visual aid that could help your readers understand your essay.

______________________

______________________

______________________

Name ______________________________

## Drafting

4. To help you organize your material and determine the format of your essay, list the following information:

   a) Equipment needed ______________________________

   ______________________________.

   b) Ingredients ______________________________

   ______________________________.

   c) Steps, from beginning to end, for preparing the food ______________________________

   ______________________________

   ______________________________.

5. On a separate sheet of paper, draft your how-to essay using your notes and information from the graphic organizer.

## Revising

6. Review your essay, checking for main steps and substeps. Is there anything you could do to make the steps clearer? If so, explain the changes you wish to make on the lines below.

   ______________________________

   ______________________________

7. Find a step that you could make more informative by adding an adverb clause or adverb phrase. Fix the step, and then write the new version. If you have already used adverb clauses or phrases to make your steps informative, write one example below.

   ______________________________

   ______________________________

## Editing and Proofreading

8. In the following sentence, add commas where needed to separate items in a series. Then, review your draft for incorrect punctuation of items in a series. Indicate your corrections on the lines below. If your draft does not contain this type of error, write *none*.

   Some recipes—such as brownies scrambled eggs and pasta—are easy for a beginner to tackle.

   ______________________________

   ______________________________

Name ______________________________

9. Evaluate your draft according to the criteria in the following rubric. List any changes that you may need to make to improve your essay.

| | Score 4 | Score 3 | Score 2 | Score 1 |
|---|---|---|---|---|
| Audience and Purpose | Clearly focuses on procedures leading to a well-defined end | Focuses on procedures leading to a well-defined end | Includes procedures related to an end, but presents some vaguely | Includes only vague descriptions of procedures and results |
| Organization | Gives instructions in logical order; subdivides complex actions into steps | Gives instructions in logical order; subdivides some complex actions into steps | For the most part, gives instructions in logical order | Gives instructions in a scattered, disorganized manner |
| Elaboration | Provides appropriate amount of detail; gives needed explanations | Provides appropriate amount of detail; gives some explanations | Provides some detail; gives few explanations | Provides few details; gives few or no explanations |
| Use of Language | Shows overall clarity and fluency; uses transitions effectively; contains few mechanical errors | Shows some sentence variety; uses some transitions; includes few mechanical errors | Uses awkward or overly simple sentence structures; contains many mechanical errors | Contains incomplete thoughts and confusing mechanical errors |

______________________________

______________________________

______________________________

______________________________

______________________________

**Publishing and Presenting**

10. List one way that you might share your how-to essay with others. Then, note one new thing you learned about writing by completing this assignment.

______________________________

______________________________

______________________________

Name ______________________ Date ______________

# Assessment for Chapter 10: Exposition: How-to Essay
## Test 2

In this test, you will write a how-to essay about something you can paint, decorate, or build.

**Prewriting**

1. Brainstorm about your topic by writing one or two details for each category in the following web. Then, complete the sentences that follow.

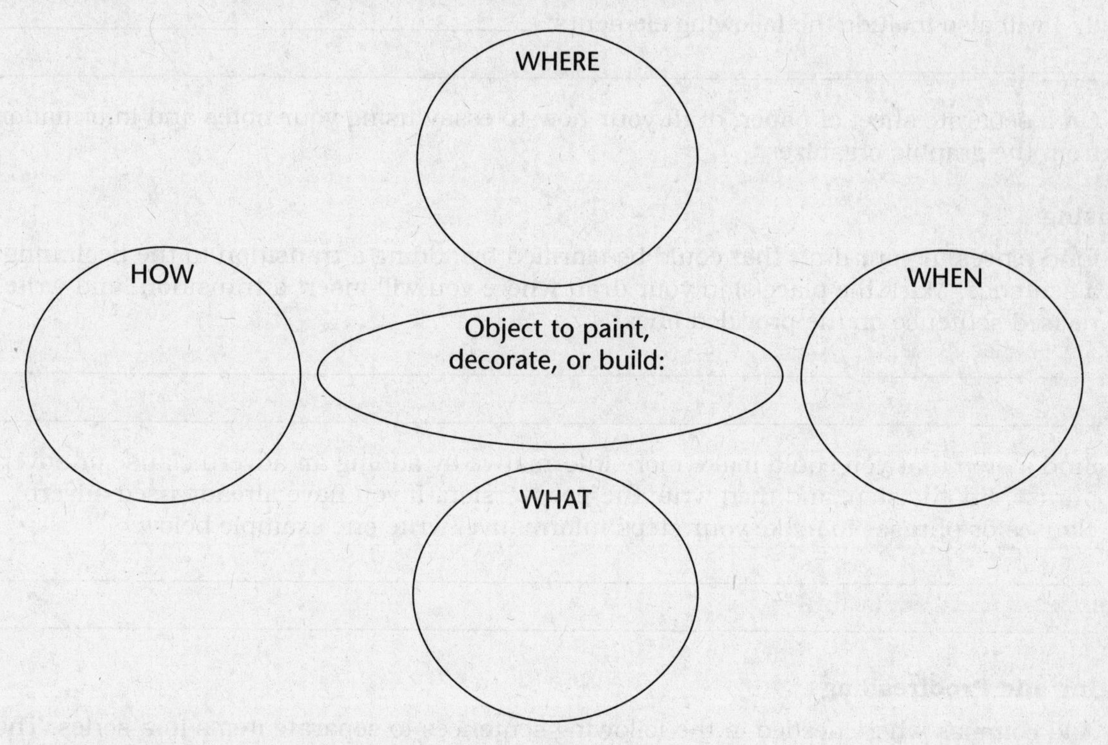


   a) I have chosen to write a how-to essay about ______________________.

   b) I will narrow the focus of my essay by limiting it to ______________________.

2. Prepare to address the needs of your audience by filling out the following audience profile questions.

   What is the age of my audience? ______________________

   How much does my audience know about my topic? ______________________

   What skills do my readers have that relate to my topic? ______________________

   ______________________

3. Describe a visual aid that could help your readers understand your essay. Write labels or a caption to accompany the visual aid.

   ______________________

   ______________________

   ______________________

Name ______________________________

## Drafting

4. Shape your essay by planning your organization and format.

   a) My introductory paragraph will contain the following: ______________________________
   ______________________________________________.

   b) I will use this method to organize and explain the steps: ______________________.

   c) My closing paragraph will contain the following: ______________________________
   ______________________________________________.

   d) I will also include the following elements: ______________________________
   ______________________________________________.

5. On a separate sheet of paper, draft your how-to essay using your notes and information from the graphic organizer.

## Revising

6. Find places in your draft that could be clarified by adding a transition to the beginning of a sentence. Mark the place(s) in your draft where you will insert a transition, and write a revised sentence on the provided lines.

   ______________________________________________

   ______________________________________________

7. Find a step that you could make more informative by adding an adverb clause or adverb phrase. Fix the step, and then write the new version. If you have already used adverb clauses or phrases to make your steps informative, write one example below.

   ______________________________________________

   ______________________________________________

## Editing and Proofreading

8. Add commas where needed in the following sentences to separate items in a series. Then, review your draft for incorrect usage of commas to separate items in a series. Make any corrections on the lines provided. If your draft does not contain this type of error, write *none.*

   Some kinds of finishes are wax shellac and polyurethane. Spray finishes are best for such small pieces as pencil cups jewelry boxes and doll furniture.

   ______________________________________________

   ______________________________________________

Name ______________________________

9. Evaluate your draft according to the criteria in the following rubric. List any changes that you may need to make to improve your essay.

| | Score 4 | Score 3 | Score 2 | Score 1 |
|---|---|---|---|---|
| Audience and Purpose | Clearly focuses on procedures leading to a well-defined end | Focuses on procedures leading to a well-defined end | Includes procedures related to an end, but presents some vaguely | Includes only vague descriptions of procedures and results |
| Organization | Gives instructions in logical order; subdivides complex actions into steps | Gives instructions in logical order; subdivides some complex actions into steps | For the most part, gives instructions in logical order | Gives instructions in a scattered, disorganized manner |
| Elaboration | Provides appropriate amount of detail; gives needed explanations | Provides appropriate amount of detail; gives some explanations | Provides some detail; gives few explanations | Provides few details; gives few or no explanations |
| Use of Language | Shows overall clarity and fluency; uses transitions effectively; contains few mechanical errors | Shows some sentence variety; uses some transitions; includes few mechanical errors | Uses awkward or overly simple sentence structures; contains many mechanical errors | Contains incomplete thoughts and confusing mechanical errors |

______________________________

______________________________

______________________________

______________________________

______________________________

**Publishing and Presenting**

10. Think of a group to which you could demonstrate the activity described in your how-to essay. Then, note how doing a demonstration might help you improve your essay.

______________________________

______________________________

______________________________

Name ______________________ Date ______________

# Assessment for Chapter 10: Exposition: How-to Essay

## Test 3

In this test, you will write a how-to essay about something you've learned to do or make in the past year.

**Prewriting**

1. Brainstorm about your topic by writing one or more details for each category in the following web. Then, complete the sentences that follow.

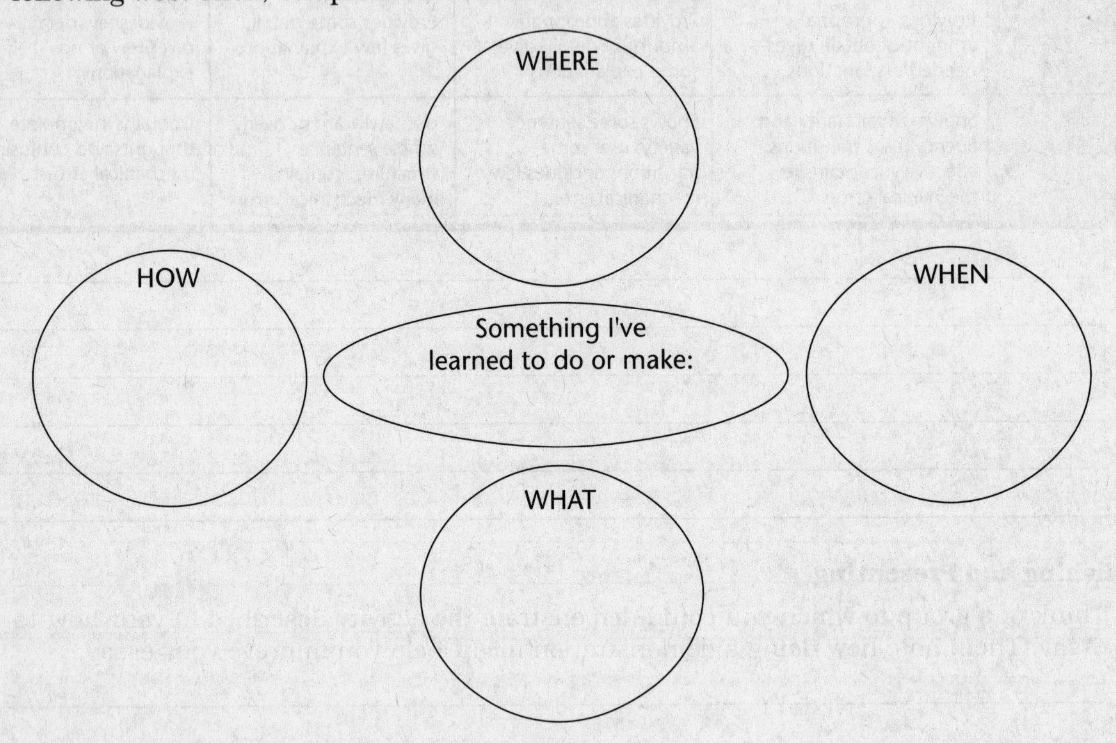


a) I have chosen to write a how-to essay about ______________________.

b) I will narrow the focus of my essay by limiting it to ______________________.

2. Prepare to address the needs of your audience by filling out the following audience profile questions.
   - What is the age of my audience? ______________
   - How much does my audience know about my topic? ______________
   - What skills do my readers have that relate to my topic? ______________
   - Now describe one way this profile will help you determine how to focus your essay.

   ______________________________________________

3. Describe one or more visual aids that could help your readers understand your essay. Write labels or a caption to accompany the visual aid(s).

   ______________________________________________

   ______________________________________________

   ______________________________________________

 

Name ____________________

**Drafting**

4. Shape your essay by planning your organization and format.
   a) My introductory paragraph will contain the following: ____________________
   ____________________.
   b) I will use this method to organize and explain the steps: ____________________.
   c) My closing paragraph will contain the following: ____________________
   ____________________.
   d) I will also include the following elements: ____________________
   ____________________.
5. On a separate sheet of paper, draft your how-to essay using your notes and information from the graphic organizer.

**Revising**

6. Find words in your draft that you repeat often. Then, choose a sentence that needs revision to avoid unnecessary repetition. Revise it and write the new version on the lines provided.
   ____________________
   ____________________
7. Find a step or description that could be made more informative by adding an adverb clause or adverb phrase. Fix the step or description, and then write the new version. If you have already used adverb clauses or phrases to make your writing informative, write one example below.
   ____________________
   ____________________

**Editing and Proofreading**

8. Review your draft for proper usage of commas and semicolons to separate items in a series. Find a sentence that needs correction, and write the sentence and your revision on the lines that follow.
   ____________________
   ____________________

Name ______________________________

9. Evaluate your draft according to the criteria in the following rubric. List any changes that you may need to make to improve your essay.

| | Score 4 | Score 3 | Score 2 | Score 1 |
|---|---|---|---|---|
| Audience and Purpose | Clearly focuses on procedures leading to a well-defined end | Focuses on procedures leading to a well-defined end | Includes procedures related to an end, but presents some vaguely | Includes only vague descriptions of procedures and results |
| Organization | Gives instructions in logical order; subdivides complex actions into steps | Gives instructions in logical order; subdivides some complex actions into steps | For the most part, gives instructions in logical order | Gives instructions in a scattered, disorganized manner |
| Elaboration | Provides appropriate amount of detail; gives needed explanations | Provides appropriate amount of detail; gives some explanations | Provides some detail; gives few explanations | Provides few details; gives few or no explanations |
| Use of Language | Shows overall clarity and fluency; uses transitions effectively; contains few mechanical errors | Shows some sentence variety; uses some transitions; includes few mechanical errors | Uses awkward or overly simple sentence structures; contains many mechanical errors | Contains incomplete thoughts and confusing mechanical errors |

______________________________

______________________________

______________________________

______________________________

______________________________

## Publishing and Presenting

10. Describe a multimedia display that would enhance your how-to essay. Then, explain how organization can affect the clarity of a how-to essay.

______________________________

______________________________

______________________________

Name ______________________________ Date ______________

# Assessment for Chapter 11: Research: Research Report

## Test 1

In this test, you'll use the work of Marc, a student like you, who is writing a research paper about the moons of Jupiter.

**Prewriting**

Marc used a variety of sources. Here are some note cards he made:

**Note Card #1**

Jupiter itself is a giant planet made of gas. Its diameter is 88,700 miles across, compared to Earth's diameter of 7,926 miles. Its volume, or total weight is 1,312 times that of Earth. It is so big that 1,300 Earths could fit inside it.

Our Solar System, p.3

**Note Card #2**

"Io, the innermost, is slightly larger than the Moon. It has a red, volcanic surface"

1000 Facts About Space, p.25

**Note Card #3**

Jupiter has 16 moons. The largest are Callisto, Ganymede, Io, and Europa. They travel in different directions.

http//:www.sel.co.kr/tech/Demo/player/jupiter/info.html

**Note Card #4**

Ganymede is larger than Mercury; Callisto is bigger than Earth's Moon.

"Moons and Rings, Companions to the Planets"

1. Which note card contains a direct quotation? How do you know?

_______________________________________________

_______________________________________________

2. What information did Marc forget to include on Note Card #4?

_______________________________________________

3. What is the source for Note Card #3?

_______________________________________________

Name ______________________________

**Drafting**

4. Marc is developing his thesis statement for his report on Jupiter's moons and has written four possibilities. Circle the one you think is best. On the lines provided, explain your choice.

   a) One of Jupiter's moons, Europa, is covered in ice.

   b) Jupiter is surrounded by sixteen natural satellites, or moons.

   c) The most interesting fact about Jupiter is its size.

   d) I am going to write about the moons of Jupiter.

   ______________________________

   ______________________________

5. Marc must now group his note cards by category. Circle the method of organization that will better suit his topic and explain your choice on the lines provided.

   CHRONOLOGICAL ORDER　　　　ORDERING BY TYPE

   ______________________________

   ______________________________

Here are the main headings of Marc's outline. Use the outline and the note cards on the previous page to answer questions 6–8.

I. Introduction
II. Jupiter Basics
III. Natural Satellites
IV. Four Largest Moons
V. Conclusion

6. Which section does Note Card #1 support? ______________

7. Which section does Note Card #2 support? ______________

8. Which section does Note Card #3 support? ______________

**Revising**

Read the following introductory paragraph of Marc's draft. Use it to answer questions 9–11 below.

> Imagine shifting into hyperspeed and traveling to the planet Jupiter. We shut down the warp drive. Then we slide into orbit around the planet. The first thing we notice is that we're not alone. At least sixteen other objects are circling Jupiter with us. *(Beasant, 25)*

9. Using the information in the note below, think of an opening sentence for Marc's second paragraph; be sure it is clearly connected to the introductory paragraph. Write the new sentence on the lines provided, and circle the word or phrase that acts as the transition.

   Detail: The closest group of moons orbits one way, with the next group traveling in the opposite direction.

   ______________________________

   ______________________________

Name ______________________________

Continue to refer to Marc's introductory paragraph as you answer the following question.

10. A peer reviewer tells Marc that he needs to vary his sentence structure. How could he do this in his first paragraph? Revise one of his sentences and write it here.

11. What does *(Beasant, 25)* mean in the introductory paragraph? Be specific.

**Editing and Proofreading**

Below are two entries from the list of works Marc cited. Use them to answer questions 12 and 13.

Simon, Seymour. Our Solar System. New York: Morrow Junior Books, 1992.

Beasant, Pam. 1000 Facts About Space. New York: Kingfisher Books.

12. Write the last names of the authors of these two entries in the order they should appear on Marc's final list of works cited.

13. One of the entries contains two mistakes. Specify them on the lines below.

**Publishing and Presenting**

14. Marc is writing his research paper for an audience of eight- to ten-year-olds. Name one place he might publish his work in order to reach this audience.

15. Name one visual aid that Marc could include to enhance his research paper.

Name ______________________ Date ______________

# Assessment for Chapter 11: Research: Research Report

## Test 2

In this test, you'll use the work of Katy, a student like yourself, who is writing a research paper about the baseball player Babe Ruth.

**Prewriting**

A biography can encompass a subject's entire lifetime, so Katy knew she must narrow her topic. Name three Classical Invention questions she might have asked herself in order to focus her general topic: Babe Ruth.

1. ______________________

2. ______________________

3. ______________________

Katy used a variety of sources. Below are some note cards she made:

**Note Card #1**

In 2,503 major league games, and 8,399 times at bat, Babe Ruth made 2,873 hits, scored 2,174 runs, drove in 2,209 runs, and had a life time batting average of .343.

100 Greatest Baseball Heroes, p.6

**Note Card #2**

Babe Ruth said,
"Gee, it's lonesome in the outfield. It's hard to keep awake with nothing to do."

http://baseball-almanac. com/players/p_bruth

**Note Card #3**

When Ruth died, he was still seen as baseball's greatest hero. His body lay in state in Yankee Stadium, and more than 200,000 fans paid him tribute there.

Sultan of Swat, p.97

**Note Card #4**

During the Depression, "What did the Babe do today?" was a question asked each day all over America.

Babe Ruth and Hank Aaron

4. Which note card contains a direct quotation? How can you tell?

______________________

______________________

5. What key information is not included on Note Card #4?

______________________

6. Do Katy's note cards reflect a variety of sources? Explain.

______________________

 

Name ______________________________

**Drafting**

7. Katy is trying to develop her thesis statement and has written four possibilities. Circle the one you think is best. On the lines below, explain your choice.

   a) Babe Ruth went to a reform school.
   b) The Babe began with the Boston Red Sox, but spent most of his career with the New York Yankees.
   c) Babe Ruth's most important contribution was the inspiration he provided to a nation whose spirit was weakened by the Great Depression.
   d) During May of 1920, the Babe slammed 12 home runs.

   ______________________________

   ______________________________

The main sections of Katy's outline follow. Use this outline and the note cards on the previous page to answer questions 8–10.

I. Introduction
II. Babe's Early Years
III. A Major League Smash
IV. The Nation's Hero
V. Conclusion

8. Which section does Note Card #1 support? ______________

9. Which section does Note Card #3 support? ______________

10. Which section does Note Card #4 support? ______________

**Revising**

The introductory paragraph of Katy's draft follows. Use it to answer question 11.

Most people remember Babe Ruth as home run hero. He was a man who slugged 714 home runs. But those who remember him recall that he was more than a baseball champion. When he was young, he went to reform school. Perhaps Ruth's greatest contribution was as a champion of the spirit. To a nation weary and downtrodden by the Great Depression, he gave people back a sense of hope and the possibility of victory.

11. a) What is the focus of Katy's paragraph?

    ______________________________

    b) Name one detail from the paragraph that relates to the focus.

    ______________________________

    c) Name one detail that does not relate to the focus.

    ______________________________

12. A peer reviewer tells Katy that the first two sentences of her introductory paragraph are short and choppy. How can she combine these into one longer sentence? Write the revised sentence on the lines that follow.

    ______________________________

    ______________________________

Name ______________________________

**Editing and Proofreading**

Three entries from Katy's list of works cited follow. Use them to answer question 13.

a) Macht, Norman L. <u>Baseball Legends: Babe Ruth</u>. New York: Chelsea House, 1991.
b) Nicholson, Lois P. Babe Ruth: Sultan of Swat. Woodbury, CT: Goodwood Press.
c) Sanford, William R. <u>Sport Immortals: Babe Ruth.</u> New York: MacMillan Publishing, 1992.

13. Which entry contains mistakes? ____________ List the mistakes on the following lines.

______________________________

______________________________

**Publishing and Presenting**

14. Katy is writing her research paper for an audience of sports enthusiasts. Suggest one place she might publish her work in order to reach this audience.

______________________________

15. Name one visual aid that Katy could include to enhance her research paper.

______________________________

 

Name ______________________ Date __________

# Assessment for Chapter 11: Research: Research Report

## Test 3

In this test you'll use the work of Ashley, a student like yourself, who is writing a research paper on the origin of the dog.

**Prewriting**

Help Ashley narrow her topic by naming three Classical Invention questions she might ask herself.

1. ______________________
2. ______________________
3. ______________________

Ashley used a variety of sources. Below are some note cards she made:

**Note Card #1**

Today's domestic dogs are the product of centuries of selective breeding.

www.science.com/features/dogs

**Note Card #2**

If a Pekingese dog were stranded in the woods, it might have a hard time surviving.

Understanding Man's Best Friend, p.105

**Note Card #3**

Researchers have based their ideas about the origin of the domestic dog on archaeological evidence.

Science News, 6/28/1997

**Note Card #4**

Scientists think wolves and dogs developed from a Miacis, a weasel-like animal that lived 40 million years ago.

World Book, Volume 5, p. 230

4. Which note card does not support Ashley's intended focus: the origin of the dog? Explain your answer.

______________________

______________________

5. What information did Ashley forget to include on Note Card #3?

______________________

6. Explain whether Ashley's note cards reflect a variety of sources. Then, explain why it is important to use a variety of sources when writing a research report.

______________________

______________________

Name ______________________________

## Drafting

7. Ashley is trying to develop her thesis statement and has written four possibilities. Circle the one you think is best. On the lines that follow, explain your choice.

   a) One of the oldest present-day dog breeds, the Saluki, originated in the Middle East around 7,000 B.C.
   b) Although dog breeds vary widely, scientists believe they all have a common ancestor: the wolf.
   c) Humans first began to domesticate wolves by adopting the pups and training them.
   d) Wolves live in packs with a leadership structure and rules of behavior.

______________________________

______________________________

Below are the main sections of Ashley's outline. Use the outline and the note cards on the previous page to answer questions 8–10.

I. Introduction
II. How Scientists Have Studied Dog Origins
III. From Wolf Pup to Domesticated Dog
IV. Other Distant Relatives
V. Conclusion

8. Which section does Note Card #1 support? ______________________________
9. Which section does Note Card #3 support? ______________________________
10. Which section does Note Card #4 support? ______________________________

## Revising

The introductory paragraph of Ashley's draft follows. Use it to answer questions 11–12.

What do a pug and a Great Dane have in common? Both of these dogs are descended from the wolf. There are also true wild dogs living in areas of Australia, Asia, and Africa. It may seem impossible that a Chihuahua and a German Shepherd have a common ancestor. But archaeologists and other scientists have gathered enough evidence to prove that the family trees of all the breeds have the same roots.

11. a) State the focus of Ashley's paragraph.

    ______________________________

    b) Name one detail from the paragraph that relates to the focus.

    ______________________________

    c) Name one detail that does not relate to the focus.

    ______________________________

12. Two sentences from Section II of Ashley's report follow:

    "Scientists have studied teeth fossils. They have classified the dog as part of the family *Canidae*."

    A peer reviewer suggests that Ashley revise the above to form one sentence, using a participial phrase to show the relationship between the two ideas. Suggest a revision.

    ______________________________

    ______________________________

Name ___________________________________

**Editing and Proofreading**

Three entries from Ashley's list of works cited follow. Use them to answer question 13.

a) Fogle, Bruce, D.V.M. The Encyclopedia of the Dog. New York: DK Publishing Inc., 1992.

b) Kojima, Toyoharu. Legacy of the Dog. San Francisco: Chronicle Books, 1995.

c) McGinnis, Terri, D.V.M. "The Dog." World Book Encyclopedia, CD-ROM.

13. Which entry is correct? ____________ Which entries contain errors? ____________

Identify the mistakes. ___________________________________

___________________________________

___________________________________

**Publishing and Presenting**

14. Ashley is writing her research paper for an audience of dog owners. Name one place she might publish her work in order to reach this audience.

___________________________________

15. Name one visual aid that Ashley could include to enhance her research paper.

___________________________________

Name ____________________ Date ____________

# Assessment for Chapter 12: Response to Literature

## Test 1

In this test, you will draft a response to the following poem. Your response should be at least three paragraphs long.

**If I can stop one Heart from breaking**

By *Emily Dickinson*

If I can stop one Heart from breaking
I shall not live in vain
If I can ease one Life the Aching
Or cool one Pain

Or help one fainting Robin
Unto his Nest again
I shall not live in Vain.

**Prewriting**

1. Use the following pentad to explore Dickinson's poem and your response to it. Answer each question using details from the poem.

*Who performs the action or thinks the thoughts?* ____________________

*What is done or thought about?* ____________________

*Why will it be done?* ____________________

Actors

Purposes

Acts

Agencies

Scenes

*How will it be done?* ____________________

*When or where will it be done?* ____________________

2. Circle the details in the pentad that interest you most. Then, summarize them below to create a focus for your response. Remember that your response to the poem should discuss what is of value in it.

Focus: ____________________

Name ____________________

3. Elaborate on your focus by analyzing patterns in the poem's characters, images, and words. What themes do these patterns suggest?

   a) Characters: ____________________
      Theme: ____________________

   b) Images: ____________________
      Theme: ____________________

   c) Words: ____________________
      Theme: ____________________

**Drafting**

4. Extend your focus statement into an insight about the poem. Your insight might be an evaluation of the poem, an interpretation of its theme, or an analysis of how the parts of the poem work together. Elaborate on this insight as you draft.

   Insight: ____________________

5. On a separate sheet of paper, draft your response to the poem using your notes and information from the graphic organizer.

**Revising**

6. Review your draft and write down your strongest point. Then, answer the questions that follow.

   Strongest point: ____________________

   Where in your draft does this point appear?

   Is this placement effective? If so, explain why. If not, suggest a better place for it and explain why you want to move it.

7. Find two points you make in your draft and write them on the lines provided. Next, write the detail from the poem that supports each point. If a point does not contain a supporting detail, choose an appropriate detail from the poem. Write it on the line and add it to your draft.

   Point 1: ____________________
   Supporting Detail 1: ____________________
   Point 2: ____________________
   Supporting Detail 2: ____________________

Name ______________________________

**Editing and Proofreading**

8. Read the sentence below and correct any errors in presenting a quotation from a literary work. Then, review your draft, checking to see that you have punctuated quotations correctly. Make necessary revisions to your draft and write the revised sentences on the lines provided.

 Moore uses repetition to create a mood of hopelessness, as when she writes and the colors lingered, unchanging."

______________________________

______________________________

9. Evaluate your essay according to the criteria in the following rubric. List any changes that you may need to make to improve your essay.

| | Score 4 | Score 3 | Score 2 | Score 1 |
|---|---|---|---|---|
| Audience and Purpose | Presents sufficient background on the work(s); presents the writer's reactions forcefully | Presents background on the work(s); presents the writer's reactions clearly | Presents some background on the work(s); presents the writer's reactions at points | Presents little or no background on the work(s); presents few of the writer's reactions |
| Organization | Presents points in logical order, smoothly connecting them to the overall focus | Presents points in logical order and connects many to the overall focus | Organizes points poorly in places; connects some points to an overall focus | Presents information in a scattered, disorganized manner |
| Elaboration | Supports reactions and evaluations with elaborated reasons and well-chosen examples | Supports reactions and evaluations with specific reasons and examples | Supports some reactions and evaluations with reasons and examples | Offers little support for reactions and evaluations |
| Use of Language | Shows overall clarity and fluency; uses precise, evaluative words; makes few mechanical errors | Shows good sentence variety; uses some precise evaluative terms; makes some mechanical errors | Uses awkward or overly simple sentence structures and vague evaluative terms; makes many mechanical errors | Presents incomplete thoughts; makes mechanical errors that create confusion |

______________________________

______________________________

______________________________

______________________________

**Publishing and Presenting**

10. Explain one way that writing this response helped enhance your understanding of Dickinson's poem.

______________________________

______________________________

Name ______________________________ Date ______________

# Assessment for Chapter 12: Response to Literature
## Test 2

In this test, you will draft a response to the following poem. Your response should be at least three paragraphs long.

**The Road Not Taken**
By *Robert Frost*

Two roads diverged in a yellow wood,
And sorry I could not travel both
And be one traveler, long I stood
And looked down one as far as I could
To where it bent in the undergrowth;

Then took the other, as just as fair,
And having perhaps the better claim,
Because it was grassy and wanted wear;
Though as for that the passing there
Had worn them really about the same,

And both that morning equally lay
In leaves no step had trodden black.
Oh, I kept the first for another day!
Yet knowing how way leads on to way,
I doubted if I should ever come back.

I shall be telling this with a sigh
Somewhere ages and ages hence:
Two roads diverged in a wood, and I—
I took the one less traveled by,
And that has made all the difference.

**Prewriting**

1. Use the following pentad to explore Frost's poem and your response to it. Answer each question using details from the poem.

Actors — *Who performs the action or thinks the thoughts?* ______________________________

Acts — *What is done or thought about?* ______________________________

Scenes — *When or where will it be done?* ______________________________

Agencies — *How will it be done?* ______________________________

Purposes — *Why will it be done?* ______________________________

Name ______________________

2. Circle the details from the pentad that interest you most. Then, summarize them below to create a focus for your response. Remember that your response to the poem should discuss what is of value in it.

   Focus: ______________________

3. Help focus your response further by considering your audience and your purpose for writing.

   a) I am writing for an audience that has the following characteristics: ______________________.

   b) My purpose for writing is to ______________________.

**Drafting**

4. Define and develop your focus statement by naming three details from the poem that connect to it. Use these details to elaborate on your focus statement as you draft.

   Detail 1: ______________________

   Detail 2: ______________________

   Detail 3: ______________________

5. On a separate sheet of paper, draft your response to the poem using your notes and information from the graphic organizer.

**Revising**

6. Review your draft. Write down your strongest point—the one that is most interesting or that summarizes your other ideas. Then, answer the questions that follow.

   My Strongest Point:

   ______________________

   a) Where in your draft does this point appear? ______________________
   b) Is this placement effective? If so, explain why. If not, suggest a better place for it and explain why you want to move it. ______________________

7. Find two points you make in your draft and write them on the lines provided. Next, write the detail from the poem that supports each point. If a point does not contain a supporting detail, choose an appropriate detail from the poem. Write it on the line and add it to your draft.

   Point 1: ______________________.

   Supporting Detail 1: ______________________.

   Point 2: ______________________.

   Supporting Detail 2: ______________________.

 

Name ____________________________________________

**Editing and Proofreading**

8. Read the following sentence and correct any errors in presenting a quotation from a literary work. Then, review your draft, checking to see that you have punctuated quotations correctly. Make necessary revisions to your draft and write the revised sentences on the lines below.

   Heller emphasizes this point when she writes The air had even taken on a grayish tinge.''

   ____________________________________________

   ____________________________________________

9. Evaluate your essay based on the criteria in the following rubric. List any changes you may need to make to improve your essay.

| | Score 4 | Score 3 | Score 2 | Score 1 |
|---|---|---|---|---|
| Audience and Purpose | Presents sufficient background on the work(s); presents the writer's reactions forcefully | Presents background on the work(s); presents the writer's reactions clearly | Presents some background on the work(s); presents the writer's reactions at points | Presents little or no background on the work(s); presents few of the writer's reactions |
| Organization | Presents points in logical order, smoothly connecting them to the overall focus | Presents points in logical order and connects many to the overall focus | Organizes points poorly in places; connects some points to an overall focus | Presents information in a scattered, disorganized manner |
| Elaboration | Supports reactions and evaluations with elaborated reasons and well-chosen examples | Supports reactions and evaluations with specific reasons and examples | Supports some reactions and evaluations with reasons and examples | Offers little support for reactions and evaluations |
| Use of Language | Shows overall clarity and fluency; uses precise, evaluative words; makes few mechanical errors | Shows good sentence variety; uses some precise evaluative terms; makes some mechanical errors | Uses awkward or overly simple sentence structures and vague evaluative terms; makes many mechanical errors | Presents incomplete thoughts; makes mechanical errors that create confusion |

   ____________________________________________

   ____________________________________________

   ____________________________________________

   ____________________________________________

**Publishing and Presenting**

10. Explain one way that writing this response helped you understand or appreciate Frost's poem more completely.

   ____________________________________________

   ____________________________________________

Name ______________________________ Date ______________

# 12 Assessment for Chapter 12: Response to Literature

## Test 3

In this test, you will draft a response to the following poem. Your response should be at least three paragraphs long.

**Mushrooms**
By *Sylvia Plath*

Overnight, very
Whitely, discreetly,
Very quietly

Our toes, our noses
Take hold on the loam,
Acquire the air.

Nobody sees us,
Stops us, betrays us;
The small grains make room.

Soft fists insist on
Heaving the needles,
The leafy bedding,

Even the paving.
Our hammers, our rams,
Earless and eyeless,

Perfectly voiceless,
Widen the crannies,
Shoulder through holes. We

Diet on water,
On crumbs of shadow,
Bland-mannered, asking

Little or nothing.
So many of us!
So many of us!

We are shelves, we are
Tables, we are meek,
We are edible,

Nudgers and shovers
In spite of ourselves.
Our kind multiplies:

We shall by morning
Inherit the earth.
Our foot's in the door.

**Prewriting**

1. a) Use the following pentad to explore Plath's poem and your response to it. Answer each question using details from the poem.

Actors — *Who performs the action or thinks the thoughts?* ______________________________

Acts — *What is done or thought about?* ______________________________

Scenes — *When or where will it be done?* ______________________________

Agencies — *How will it be done?* ______________________________

Purposes — *Why will it be done?* ______________________________

b) Circle the details from the pentad that interest you most. Then, summarize them to create a focus for your response. Remember that your response to the poem should discuss what is of value in it.

Focus: ______________________________

Name ______________________________

2. Elaborate on your focus by analyzing patterns in the poem's "characters," images, and words. What themes do these patterns suggest?

   a) Characters: ______________________________
      Theme: ______________________________

   b) Images: ______________________________
      Theme: ______________________________

   c) Words: ______________________________
      Theme: ______________________________

**Drafting**

3. Extend your focus statement into an insight about the poem. Your insight might be an evaluation of the poem, an interpretation of its theme, or an analysis of how the parts of the poem work together. Elaborate on this insight as you draft.

   Insight: ______________________________

4. Consider other insights by turning your perspective upside down. Review the insight you identified in Question 3 and look for an opposite or "upside-down" perspective. Then, tell whether you will include this new perspective in your draft and explain why.

   a) Upside-Down Perspective: ______________________________

   b) I will/will not include this perspective in my draft because ______________________________.

5. On a separate sheet of paper, draft your response to the poem using your notes and information from the graphic organizer.

**Revising**

6. Review your draft and write your strongest point on the lines provided. Then, answer the questions that follow.

   Strongest Point: ______________________________

   a) Where in your draft does this point appear? ______________________________
   b) Is this placement effective? If so, explain why. If not, suggest a better place for it and explain why you want to move it. ______________________________

7. Review your draft for two or more sentences that make either related points or contrasting points. Make your writing smoother and clearer by combining the sentences into a compound or complex sentence. Write the revised sentence on the following lines.

Name ______________________________

**Editing and Proofreading**

8. Review your draft, checking to see that you have presented quotations correctly. Make any necessary revisions and write the revised sentences on the lines provided. If you have no errors in punctuating or formatting quotations, write a correctly punctuated quotation on the lines below.

9. Evaluate your essay according to the criteria in the following rubric. List any changes that you may need to make to improve your essay.

| | Score 4 | Score 3 | Score 2 | Score 1 |
|---|---|---|---|---|
| Audience and Purpose | Presents sufficient background on the work(s); presents the writer's reactions forcefully | Presents background on the work(s); presents the writer's reactions clearly | Presents some background on the work(s); presents the writer's reactions at points | Presents little or no background on the work(s); presents few of the writer's reactions |
| Organization | Presents points in logical order, smoothly connecting them to the overall focus | Presents points in logical order and connects many to the overall focus | Organizes points poorly in places; connects some points to an overall focus | Presents information in a scattered, disorganized manner |
| Elaboration | Supports reactions and evaluations with elaborated reasons and well-chosen examples | Supports reactions and evaluations with specific reasons and examples | Supports some reactions and evaluations with reasons and examples | Offers little support for reactions and evaluations |
| Use of Language | Shows overall clarity and fluency; uses precise, evaluative words; makes few mechanical errors | Shows good sentence variety; uses some precise evaluative terms; makes some mechanical errors | Uses awkward or overly simple sentence structures and vague evaluative terms; makes many mechanical errors | Presents incomplete thoughts; makes mechanical errors that create confusion |

**Publishing and Presenting**

10. Suggest a descriptive title for your response that suggests your thoughts about the poem. What insights did you gain into the poem "Mushrooms" by writing this response?

Name ____________________ Date ____________

# Assessment for Chapter 13: Writing for Assessment

## Test 1

In this test, you will draft an essay of at least three paragraphs. Imagine that you are writing this essay as part of a health class test on exercise and nutrition.

**Prewriting**

1. For one essay question, you have been given a choice of three topics. Read the topics and explain which one you would select—and why—on the following lines.
   a) Should physical education be mandatory for junior-high-school students? Write a brief persuasive essay that explains your position.
   b) Give an example of a team sport and a more solitary form of exercise. Then, compare and contrast these two physical activities.
   c) Write a brief cause-and-effect essay in which you analyze why some teenagers decide to follow a plan for healthy eating and regular exercise. Identify at least two causes, giving an illustration for each one.

   ____________________

   ____________________

2. Reread the three prompts in Question 1. On the lines below, indicate the type of writing that each response must take.

   a) ____________________

   b) ____________________

   c) ____________________

3. Identify another way you can analyze a test prompt to help clarify and narrow your topic before you begin to write.

   ____________________

**Drafting**

4. Indicate your chosen topic (a, b, or c) on the line provided. Then, choose what you feel is the best organizational method for the topic by writing either "order of importance" or "chronological order" in the space provided.

   My topic: __________

   Order: ____________________

5. On a separate sheet of paper, draft your response to the essay question using your notes.

**Revising**

6. Pick one paragraph from your essay and answer these questions about it.
   a) What is the main idea of the paragraph?

   ____________________

   b) Do all the details support this main idea? If not, write the detail(s) that do not support the main idea below, and delete them from the paragraph.

   ____________________

Name ______________________________

7. Explain what the conclusion of an essay should accomplish. Then, evaluate your own conclusion and tell whether it accomplishes this task by circling the appropriate answer. If necessary, revise your conclusion on the lines provided.

   A conclusion should ______________________________

   ______________________________.

   My conclusion does/does not accomplish this purpose.

   My revised conclusion: ______________________________

   ______________________________.

**Editing and Proofreading**

8. Circle the comma splice below and correct the error. Then, review your essay for comma splices and make any necessary corrections. Write both the old and new versions on the lines provided. If you have no comma splices, write *none*.

   Many health professionals are worried about the lifestyles of today's teenagers, scientists claim that teenagers watch too much TV.

   ______________________________

   ______________________________

9. Evaluate your essay according to the criteria in the following rubric. List any changes that you may need to make to improve your essay.

| | Score 4 | Score 3 | Score 2 | Score 1 |
|---|---|---|---|---|
| Audience and Purpose | Uses word choices and supporting details appropriate to the specified audience; clearly addresses writing prompt | Mostly uses word choices and supporting details appropriate to the specified audience; adequately addresses prompt | Uses some inappropriate word choices and details; addresses writing prompt | Uses inappropriate word choices and details; does not address writing prompt |
| Organization | Presents a clear, consistent organizational strategy | Presents a clear organizational strategy with few inconsistencies | Presents an inconsistent organizational strategy | Shows a lack of organizational strategy |
| Elaboration | Adequately supports the thesis; elaborates on each idea; links all details to the thesis | Supports the thesis; elaborates on most ideas; links most information to the thesis | Partially supports the thesis; does not elaborate on some ideas | Provides no thesis; does not elaborate on ideas |
| Use of Language | Uses excellent sentence variety and vocabulary; includes very few mechanical errors | Uses adequate sentence variety and vocabulary; includes few mechanical errors | Uses repetitive sentence structure and vocabulary; includes some mechanical errors | Demonstrates poor use of language; includes many mechanical errors |

______________________________

______________________________

______________________________

______________________________

**Publishing and Presenting**

10. Explain one new strategy for writing for assessment that you learned from this test.

    ______________________________

    ______________________________

Name ______________________ Date ____________

# Assessment for Chapter 13: Writing for Assessment
## Test 2

In this test, you will draft an essay of at least three paragraphs. Imagine that you are taking a social studies test on fairness and justice.

**Prevriting**

1. For one essay question, you have been given a choice of three topics. Read the topics and explain which one you would select—and why—on the lines that follow.
   a) Should teenagers be able to choose their own bedtimes? Write a brief persuasive essay that explains your position.
   b) Give an example of an injustice with which you are familiar, or have experienced yourself. Describe the injustice and analyze its causes. Then, propose at least one possible solution.
   c) Are teenagers sometimes treated unfairly? Compare and contrast three ways in which teenagers are treated differently from adults.

   ______________________

   ______________________

2. Reread the three prompts in Question 1. On the lines below, indicate the type of writing that each response must take.

   a) ______________________

   b) ______________________

   c) ______________________

3. Name two other ways you can analyze a test prompt before you begin to write.

   ______________________

**Drafting**

4. Choose the best organizational method for the test topic you selected by checking either "order of importance" or "chronological order." Then, map out your essay by filling out the corresponding graphic organizer.

Order of Importance

I. Introduction ______________________

______________________

II. Second most important point ______________________

______________________

III. Remaining points, in decreasing order of importance

______________________

______________________

______________________

IV. Most important point ______________________

______________________

V. Conclusion ______________________

______________________

______________________

Chronological Order

< timeline → → → → →

______________________

______________________

______________________

______________________

______________________

______________________

______________________

______________________

______________________

______________________

______________________

Name ______________________

5. On a separate sheet of paper, draft your response to the essay question using your notes and information from the graphic organizer.

**Revising**

6. Pick one paragraph from your essay and answer these questions about it.
   a) What is the main idea of this paragraph?

   ______________________

   b) Do all the details support this main idea? If not, write the detail(s) that do not support the main idea below, and delete them from your paragraph. ______________________

   ______________________

   ______________________

7. Reread your draft, referring to the following checklist. Then, choose two things you'd like to revise. Write both the old and the new versions on the lines that follow.

**Revision Checklist**

_______ Does my introduction support the writing prompt instructions?
_______ Does my conclusion restate what I have written?
_______ Does each paragraph contain a main idea?
_______ Does each sentence support the paragraph topic?
_______ Does my writing contain any fragments or run-ons?
_______ Have I chosen precise and vivid words?

______________________

______________________

______________________

______________________

**Editing and Proofreading**

8. Correct the following comma splice by inserting your correction above the line. Then, review your essay for comma splices and make corrections. Write both the old and new versions on the lines that follow.

   "Adults are treated with respect when they enter a store, clerks watch teens with suspicion."

______________________

______________________

______________________

 

Name ____________________

9. Evaluate your essay according to the criteria in the following rubric. List any changes that you may need to make to improve your essay.

| | Score 4 | Score 3 | Score 2 | Score 1 |
|---|---|---|---|---|
| Audience and Purpose | Uses word choices and supporting details appropriate to the specified audience; clearly addresses writing prompt | Mostly uses word choices and supporting details appropriate to the specified audience; adequately addresses prompt | Uses some inappropriate word choices and details; addresses writing prompt | Uses inappropriate word choices and details; does not address writing prompt |
| Organization | Presents a clear, consistent organizational strategy | Presents a clear organizational strategy with few inconsistencies | Presents an inconsistent organizational strategy | Shows a lack of organizational strategy |
| Elaboration | Adequately supports the thesis; elaborates on each idea; links all details to the thesis | Supports the thesis; elaborates on most ideas; links most information to the thesis | Partially supports the thesis; does not elaborate on some ideas | Provides no thesis; does not elaborate on ideas |
| Use of Language | Uses excellent sentence variety and vocabulary; includes very few mechanical errors | Uses adequate sentence variety and vocabulary; includes few mechanical errors | Uses repetitive sentence structure and vocabulary; includes some mechanical errors | Demonstrates poor use of language; includes many mechanical errors |

____________________

____________________

____________________

____________________

## Publishing and Presenting

10. Which stage of the writing process did you find most useful as you wrote for assessment? Explain.

____________________

____________________

Name ____________________ Date ____________

# Assessment for Chapter 13: Writing for Assessment

## Test 3

In this test, you will draft an essay of at least three paragraphs. Imagine that you are taking a social studies test on conflict resolution.

**Prewriting**

1. For one essay question, you have been given a choice of three topics. Read the topics and explain which one you would select—and why—on the lines that follow.
   a) Write a letter to the school community that apologizes for a fight you had with another student during assembly. Include a suggestion for a way you might have resolved the conflict more peacefully.
   b) Describe a conflict in a favorite play or novel. What events occur as a result of this conflict?
   c) Explain how you handle conflict in your daily life. What conflicts arise? Do you shy away from them, or jump right in? Evaluate your methods for resolving conflict.

   ____________________

   ____________________

2. Reread the three prompts in Question 1. On the lines below, indicate the type of writing that each response might take.
   a) ____________________
   b) ____________________
   c) ____________________
3. Name two other ways you can analyze a test prompt before you begin to write.

   ____________________

**Drafting**

4. Choose the best organizational method for the test topic you selected by checking either "order of importance" or "chronological order." Then, map out your essay by filling out the corresponding graphic organizer.

Order of Importance

I. Introduction ____________________

____________________

II. Second most important point ____________________

____________________

III. Remaining points, in decreasing order of importance

____________________

____________________

____________________

IV. Most important point ____________________

____________________

V. Conclusion ____________________

____________________

____________________

Chronological Order

< timeline ——→——→——→——→——→

____________________

____________________

____________________

____________________

____________________

____________________

____________________

____________________

____________________

____________________

____________________

Name ____________________

5. On a separate sheet of paper, draft your response to the essay question using your notes and information from the graphic organizer.

**Revising**

6. Find a paragraph in your draft in which at least one sentence does not support the main idea. Then complete the following sentences.

   The main idea of the paragraph is ____________________

   ____________________.

   The following sentence does not fit: ____________________

   ____________________.

7. Reread your draft, referring to the following checklist. Then, choose two things you'd like to revise. Write both old and new versions on the lines provided.

**Revision Checklist**

_______ Does my introduction support the writing prompt instructions?
_______ Does my conclusion restate what I have written?
_______ Does each paragraph contain a main idea?
_______ Does each sentence support the paragraph topic?
_______ Does my writing contain any fragments or run-ons?
_______ Have I chosen precise and vivid words?

____________________

____________________

____________________

____________________

Name ______________________________

## Editing and Proofreading

8. Define a *comma splice*. Then, review your essay for comma splices and make corrections. Write both old and new versions on the lines that follow.

______________________________

______________________________

______________________________

9. Evaluate your essay according to the criteria in the following rubric. List any changes that you may need to make to improve your essay.

| | Score 4 | Score 3 | Score 2 | Score 1 |
|---|---|---|---|---|
| Audience and Purpose | Uses word choices and supporting details appropriate to the specified audience; clearly addresses writing prompt | Mostly uses word choices and supporting details appropriate to the specified audience; adequately addresses prompt | Uses some inappropriate word choices and details; addresses writing prompt | Uses inappropriate word choices and details; does not address writing prompt |
| Organization | Presents a clear, consistent organizational strategy | Presents a clear organizational strategy with few inconsistencies | Presents an inconsistent organizational strategy | Shows a lack of organizational strategy |
| Elaboration | Adequately supports the thesis; elaborates on each idea; links all details to the thesis | Supports the thesis; elaborates on most ideas; links most information to the thesis | Partially supports the thesis; does not elaborate on some ideas | Provides no thesis; does not elaborate on ideas |
| Use of Language | Uses excellent sentence variety and vocabulary; includes very few mechanical errors | Uses adequate sentence variety and vocabulary; includes few mechanical errors | Uses repetitive sentence structure and vocabulary; includes some mechanical errors | Demonstrates poor use of language; includes many mechanical errors |

______________________________

______________________________

______________________________

______________________________

______________________________

______________________________

______________________________

## Publishing and Presenting

10. What are your strengths at writing for assessment? What is one thing you would like to improve?

______________________________

______________________________

# Part 2: Grammar, Usage, and Mechanics

Name ______________________ Date ______________

# Grammar, Usage, and Mechanics: Cumulative Diagnostic Test

**Part 1: Identifying Parts of Speech**
On the lines, write the part of speech of each underlined word: *noun, pronoun, verb, adjective, adverb, preposition, conjunction,* or *interjection.*

1. My little sister, Annie, pretends to be a princess. ______________
2. She can play make-believe games for hours. ______________
3. Her friend Tasha plays with her. ______________
4. Annie and Tasha are best friends. ______________
5. They play together well. ______________
6. When I was little, I pretended to be a knight. ______________
7. I built a castle out of cardboard boxes. ______________
8. Well, it seemed very exciting back then. ______________
9. That was my favorite game. ______________
10. I had such a vivid imagination. ______________

**Part 2: Identifying Subjects and Verbs**
Identify the simple subject and the verb in each sentence below.

11. The games on this shelf are very old.
    S: ______________ V: ______________
12. When did we get them?
    S: ______________ V: ______________
13. There are so many missing pieces!
    S: ______________ V: ______________
14. Take some of these to the basement.
    S: ______________ V: ______________
15. In the spring, maybe we will have a garage sale.
    S: ______________ V: ______________

**Part 3: Identifying Complements**
Write the complements in the following sentences and label each one *direct object, indirect object, predicate noun,* or *predicate adjective.*

16. Spring is my favorite season.
    ______________________________
17. I really enjoy the tulips and daffodils.
    ______________________________
18. We always give our neighbors flowers on May Day.
    ______________________________
19. The red tulips are the prettiest.
    ______________________________

Name ______________________________

20. My grandmother sent us pictures of her garden.

**Part 4: Identifying Phrases and Clauses**

Write all the phrases in the following sentences and label each one *adjective phrase, adverb phrase, appositive phrase, participial phrase, gerund phrase,* or *infinitive phrase.* Then, write any subordinate clauses in the sentences and label them *adjective* or *adverb.*

21. The boy in this picture is an old friend whom I haven't seen lately.

22. Jeremy, my closest childhood friend, moved to Texas when we were twelve.

23. Sending him e-mail is lots of fun because it is so inexpensive.

24. He and I like to play on-line computer games together, too.

25. Communicating this way, we can still share all the things that interest both of us.

**Part 5: Correcting Sentence Structure Errors**

Revise each of the following items, correcting all errors in sentence structure. To complete the fragments, add any information you like.

26. Making a loud grinding noise in the gears, Dad took the car to a mechanic.

27. The mechanic took a test drive, he also looked under the hood and tested all the engine parts, then he finally told Dad what the problem was.

28. Because the repair would be very expensive. Dad thinking about a new car.

29. Dad, the next day deciding to buy a new car.

30. Getting my license next year, the new car will be fun to drive.

 

Name ______________________________

**Part 6: Choosing the Correct Usage**
For each sentence, write the correct form from the pair of words or phrases in parentheses.

31. Everyone (accept, except) me arrived at the game on time.

_______________________________________________

32. I hadn't (ever, never) been late for a game before.

_______________________________________________

33. The reason I was late is (because, that) my uniform was still in the washing machine.

_______________________________________________

34. (Beside, Besides) that, I couldn't find my sneakers.

_______________________________________________

35. I suppose I'm (kind of, somewhat) disorganized.

_______________________________________________

36. (There, Their) are several things I need to do to get organized.

_______________________________________________

37. My friend Nick is having a good (affect, effect) on me.

_______________________________________________

38. His personality is very different (from, than) mine.

_______________________________________________

39. He's very organized at school, and he's organized at home, (to, too).

_______________________________________________

40. He's helping me schedule my time so that I don't get into any (farther, further) trouble with the coach.

_______________________________________________

**Part 7: Using Irregular and Troublesome Verbs**
For each sentence, choose the correct verb form in parentheses.

41. I (saw, seen) a great video last night.

_______________________________________________

42. After she (did, done) her homework, Haley called a friend.

_______________________________________________

43. We arrived five minutes after the movie had (began, begun).

_______________________________________________

44. My dad said that the game I wanted (cost, costed) too much.

_______________________________________________

45. We (buyed, bought) a cheaper one instead.

_______________________________________________

46. My dad is trying to (learn, teach) me to save my own money.

_______________________________________________

47. Yesterday he (says, said) that I (ain't, am not) responsible with my money.

_______________________________________________

Name ______________________________

48. He already (raised, rose) my allowance once this year.

______________________________

49. I guess I (should of, should have) saved the extra money.

______________________________

50. I'll just have to (sit, set) at home tonight, instead of going out to the movies.

______________________________

**Part 8: Using Pronouns**
Choose the correct pronoun from each pair in parentheses.

51. Rosa and (she, her) are both running for class president.

______________________________

52. For (who, whom) will you vote?

______________________________

53. (Its, It's) hard to choose the best candidate.

______________________________

54. I told Kyle and (he, him) to run for vice president.

______________________________

55. I think that the best candidates are Shawna and (she, her).

______________________________

56. Whose speech did you like better, Kyle's or (her's, hers)?

______________________________

57. (Who, Whom) will do the best job on the student council?

______________________________

58. If the job were (yours, your's), what would you do?

______________________________

59. Ben made posters with Rosa and (I, me).

______________________________

60. (Who, Whom) did you ask to put up the posters?

______________________________

**Part 9: Making Words Agree**
For each sentence, choose the correct verb or pronoun in parentheses. Verbs should agree with their subjects, and pronouns should agree with their antecedents.

61. Each of the girls (is, are) finishing (her, their) science project.

______________________________

62. Danny and Chad (is, are) working together on (his, their) project.

______________________________

63. Emma knows that (she, you) must work very hard to win a prize.

______________________________

64. (Here's, Here are) the materials we need to make our weather station.

______________________________

 

Name ______________________________

65. Working quietly in the corner (is, are) the girls who won the competition last year.

66. Either Danny or Chad (was, were) working after school yesterday.

67. One of the boys (needs, need) to improve (his, their) grades.

68. Some of the students (is, are) using (his or her, their) computers to do research.

69. (There's, There are) very strict rules for the competition.

70. Neither parents nor teachers (is, are) allowed to help.

**Part 10: Using Modifiers**
Choose the correct form of the modifiers in parentheses.

71. Jake swims (faster, more faster) than Ben.

72. Jamahl is the (best, bestest) swimmer on the team.

73. He swims faster than (anyone, anyone else) on the team.

74. Alberto is the (better, best) of those two divers.

75. He does the (difficultest, most difficult) dives in the whole competition.

76. That diving board is (higher, more higher) than this one.

77. Tyler practices his dives more than (any, any other) diver.

78. He makes (less, fewer) mistakes than I do.

79. I dive very (good, well), but he usually does (better, more better) at competitions.

80. I felt (bad, badly) when I didn't win a medal, but I will be (relaxeder, more relaxed) at the next competition.

Name ______________________________

**Part 11: Punctuation**

Copy the following sentences, adding commas, semicolons, colons, quotation marks, underlining, hyphens, and apostrophes where they are needed.

81. Johnny Tremain a novel about the Revolutionary War was written by Esther Forbes.

82. This novel which you can find in most libraries won the Newbery Medal when it was first published.

83. Among the characters in the novel are such well loved historical figures as Samuel Adams Paul Revere and John Hancock.

84. In the beginning of the novel Johnny is the kind of person who cares very little about politics.

85. When some Boston patriots help him out in a time of desperate need however he changes his mind and soon he is participating in the Boston Tea Party.

86. The novel also describes the Battle of Lexington this was the battle that occurred after Paul Revere warned the colonists that British troops were approaching.

87. In my opinion a good novel needs three elements a good plot interesting characters and an important message about life.

88. Many peoples favorite poem is Paul Reveres Ride.

89. I like that poem, Joanna said because it tells a true story in an exciting way.

90. She said Its also fun to read this poem aloud because it has such a great rhythm to it. Would you like to read it with me Michael?

Name ______________________

**Part 12: Capitalization**

Copy each of the following sentences, adding capital letters where they are needed.

91. a speaker named professor eleni andropoulos talked to all the classes at roosevelt middle school on friday.

92. she teaches courses about the history of greece at morgan college in steelton, pennsylvania.

93. she talked about greek history and culture, and she showed slides of places such as mount olympus and a famous building called the parthenon.

94. professor andropoulos explained that greece is located on a peninsula, surrounded by the aegean sea, the ionian sea, and the mediterranean sea.

95. long ago, the greeks worshiped gods such as zeus, apollo, and athena.

96. today, most greeks follow the greek orthodox religion.

97. many greeks understand english and french, as well as their own greek language.

98. greek independence day is celebrated every spring on march 25.

99. when i got home, i told my mom what we had learned about this fascinating country.

100. "did your speaker talk about the island called crete?" mom asked. "it's one of my favorite places."

Name ______________________ Date ____________

# Assessment for Chapter 14: Nouns and Pronouns

**Part 1: Identifying Nouns**

Write all the nouns in each of the following sentences.

1. Bravery and intelligence are important qualities for an astronaut.

______________________

2. Most of the first astronauts were jet pilots before they joined the space program.

______________________

3. Before blasting into the unknown, these men were tested to make certain their health was good and they could handle stress.

______________________

4. No one was certain what skills or aptitudes were needed to ensure success.

______________________

5. Excitement and fear were emotions everyone in the space program felt before the first launch.

______________________

**Part 2: Identifying Collective and Compound Nouns**

Identify each underlined noun as a *collective noun* or a *compound noun*.

6. Large teams were involved at every stage of the process.

______________________

7. Everyone in the National Aeronautics and Space Administration (NASA) had a part to play.

______________________

8. Committees met to discuss the cost of the program.

______________________

9. A vast network of computers connected radar installations with NASA headquarters.

______________________

10. The Air Force recommended its best pilots for the program.

______________________

11. This band of brave men inspired many to dream of space travel.

______________________

12. Cape Canaveral was the site from which the first American rocket ship would attempt to escape Earth's gravity.

______________________

13. One thing that made this launch so important was the Cold War.

______________________

14. It was feared that the Communists, who had said that they would bury the United States, could launch attacks from outer space.

______________________

Name ______________________________

15. How would our <u>army</u> fight such an attack?

______________________________

**Part 3: Identifying Common and Proper Nouns**
Write the nouns in the following sentences. Place a *C* after each common noun and a *P* after each proper noun.

16. The Soviet Union had taken the lead in the "space race."

______________________________

17. They had launched a satellite called *sputnik*, which is Russian for "fellow traveler."

______________________________

18. Americans listened in amazement as the Soviets put live animals in their satellites.

______________________________

19. Soon, Moscow wanted to send men, whom they called "cosmonauts," into space.

______________________________

20. Yuri Gagarin was the first person to travel in space, and he became a hero in Russia.

______________________________

**Part 4: Identifying Personal Pronouns and Their Antecedents**
Write the personal pronouns in each sentence. Next to each pronoun, write its antecedent.

21. Americans wanted to see their own space program making progress.

______________________________

22. President Kennedy set his goal to promote space exploration, and he promised that Americans would be first to the moon.

______________________________

23. Television demonstrated its power during important moments of America's space program.

______________________________

24. News programs and special reports kept the country informed, as they presented images that would become part of our cultural consciousness.

______________________________

25. When Neil Armstrong first placed his feet on the moon in 1969, a camera relayed the image back to earth.

______________________________

26. Americans watched their televisions in amazement and heard Neil Armstrong's words as he took his historic "giant leap for mankind."

______________________________

27. The space program has been documented carefully through the years, with reporters and camera crews following its progress.

______________________________

28. Television was there when Sally Ride made her mark on history as the first American woman in space.

______________________________

Name ______________________

29. The program's successes and tragedies have had their impact on how Americans continue to pursue their dreams of space exploration.

______________________

30. Today, the space program continues, but there have been so many successes that it no longer seems like news when we blast into space.

______________________

**Part 5: Identifying Types of Pronouns**

Identify each underlined pronoun as *demonstrative, relative, interrogative*, or *indefinite*.

31. <u>Who</u> could have predicted the dramatic impact of the Internet?

______________________

32. <u>This</u> is a technology <u>that</u> has brought together individuals and organizations from all over the world.

______________________

33. Small companies, <u>which</u> could reach only local customers in the past, now sell to a worldwide market.

______________________

34. <u>Many</u> of these companies can now sell directly to <u>anyone who</u> has access to their Web sites.

______________________

35. The World Wide Web also offers support groups for people <u>who</u> share common problems or interests.

______________________

36. <u>That</u> means a lot to people in small towns <u>whose</u> opportunities for support are otherwise limited.

______________________

37. <u>What</u> happens to people <u>who</u> live in countries with censorship?

______________________

38. <u>Those</u> are the people who can now find freedom of expression on the Web.

______________________

39. <u>Some</u> of their censored writing has been published on the Web.

______________________

40. <u>All</u> of <u>these</u> are important effects <u>that</u> have changed the way people live.

______________________

**Part 6: Revising to Avoid Repetition**

Rewrite the following sentences, replacing any repeated words or phrases with personal pronouns.

41. My grandparents are rediscovering my grandparents' favorite old movies, thanks to cable TV and videos.

______________________

______________________

 

Name ____________________________________________

42. Last weekend my grandparents rented an old movie. The old movie was one my grandparents had last seen before my grandparents were married.

_______________________________________________

_______________________________________________

_______________________________________________

43. Grandpa loved seeing the movie again. Grandpa watched the movie twice.

_______________________________________________

_______________________________________________

44. Grandma watches the TV schedule for Grandma's favorite old movies. Grandma doesn't want to miss any of the favorite old movies.

_______________________________________________

_______________________________________________

45. Grandma and I watch old musicals together. Grandma and I make popcorn and curl up on Grandma's couch together.

_______________________________________________

_______________________________________________

**Part 7: Standardized Test Preparation**

Read the passage, then read the items that follow. Choose the best rewrite of the sentence in each instance, or, if the sentence should not be rewritten, choose "Best as is." Circle the letter of the response you have chosen.

(46) Alexander Graham Bell and Alexander Graham Bell's assistant, Thomas Watson, worked together on making the world's first telephone. (47) In 1876, the year Bell patented the telephone, he and Watson were both young men in their twenties. (48) The telephone achieved the telephone's first commercial success in New England. (49) George Coy was one of the first telephone operators, and George Coy welcomed George Coy's customers with the greeting "Ahoy!" (50) By 1887, there were 150,000 customers who had paid to have their homes connected by telephones.

46. **A** Alexander Graham Bell and Alexander Graham Bell's assistant, Thomas Watson, they worked together on making the world's first telephone.
    **B** Alexander Graham Bell and his assistant, Thomas Watson, worked together on making the world's first telephone.
    **C** He and his assistant, they worked together on making the world's first telephone.
    **D** Best as is.

47. **F** In 1876, the year he patented the telephone, Bell and Watson were both in their twenties.
    **G** In 1876, the year Bell patented the telephone, he was in their twenties, and so was Watson.
    **H** In 1876, the year Bell and Watson were both in their twenties, he patented the telephone.
    **J** Best as is.

48. **A** The telephone achieved its first commercial success in New England.
    **B** It, the telephone, achieved first commercial success in New England.
    **C** The telephone achieved first commercial success in its New England.
    **D** Best as is.

Name ____________________

49. F George Coy was one of the first telephone operators, and he welcomed George Coy's customers with the greeting "Ahoy!"
    G He was one of the first telephone operators, and he welcomed George Coy's customers with the greeting "Ahoy!"
    H George Coy was one of the first telephone operators, and he welcomed his customers with the greeting "Ahoy!"
    J Best as is.

50. A By 1887, there were 150,000 customers who had paid to have the customers' homes connected by telephones.
    B By 1887, there were 150,000 customers who had paid to have their homes connected by it.
    C By 1887, there were 150,000 customers who had paid their customers to have the customers' homes connected by it.
    D Best as is.

Name ______________________ Date ____________

# Assessment for Chapter 15: Verbs

**Part 1: Identifying Transitive Verbs and Intransitive Verbs**
Write the action verb(s) in each sentence. Then, identify each verb as *transitive* or *intransitive.*

1. Stephen Crane wrote *The Red Badge of Courage*, a novel about the Civil War.
______________________
2. In the novel, a young soldier fights his fears of battle.
______________________
3. Henry Fleming dreams of heroic deeds.
______________________
4. During his first battle, though, Henry turns and runs.
______________________
5. Later, he conquers his fears and returns to the battle.
______________________
6. He fights on, but his view of war has changed forever.
______________________
7. Crane writes brilliantly about the feelings of soldiers.
______________________
8. Crane created a realistic view of war.
______________________
9. Crane's novel about the Civil War established his reputation as a great American writer.
______________________
10. Many people today still read and admire *The Red Badge of Courage.*
______________________

**Part 2: Identifying Linking Verbs**
For each sentence, circle the linking verb and underline the words the linking verb connects.

11. The Civil War was devastating.
12. It seemed important to the South to preserve states' rights.
13. President Lincoln remained determined to keep the states united.
14. The situation turned ugly, and soon shots were being fired.
15. This war became the cause of more American deaths than any other war.

Name ______________________

**Part 3: Identifying Action Verbs and Linking Verbs**

Write the verb(s) in each sentence. Then, identify each verb as an action verb or a linking verb.

16. Ambrose Bierce wrote several stories about the Civil War.

17. One of his famous stories is "A Horseman in the Sky."

18. Carter Druse, a Union soldier on guard duty, looks along a mountain road to a nearby cliff.

19. Suddenly, an enemy soldier appears on the cliff.

20. The Confederate soldier on horseback looks very heroic.

21. The Confederate soldier remains very still.

22. Carter Druse grows pale.

23. He feels torn and confused.

24. He feels the rifle in his hand.

25. Carter Druse shoots, and the horse and rider fall through the sky.

26. At the end of the story, the reader learns the truth.

27. Carter Druse grew up in Virginia.

28. A few years earlier, he had become a Union soldier.

29. His father, however, remained loyal to the Confederacy.

30. The enemy on horseback was actually Carter Druse's father.

**Part 4: Identifying Verb Phrases and Their Parts**

Write the complete verb phrase from each sentence. Then, label the *helping verbs* and the *main verbs*.

31. Our class has been studying the role of women during the Civil War.

Name ____________________________________________

32. Until recently, many of these women had not received much recognition.

_______________________________________________

33. Most people probably have heard of Clara Barton.

_______________________________________________

34. Did you know of her accomplishments during the Civil War?

_______________________________________________

35. Barton was not actually trained as a nurse.

_______________________________________________

36. Still, she would bring medicine and supplies to Union soldiers on the front lines.

_______________________________________________

37. Soon she was nursing wounded soldiers.

_______________________________________________

38. Do you recognize the name of Sally Louisa Tompkins?

_______________________________________________

39. Early in the war, she had opened a hospital for wounded Confederate soldiers.

_______________________________________________

40. Later, she would be awarded the military rank of captain by Jefferson Davis, the president of the Confederacy.

_______________________________________________

**Part 5: Standardized Test Preparation**

Read the passage and circle the letter of the verb or verb phrase that belongs in each space.

I ___(41)___ a trip to Australia next year. To prepare, I ___(42)___ for months now. Because of my studying, I ___(43)___ so much already. Aborigines ___(44)___ in Australia for thousands of years. Animals in Australia, like the kangaroo and koala, ___(45)___ strategies to survive.

**41.** **A** will plan
**B** am planning
**C** will have planned
**D** plan

**42.** **F** have been reading
**G** will read
**H** read
**J** am reading

**43.** **A** learned
**B** will learn
**C** learn
**D** have learned

**44.** **F** will live
**G** live
**H** have been living
**J** are living

**45.** **A** have developed
**B** must develop
**C** are developing
**D** develop

Name ________________________________________

When I get to Australia, I ____(46)____ an animal park. My whole life, I ____(47)____ to pet a koala. I know that I ____(48)____ careful when handling the koala, however. I also ____(49)____ to see a duck-billed platypus. By the time I leave, I hope that I ____(50)____ everything that I have planned.

**46.** **F** would visit
**G** have been visiting
**H** visited
**J** will visit

**47.** **A** did want
**B** have wanted
**C** might want
**D** should want

**48.** **F** must be
**G** could be
**H** was
**J** have been

**49.** **A** like
**B** did like
**C** would like
**D** have liked

**50.** **F** did
**G** will have done
**H** must do
**J** might have done

Name ______________________ Date ____________

# Assessment for Chapter 16: Adjectives and Adverbs

**Part 1: Identifying Adjectives and the Words They Modify**
Write the underlined adjectives and label each one *adjective, proper adjective, compound adjective, noun used as adjective, definite article*, or *indefinite article*. Next to each adjective, write the noun it modifies.

1. The Constitution of the United States is a well-crafted document.
2. Our constitution provides for a strong central government.
3. In 1791, ten amendments, called the Bill of Rights, were added to the constitution.
4. The Bill of Rights protects the freedoms of the American people.
5. According to the Bill of Rights, all trials and punishments must be fair and reasonable.
6. The Bill of Rights was based on ideas found in British laws.
7. Our constitution also reserves some powers for the individual states.
8. State laws regulate matters such as public schools and sales taxes.
9. A Minnesota law can be quite different from a Texas law.
10. Today, the United States Constitution remains a much-admired document to people around the world.

**Part 2: Identifying Pronouns and Adjectives**
Label each underlined word in the following sentences *pronoun* or *adjective.*

11. All Americans should understand how their government works.
12. This is an important responsibility of being a citizen.
13. What do you know about the United States Constitution?
14. The three branches of government must obey this document.
15. Each has some power over the other branches.

Name ______________________________

16. Which branch of the government makes the laws?

______________________________

17. What powers does the president have?

______________________________

18. These are identified in our Constitution.

______________________________

19. Whose job involves interpreting the laws?

______________________________

20. That is also explained in the Constitution.

______________________________

**Part 3: Identifying Types of Adjectives**

Write the underlined adjectives in the following sentences and label each one as *possessive*, *demonstrative*, *interrogative*, or *indefinite*.

21. Whose responsibility is it to make certain the Constitution continues to be interpreted correctly?

______________________________

22. That job falls to the American people.

______________________________

23. Many people in other countries are envious of our right to participate in our government.

______________________________

24. Every American should read this important document.

______________________________

25. It is our responsibility to know what the Constitution says, and to vote for representatives that truly uphold our rights and freedom.

______________________________

26. This knowledge can also make it possible for voters to hold their representatives accountable.

______________________________

27. Representatives must be responsive to their constituents.

______________________________

28. Government "by the people and for the people" functions best when each American does his or her duty, learning what the Constitution says and participating in the government process.

______________________________

29. What results can we expect if people do not take this responsibility seriously?

______________________________

30. Some representatives will not operate in the best interest of those they are supposed to represent.

______________________________

Name ____________________________________________

**Part 4: Identifying Adverbs and the Words They Modify**
Write the adverbs in the following sentences. Then, write the word that each adverb modifies.

31. Wetlands often reduce the risk of floods.

______________________________________________________________

32. They greedily absorb heavy rains.

______________________________________________________________

33. They then release the water slowly, preventing floods.

______________________________________________________________

34. Wetlands are very useful for removing pollution.

______________________________________________________________

35. Wetland soils and plants can filter away poisons.

______________________________________________________________

36. Wetlands are vitally important to many animals.

______________________________________________________________

37. The ice in shallow wetlands melts quite early.

______________________________________________________________

38. Spring plants grow easily there.

______________________________________________________________

39. These plants provide urgently needed food for many animals.

______________________________________________________________

40. People hardly ever think of the benefits provided by wetlands.

______________________________________________________________

**Part 5: Distinguishing Between Adverbs and Adjectives.**
Label the underlined word in each sentence *adverb* or *adjective*.

41. Wetlands support a <u>lively</u> population of animals.

______________________________________________________________

42. Wetlands are the <u>only</u> places some animals can survive.

______________________________________________________________

43. <u>Only</u> recently have we begun protecting our wetlands.

______________________________________________________________

44. Some wetlands are <u>less</u> protected than others.

______________________________________________________________

45. There is <u>less</u> support for protecting smaller wetlands.

______________________________________________________________

Name ______________________________

**Part 6: Revising Sentences With Adjectives and Adverbs**
Revise each of the following sentences by adding at least one adjective and one adverb.

46. Animals run.

_______________________________________________

47. The book describes wetlands.

_______________________________________________

48. My friend works.

_______________________________________________

49. The cookies are good.

_______________________________________________

50. The boy answered the question.

_______________________________________________

**Part 7: Standardized Test Practice**
Read the passage and circle the letter of the word or group of words that belongs in each space.

My mother always drives very ___(51)___. ___(52)___, she doesn't pass anyone unless she needs to. She stays very ___(53)___ while she drives. Sometimes she sings ___(54)___ along with the radio. She ___(55)___ ever talks while she drives.

**51.** **A** cautious
**B** cautiously
**C** sometimes
**D** lately

**52.** **F** Usual
**G** Usually
**H** Slowly
**J** Nearly

**53.** **A** calm
**B** calmly
**C** calmer
**D** calms

**54.** **F** very
**G** hardly
**H** soft
**J** softly

**55.** **A** hard
**B** hardly
**C** harder
**D** hardlier

Name ______________________ Date ______________

# Assessment for Chapter 17: Prepositions

**Part 1: Identifying Prepositions**
Write the preposition(s) in each sentence.

1. Nearly every culture has sports, but the sports vary from one country to the next.

 ______________________

2. Soccer is the most widely played game in the world.

 ______________________

3. In countries of the British Commonwealth, cricket is near soccer in popularity.

 ______________________

4. *Jai alai* is a Basque game that is popular among the people of Spain and Latin America.

 ______________________

5. Through the years, games with balls have been the most popular.

 ______________________

6. If you read about sports, you'll find that many have interesting histories.

 ______________________

7. The old British game of rounders appears to have turned into baseball after it came across the Atlantic Ocean.

 ______________________

8. The game of rugby was named for a school in England.

 ______________________

9. Within the tradition of sports that involve kicking balls are rugby, soccer, American football, and Australian Rules football.

 ______________________

10. Besides the kicking, there is a lot of running during these games.

 ______________________

**Part 2: Identifying Compound Prepositions**
Write the compound preposition(s) in each sentence.

11. In addition to games that involve kicking are games that involve hitting the ball with a stick.

 ______________________

12. With cricket, the batter stands in front of the wicket.

 ______________________

13. For hockey, in place of a ball there is a puck, which is moved by means of a stick.

 ______________________

14. In spite of the best efforts of the goalie, the skaters still score because of their speed and skill.

 ______________________

15. In polo, instead of wearing ice skates, players are on top of horses.

 ______________________

Name ______________________________

**Part 3: Identifying Prepositional Phrases and Objects of the Preposition**
Write the prepositional phrase(s) in each sentence. Underline the object of the preposition in the phrase. Some sentences contain compound prepositions.

16. In the bottom of the ninth inning, Sarah was batting.

____________________________________________

17. She hit the ball over the fence.

____________________________________________

18. Sarah ran around the bases and back to home plate.

____________________________________________

19. Fans in the bleachers rose to their feet with a loud cheer.

____________________________________________

20. Because of her home run, the game was tied and went into extra innings.

____________________________________________

21. Between innings, our coach spoke confidently to us.

____________________________________________

22. During the next inning, our opponents scored against us, in spite of my great work at the pitcher's mound.

____________________________________________

23. Kayla batted first, ahead of me.

____________________________________________

24. She hit the ball into the outfield.

____________________________________________

25. Then I hit one out of the park, and everyone cheered on account of our great victory.

____________________________________________

**Part 4: Distinguishing Between Prepositions and Adverbs**
Label each underlined word as *preposition* or *adverb*.

26. Sam was sitting behind me at the basketball game.

____________________________________________

27. In the second quarter, our team was behind.

____________________________________________

28. Then Nick shot, and the ball went in with a swish.

____________________________________________

29. Sam and I raised our voices in a great cheer.

____________________________________________

30. Our opponents passed the ball around to the other end of the court.

____________________________________________

31. I could feel the tension all around the gym.

____________________________________________

32. Someone shot, but the ball did not go through the hoop.

____________________________________________

Name ______________________

33. I hoped we could score again before the quarter was over.

34. Then the buzzer went off at the end of the quarter.

35. The two teams ran off the court for their halftime breaks.

**Part 5: Revising Sentences With Prepositional Phrases**
Revise each of the following sentences by adding a prepositional phrase.

36. Devon ran speedily.

37. The ball flew.

38. We lost the game.

39. Someone stole the ball.

40. The end was exciting.

**Part 6: Revising Prepositions**
Revise the following sentences using a different preposition (or compound preposition) in place of the underlined prepositions. (The meaning of the sentence can change, but it must still make sense.)

41. Historically, sports were played during festivals and carnivals or because of victories.

42. Often, games ranged through the town.

43. In Italy, one goal might be set up near a town and the other could be miles away.

44. One entire village would play against another.

45. In addition to sports, there might be feasting, music, and dancing.

Name ___________________________

**Part 7: Standardized Test Preparation**

Read the passage and circle the letter of the best way to rewrite each group of sentences.

[1] Long ago, the people made masks. The people were in Latin America. The masks were gold and silver. [2] New crafts were introduced. Spanish explorers brought them. It was the 1500's. [3] People made beautiful images. The images were Spanish roses, Mexican sunflowers, sea horses, and starfish. [4] The women invented a sewing technique. They were in Panama. The technique was applique. [5] Today we truly appreciate all these crafts. We see their artistic value. We see their cultural significance.

**46.** What is the BEST way to write the sentences in section [1]?
- A Long ago, of gold and silver, the people made masks of Latin America.
- B Long ago, the people made masks of Latin America of gold and silver.
- C Long ago, the people of Latin America made masks of gold and silver.
- D Long ago, the people, of gold and silver, made masks in Latin America.

**47.** What is the BEST way to write the sentences in section [2]?
- F New crafts were introduced, in the 1500's, Spanish explorers brought them.
- G In the 1500's, new crafts were introduced by Spanish explorers.
- H New crafts in the 1500's, were introduced by Spanish explorers.
- J Spanish explorers brought new crafts because it was the 1500's.

**48.** What is the BEST way to write the sentences in section [3]?
- A People made beautiful images of Spanish roses, Mexican sunflowers, sea horses, and starfish.
- B Besides Spanish roses, Mexican sunflowers, sea horses, and starfish, people made beautiful images.
- C People made beautiful images for Spanish roses, Mexican sunflowers, sea horses, and starfish.
- D Around the Spanish roses, Mexican sunflowers, sea horses, and starfish, people made beautiful images.

**49.** What is the BEST way to write the sentences in section [4]?
- F Of applique, the women invented a sewing technique in Panama.
- G The women invented of Panama the sewing technique of applique.
- H The women, of applique, invented a sewing technique in Panama.
- J The women of Panama invented the sewing technique of applique.

**50.** What is the BEST way to write the sentences in section [5]?
- A Today, we truly appreciate all these crafts for their artistic value and for their cultural significance.
- B For their artistic value today, we truly appreciate all these crafts of their cultural significance.
- C Today, for their artistic value, we truly appreciate, for their cultural significance, these crafts.
- D All these crafts, for their artistic value and their cultural significance, we truly appreciate them today.

Name ______________________________ Date ______________

# Assessment for Chapter 18: Conjunctions and Interjections

**Part 1: Identifying Coordinating Conjunctions**
Write the coordinating conjunction in each sentence.

1. Madison Avenue and Wall Street are famous business locations in New York City.

   ______________________________

2. Many people go to New York for the theater, but there are many other things to see, as well.

   ______________________________

3. If you love art, you might want to visit the Metropolitan Museum of Art or the Guggenheim Museum.

   ______________________________

4. Many people go to New York on business, so they never get to see the sights.

   ______________________________

5. I have never walked through New York's Central Park, nor have I been to Ellis Island.

   ______________________________

**Part 2: Identifying Correlative Conjunctions**
On the line, write the part of the correlative conjunction that is missing in each sentence.

6. Both Ellis Island ______________ Liberty Island are in New York Harbor.

   ______________________________

7. We can either go shopping on Fifth Avenue ______________ go on a harbor cruise.

   ______________________________

8. ______________ is New York crowded, but it is also noisy.

   ______________________________

9. Whether we visit Greenwich Village ______________ walk through Chinatown is up to you.

   ______________________________

10. I'm afraid of heights, so ______________ the Empire State Building nor the World Trade Center appeals to me.

    ______________________________

**Part 3: Identifying Subordinating Conjunctions**
Write the dependent idea in each sentence. Underline the subordinating conjunction that connects the dependent idea to the main idea.

11. It is fun to explore New York City because there is so much variety.

    ______________________________

12. Some people want to visit Greenwich Village as soon as they reach New York.

    ______________________________

13. Others wish to visit Chinatown, even though it's not the most famous Chinatown in the U.S.

    ______________________________

Name ______________________

14. Many seek out areas related to their heritage, while others explore areas made famous in books and movies.

______________________

15. Before you go to New York, you really need to spend some time figuring out what to see.

______________________

**Part 4: Writing Sentences With Subordinating Conjunctions**
Write sentences using each of the following subordinating conjunctions.

16. although

______________________

______________________

17. after

______________________

______________________

18. as long as

______________________

______________________

19. unless

______________________

______________________

20. wherever

______________________

______________________

**Part 5: Identifying Conjunctions**
Write the conjunction(s) in each sentence. Then, label each conjunction *coordinating*, *correlative*, or *subordinating*.

21. The Brooklyn Bridge and the Statue of Liberty are two famous landmarks in New York City.

______________________

22. When it was completed in 1883, the Brooklyn Bridge was the longest bridge in the world.

______________________

23. Both John Roebling and his son, Washington Roebling, deserve credit for this brilliant engineering feat.

______________________

24. John Roebling designed the amazing suspension bridge, but he died in an accident as the construction was beginning.

______________________

25. Not only John Roebling, but also twenty-seven workers died while the bridge was being built from 1869 to 1883.

______________________

Name ______________________________

26. Although Washington Roebling took over as chief engineer, he was confined to bed with a crippling disease for the last ten years of the construction project.

_______________________________________________

27. Because he could not leave his bed, his wife, Emily, had to carry messages to the engineers and contractors at the construction site.

_______________________________________________

28. Emily Roebling was not a trained professional, yet she won great respect for her knowledge of the project and for her skill in resolving conflicts.

_______________________________________________

29. Neither political conflicts nor technical problems could overcome her determination to see the bridge completed.

_______________________________________________

30. In 1983, when the bridge was one hundred years old, New York City held a giant fireworks celebration to honor the Roeblings' achievement.

_______________________________________________

**Part 6: Revising: Combining Sentences With Conjunctions**

Use the type of conjunction specified to join the following pairs of sentences. Write your combined sentences on the lines.

31. We visited New York City. We saw many famous historic places. (subordinating conjunction)

_______________________________________________

_______________________________________________

32. We visited Ellis Island. We visited Liberty Island, too. (coordinating conjunction)

_______________________________________________

_______________________________________________

33. My great-grandfather immigrated to America from Russia. My great-uncle immigrated from Russia, too. (correlative conjunction)

_______________________________________________

_______________________________________________

34. My great-grandfather is not alive today. Neither is my great-uncle. (correlative conjunctions)

_______________________________________________

_______________________________________________

35. Many Americans visit Ellis Island. They want to see the place that welcomed their ancestors to America. (subordinating conjunction)

_______________________________________________

_______________________________________________

Name ______________________________

## Part 7: Identifying Interjections

Write the interjection in each sentence.

36. Yikes! The Statue of Liberty is enormous!

_______________________________________________

37. Hey, let's climb the stairs all the way up to the crown.

_______________________________________________

38. No way! I'm afraid of heights.

_______________________________________________

39. Well, I'll just go by myself then.

_______________________________________________

40. Wow! What an amazing view from way up here!

_______________________________________________

## Part 8: Supplying Conjunctions and Interjections

Supply a conjunction and/or interjection to complete each sentence.

41. ____________ Things are really expensive in New York.

42. ____________ Bill had more money than I did, he helped me out.

43. There was a Broadway show we wanted to see, ________ we didn't have enough money.

44. ________ I would think it would be hard to live here, ________ millions seem to be able to afford it.

45. ____________ I go back, I'll budget more carefully.

## Part 9: Standardized Test Practice

Read the passage and answer the questions that follow. Choose the best way to rewrite the sentences in each section. Circle the letter of the response you have chosen.

[1] I like Chinese kites. I like Chinese puppets, too. [2] Many Chinese kites look like flying creatures such as birds and butterflies. Others resemble fish or tortoises. [3] One of the most popular Chinese kites is the centipede kite. It is not the easiest kite to fly. [4] Hand puppets are popular in China. So are string puppets. Shadow puppets are popular, too. [5] Shadow puppets are the most amazing. They are so difficult to operate and so haunting to watch.

**46.** What is the BEST way to rewrite the sentences in section [1]?

**A** I like Chinese kites, but I like Chinese puppets.
**B** I like Chinese kites and Chinese puppets.
**C** I like Chinese kites, although I like Chinese puppets.
**D** I like Chinese kites, also Chinese puppets.

**47.** What is the BEST way to rewrite the sentences in section [2]?

**F** Many Chinese kites look like flying creatures, such as birds and butterflies, but others resemble fish and tortoises.
**G** Many Chinese kites look like flying creatures such as birds and butterflies, for others resemble fish and tortoises.
**H** Many Chinese kites look like flying creatures such as birds and butterflies, because others resemble fish and tortoises.
**J** Many Chinese kites look like flying creatures such as birds and butterflies, and others resemble fish and tortoises, though.

Name ____________________

48. What is the BEST way to rewrite the sentences in section [3]?
 A Since it is not the easiest kite to fly, the centipede is one of the most popular Chinese kites.
 B The centipede is the most popular and not the easiest Chinese kite to fly.
 C Although it is not the easiest kite to fly, the centipede is one of the most popular Chinese kites.
 D Not only the easiest to fly, but also the most popular Chinese kite, is the centipede.

49. What is the BEST way to rewrite the sentences in section [4]?
 F Hand puppets are popular in China, also string puppets and shadow puppets.
 G Hand puppets are popular in China, and so are string puppets, and shadow puppets are popular, too.
 H Popular in China are hand puppets and string puppets, shadow puppets are popular, too.
 J Hand puppets, string puppets, and shadow puppets are all popular in China.

50. What is the BEST way to rewrite the sentences in section [5]?
 A After shadow puppets are the most amazing, they are so difficult to operate and so haunting to watch.
 B Shadow puppets are the most amazing because they are so difficult to operate and so haunting to watch.
 C Shadow puppets are the most amazing, they are so difficult to operate and so haunting to watch, too.
 D Shadow puppets are the most amazing and they are so difficult to operate and they are so haunting to watch.

Name ______________________________ Date ______________

# Assessment for Chapter 19: Basic Sentence Parts

**Part 1: Identifying Subjects and Predicates**
In each of the following sentences, draw a vertical line between the complete subject and the complete predicate. Then, underline the simple subject once and the verb twice.

1. Settlers reached the Oregon Territory in the 1840's.
2. The search for gold and silver attracted miners to California in 1849.
3. Homesteaders flocked to the Great Plains in the 1870's.
4. They made fences out of barbed wire.
5. Thousands of African American homesteaders went west.
6. Many well-known cowboys were African Americans.
7. Nat Love was a cowboy famous for his skills on cattle drives.
8. Bose Ikard, a former slave, managed one of the largest ranches in Texas.
9. People on the frontier ate simple foods such as bread, beans, and meat.
10. Homesteading families on the plains amused themselves at square dances, house-raisings, and corn-husking parties.

**Part 2: Identifying Compound Subjects and Compound Verbs**
Tell whether each sentence has a *compound subject* or a *compound verb*. Then, identify the subjects or verbs in each compound part.

11. Scandinavians and other Europeans became farmers on the Great Plains.
    ______________________________
12. Some Chinese immigrants built the railroads and later opened their own small businesses.
    ______________________________
13. Wyatt Earp hunted buffalo, drove stagecoaches, and also enforced the law.
    ______________________________
14. Merchants, farmers, and soldiers all went west.
    ______________________________
15. Miners and cowboys gambled in saloons.
    ______________________________
16. Important transportation centers, such as Wichita, Kansas, grew and prospered.
    ______________________________
17. Wood and water were often scarce on the Great Plains.
    ______________________________
18. Enterprising people brought in water and sold it for several dollars a barrel.
    ______________________________
19. Prospectors carried some supplies on their burros and then returned to camp for more.
    ______________________________
20. Farmers and ranchers fought range wars over the use of barbed-wire fences.
    ______________________________

Name ______________________________

**Part 3: Identifying Hard-to-Find Subjects**
Write the subject of each of the following sentences. (Some sentences give orders, some ask questions, and some are in inverted order.)

21. There were several overland trails to the western frontier.
______________________________
22. Look at this book about the Oregon Trail.
______________________________
23. From Independence, Missouri, to the Pacific Northwest ran this rugged pathway.
______________________________
24. When did the first settlers begin their journeys on the Oregon Trail?
______________________________
25. Among the first wagon-train leaders in the 1830's was Benjamin Bonneville.
______________________________
26. Through deserts and over mountains trudged the wagons.
______________________________
27. Think of the dangers along the way!
______________________________
28. Can we imagine the courage of these pioneers?
______________________________
29. Here are some maps of the Oregon Trail.
______________________________
30. Where did most of the settlers end up?
______________________________

**Part 4: Identifying Direct Objects, Indirect Objects, and Objects of Prepositions**
In the following sentences, underline each *direct object* once. Underline each *indirect object* twice. Circle each *object of a preposition.* (Not every sentence has all three.)

31. Stagecoaches carried many people to the West.
32. Stations along the way gave passengers a chance to rest and eat.
33. Travelers faced many dangers.
34. Which stagecoach lines did most passengers use?
35. The pony express brought people their mail.
36. Our teacher told us a story about a pony express rider.
37. Wagons brought machinery and explosives to the miners.
38. Whom did the settlers call for protection from outlaws?
39. Sheriffs brought some law and order to the Wild West.
40. Judge Roy Bean protected settlers in Texas.

Name ______________________________

**Part 5: Identifying Subject Complements**

Identify each subject complement in the following sentences. Then, label each complement a *predicate noun, predicate pronoun,* or *predicate adjective.*

41. "The Luck of Roaring Camp" is a classic story of the American frontier.

______________________________

42. Its author is Bret Harte.

______________________________

43. Harte's stories of frontier life were very popular.

______________________________

44. The best-known writers about frontier life were Mark Twain and he.

______________________________

45. Their stories are humorous and often exaggerated.

______________________________

**Part 6: Revising With Compound Subjects, Compound Predicates, and Compound Complements**

Combine the following pairs of sentences by using a compound subject, compound predicate, or compound complement. You may make other minor changes as necessary.

46. *Billy the Kid* is a ballad by Aaron Copland. *Rodeo* is a ballad by Copland, too.

______________________________

______________________________

47. The main characters of the musical *Oklahoma!* are cowboys on the frontier. Frontier farmers are also main characters in the musical.

______________________________

______________________________

48. Frederic Remington painted images of the West. He sculpted them, too.

______________________________

______________________________

49. Remington painted cowboys. He also painted galloping horses and stampeding cattle.

______________________________

______________________________

50. *Stagecoach* is a classic film about the western frontier. So is *High Noon.*

______________________________

______________________________

Name ____________________________

**Part 7: Standardized Test Practice**

Read the passage and answer the questions that follow. Circle the letter of the correct answer to each question.

[1] Many settlers heading west in the 1800's. Traveled in wagon trains. [2] Wagon trains might include up to one hundred wagons. They were led and protected by men on horseback. [3] Settlers would meet in early spring. At a town near the Missouri River. [4] They would elect officers and hire guides. Buy supplies and wait for good weather. [5] Some settlers took the Oregon Trail to the Northwest. Others took the Santa Fe Trail to the Southwest.

**51.** Which is the BEST way to write section [1] of the passage?
- **A** Many settlers traveled in wagon trains. Heading west in the 1800's.
- **B** Many settlers heading west in the 1800's traveled in wagon trains.
- **C** Many settlers headed west in the 1800's. Traveling in wagon trains.
- **D** Correct as is.

**52.** Which is the BEST way to write section [2] of the passage?
- **F** Wagon trains might include up to one hundred wagons. Led and protected by men on horseback.
- **G** Wagon trains might include up to one hundred wagons. They were led and protected by men. On horseback.
- **H** Wagon trains might include up to one hundred wagons. They were led by men on horseback. Protected, too.
- **J** Correct as is.

**53.** Which is the BEST way to write section [3] of the passage?
- **A** Settlers would meet in early spring at a town near the Missouri River.
- **B** Settlers would meet. In early spring. At a town near the Missouri River.
- **C** Settlers in early spring, at a town near the Missouri River. Would meet.
- **D** Correct as is.

**54.** Which is the BEST way to write section [4] of the passage?
- **F** Electing officers, hiring guides, buying supplies. They would wait for good weather.
- **G** They would elect officers, hire guides, and buy supplies. Waiting for good weather.
- **H** They would elect officers, hire guides, buy supplies, and wait for good weather.
- **J** Correct as is.

**55.** Which is the BEST way to write section [5] of the passage?
- **A** Some settlers took the Oregon Trail. To the Northwest. Others took the Santa Fe Trail. To the Southwest.
- **B** Taking the Oregon Trail to the Northwest for some settlers. Taking the Santa Fe Trail for others.
- **C** Some settlers to the Northwest. Taking the Oregon Trail. Some settlers to the Southwest. Taking the Santa Fe Trail.
- **D** Correct as is.

Name ______________________ Date ______________

# 20 Assessment for Chapter 20: Phrases and Clauses

**Part 1: Classifying Prepositional Phrases**
Write the prepositional phrase in each sentence. Then, identify each one as an *adjective phrase* or an *adverb phrase*.

1. The Rio Grande flows through New Mexico.

______________________

2. New Mexico has many kinds of wildlife.

______________________

3. Coyotes and prairie dogs live in New Mexico.

______________________

4. Roadrunners race along New Mexico's roads.

______________________

5. Creatures of the desert include rattlesnakes and tarantulas.

______________________

6. Many movies are made in New Mexico.

______________________

7. Filmmakers love the open spaces and varied beauty of this state.

______________________

8. Recent movies shot on location in New Mexico include *Wild, Wild West*; *Armageddon*; *Contact*; and *Independence Day*.

______________________

9. Mountains in the north offer opportunities for skiing or hiking.

______________________

10. Rock hounds love New Mexico for its mineral wealth.

______________________

**Part 2: Identifying Other Phrases**
In the following sentences, write and label all of the *appositive*, *participial*, *gerund*, and *infinitive* phrases.

11. A pine tree called the piñon is the state tree of New Mexico.

______________________

12. The Zia Sun symbol, seen on the New Mexico flag, stands for peace and friendship.

______________________

13. The Navajos, the largest group of Native Americans in New Mexico, weave beautiful blankets.

______________________

14. Adobe, a type of sun-dried brick, is used in many buildings in New Mexico.

______________________

Name ____________________

15. Growing chili peppers is an important source of income in New Mexico.

16. Chili peppers are used to make spicy foods such as *pico de gallo* and salsa.

17. Albuquerque, the state's largest city, hosts the International Balloon Fiesta each fall.

18. Containing strange and beautiful rock formations, Carlsbad Caverns National Park is a major tourist attraction in New Mexico.

19. Visitors love to see the ancient pictographs on the walls of the Gila Cliff Dwellings.

20. Artists love painting New Mexico's beautiful scenery.

**Part 3: Classifying Clauses**

Identify each underlined clause as *independent* or *subordinate.* Then, label each subordinate clause an *adjective* or *adverb.*

21. Kit Carson, who forced thousands of Apaches and Navajos onto reservations in the 1860's, later tried to help the Navajos return to their own lands.

22. New Mexico native Ann Nolan Clark wrote a book called *Secret of the Andes,* which won the 1953 Newbery Medal.

23. When she was a child, Pablita Velarde studied ancient Native American rock drawings in New Mexico.

24. As an adult, she illustrated a book that celebrates Native American legends.

25. Bill Mauldin was a cartoonist who drew pictures for the soldiers serving in World War II.

26. Mauldin received a Pulitzer Prize for his cartoons after the war was over.

27. Because she taught people how to make beautiful black pottery, Maria Montoya Martinez helped her village to become prosperous.

28. Georgia O'Keeffe was a great artist who created paintings of New Mexico desert scenes.

29. You have probably seen the cartoon character Smokey Bear, which came to be associated with a real bear cub in New Mexico.

Name ___________________________________

30. Because he survived a devastating forest fire in 1950, Smokey became a hero to children and lived at the National Zoo in Washington, D.C. for many years.

_______________________________________________

**Part 4: Identifying Sentence Structure**
Label the following sentences *simple, compound, complex,* or *compound-complex.*

31. The yucca is a flowering New Mexican plant that has stiff, pointed leaves.

_______________________________________________

32. Hispanics make up about 25 percent of New Mexico's population, and Native Americans represent 9 percent.

_______________________________________________

33. New Mexico's five largest cities are Albuquerque, Santa Fe, Las Cruces, Roswell, and Farmington.

_______________________________________________

34. New Mexico has many ghost towns that were abandoned when their silver mines were depleted, and these towns are popular tourist attractions.

_______________________________________________

35. The novel *Laughing Boy,* which won the Pulitzer Prize in 1929, is a story about Navajos torn between two worlds.

_______________________________________________

**Part 5: Recognizing Elliptical Adverb Clauses**
For each of the following sentences, write out the full adverb clause, adding the understood words.

36. I can do more push-ups than you.

_______________________________________________

37. Jorge likes swimming more than running.

_______________________________________________

38. Carla is not as fast a runner as Shalonda.

_______________________________________________

39. Bill arrives as early as I.

_______________________________________________

40. I have spent more time studying than Talia.

_______________________________________________

**Part 6: Revising: Combining Sentences With Phrases and Clauses**
Combine each pair of sentences, using the type of phrase or clause indicated.

41. Amman is the capital of Jordan. The city was once known as Philadelphia. (appositive phrase)

_______________________________________________

_______________________________________________

Name ______________________________

42. Amman is home to the Jordan Museum of Popular Traditions. This museum displays exhibits of traditional clothing and jewelry. (adjective clause)

______________________________

______________________________

43. The city contains an ancient Roman theater. The theater was built in the second or third century A.D. (participial phrase)

______________________________

______________________________

44. The city of Aqaba has been a trading center for many centuries. Archaeologists can find many ancient artifacts there. (adverb clause)

______________________________

______________________________

45. A scenic route from Amman to Aqaba is the King's Highway. The King's Highway runs through ancient biblical lands. (adjective clause)

______________________________

______________________________

**Part 7: Standardized Test Preparation**

Read the passage and answer the questions that follow. Choose the best way to combine the sentences in each section. Circle the letter of the response you have chosen.

> [1] Most Brazilians speak Portuguese. Many of their customs are Indian or African. [2] São Paulo is the largest city in Brazil. It is located on the southeastern coast of the country. [3] São Paulo has many wealthy companies and splendid stores. There are also many poor people in the city. [4] There are not enough jobs or good places to live for everyone. Many families live in small huts with no running water. [5] Everyone in São Paulo enjoys *feijoada.* This dish is made with black beans, rice, and vegetables.

46. What is the BEST way to combine the sentences in section [1]?
   **A** Most Brazilians speak Portuguese because many of their customs are Indian or African.
   **B** Most Brazilians speak Portuguese, but many of their customs are Indian or African.
   **C** Most Brazilians, speaking Portuguese, have Indian or African customs.
   **D** After many Brazilians speak Portuguese, many of their customs are Indian or African.

47. What is the BEST way to combine the sentences in section [2]?
   **F** São Paulo, the largest city in Brazil, is located on the southeastern coast of the country.
   **G** Although São Paulo is the largest city in Brazil, it is located on the southeastern coast of the country.
   **H** São Paulo is located on the southeastern coast of the country because it is the largest city in Brazil.
   **J** Since being the largest city in Brazil, São Paulo is located on the southeastern coast of the country.

48. What is the BEST way to combine the sentences in section [3]?
   **A** São Paulo has many wealthy companies and splendid stores because there are also many poor people in the city.
   **B** São Paulo, having many wealthy companies and splendid stores, there are also many poor people in the city.
   **C** Having many wealthy companies and poor people, São Paulo has splendid stores.
   **D** Although São Paulo has many wealthy companies and splendid stores, there are also many poor people in the city.

Name ______________________________

49. What is the BEST way to combine the two sentences in section [4]?
   F There are not enough jobs or good places to live for everyone, yet many families live in small huts with no running water.
   G Living in small huts with no running water, there are not enough jobs or good places to live for everyone.
   H Because there are not enough jobs or good places to live for everyone, many families live in small huts with no running water.
   J Because many families live in small huts with no running water, there are not enough jobs or good places to live for everyone.

50. What is the BEST way to combine the two sentences in section [5]?
   A Everyone in São Paulo enjoys *feijoada*, a dish made with black beans, rice, and vegetables.
   B While everyone in São Paulo enjoys *feijoada*, it is a dish made with black beans, rice, and vegetables.
   C Because everyone in São Paulo enjoys *feijoada*, it is a dish made with black beans, rice, and vegetables.
   D Even though everyone in São Paulo enjoys *feijoada*, it is a dish made with black beans, rice, and vegetables.

Name ______________________ Date ____________

# Assessment for Chapter 21: Effective Sentences

**Part 1: Identifying and Punctuating Types of Sentences**
Answer each question in a few words.

1. What is the function of a declarative sentence?

2. What is the function of an interrogative sentence?

3. What is the function of an imperative sentence?

4. What is the function of an exclamatory sentence?

5. Imperative sentences can end with a period or an exclamation point; why would you choose one over the other?

**Part 2: Identifying and Punctuating Types of Sentences**
Identify each of the following sentences as *declarative, interrogative, imperative,* or *exclamatory*. Then, add the appropriate end mark.

6. How does a helicopter hover in the air

7. A helicopter has no wings

8. Watch the spinning rotor blades cut through the air

9. The rotor can generate lift without moving forward

10. What an amazing rescue that helicopter performed

**Part 3: Revising: Combining Sentences**
Combine each pair of sentences using the technique indicated in parentheses.

11. Truck drivers often sleep in their cabs. They sleep in an area behind the seats. (prepositional phrases)

12. Many cabs have bunks. They also have televisions and refrigerators. (compound direct object)

Name ______________________________

13. Trucks are an ideal means for transporting goods. They can deliver right to your door. (subordinate clause)

______________________________

______________________________

14. The caravel was a type of sailing ship. So was the galleon. (compound subject)

______________________________

______________________________

15. Small, powerful tugboats push big ships safely into harbors. They also pull ships into harbors. (compound verb)

______________________________

______________________________

16. People in Venice ride gondolas to work. They may also ride motorboats to work. (compound direct object)

______________________________

______________________________

17. Early airships such as zeppelins were filled with hydrogen. Today's blimps use helium instead. (compound sentence)

______________________________

______________________________

18. Hydrogen is flammable. Hydrogen can be very dangerous in large quantities. (subordinate clause)

______________________________

______________________________

19. In 1937, the zeppelin *Hindenberg* burst into flames. The accident killed thirty-six people. (participial phrase)

______________________________

______________________________

20. Charles Lindbergh made the first nonstop solo flight across the Atlantic Ocean in 1927. The flight took thirty-three hours. (compound sentence)

______________________________

______________________________

**Part 4: Revising: Varying Sentences**

Revise the following sentences using the techniques indicated in parentheses.

21. Lindbergh was born in Detroit and began his career as an airmail pilot between St. Louis and Chicago. (Begin with a participial phrase.)

______________________________

______________________________

22. Thousands of French citizens were waiting for Lindbergh's arrival in France. (Reverse subject-verb order.)

______________________________

______________________________

Name ______________________________

23. After his historic flight, Lindbergh was awarded the Congressional Medal of Honor, and he later pioneered some of the first commercial airline routes. (Divide into two sentences.)

______________________________

______________________________

24. He suddenly became a national hero. (Begin with an adverb.)

______________________________

______________________________

25. He was awarded a 1954 Pulitzer Prize for his autobiography, *The Spirit of St. Louis.* (Begin with a prepositional phrase.)

______________________________

______________________________

**Part 5: Revising to Correct Phrase Fragments, Clause Fragments, Run-ons, and Misplaced Modifiers**

Revise each of the following items, correcting all errors in sentence structure.

26. The first woman to fly solo across the Atlantic was Amelia Earhart, in 1932, she flew from Newfoundland to Northern Ireland in about fifteen hours.

______________________________

______________________________

27. Taking off from California five years later, with her navigator, in an attempt to fly around the world.

______________________________

______________________________

28. Reaching New Guinea in June, more than three-quarters of their journey was complete.

______________________________

______________________________

29. The next day radio messages from Earhart reporting empty fuel tanks.

______________________________

______________________________

30. When efforts to make radio contact with the plane failed.

______________________________

______________________________

31. After searching and finding no trace of the plane or crew, their fate was a mystery that couldn't be solved.

______________________________

______________________________

32. Probably crashing into the ocean and dying.

______________________________

______________________________

Name ______________________

33. During World War II, some people claimed that Earhart had been a spy, there were reports of Japanese captives resembling Earhart and her navigator.

34. No convincing evidence supporting these claims.

35. The unsolved mystery of Earhart's fate, many people have become obsessed with it.

**Part 6: Choosing the Correct Usage**

For each sentence, write the correct form from the pair of words in parentheses.

36. Small airplanes are different (than, from) larger passenger planes in an important way.

37. (Beside, Besides) their smaller size, they also have propellers instead of jet engines.

38. Larger planes, of course, can fly (farther, further) without stopping to refuel.

39. Smaller planes are better when you need to fly (in, into) a remote area.

40. The reason is (because, that) small planes can land safely on a short runway.

41. (They're, Their) able to take off again more safely, (to, too).

42. This advantage is (kind of, quite) important in emergency rescue situations.

43. I haven't (ever, never) traveled on an airplane before.

44. Everyone in my class (accept, except) me has gone on airplane trips.

45. I wonder what (affects, effects) my first airplane trip will have on me.

Name ______________________

**Part 7: Standardized Test Practice**

For each sentence, find the line that has an error in usage. If the sentence has no errors, choose *No mistakes.* Circle the letter of the response you have chosen.

**46.** **A** Their are two reasons
**B** that you should
**C** accept my advice.
**D** *No mistakes.*

**47.** **F** The effects of the law
**G** may depend on
**H** where you live at.
**J** *No mistakes.*

**48.** **A** I don't know nothing
**B** about the kind of machines
**C** used to make roads.
**D** *No mistakes.*

**49.** **F** The people who live
**G** farther down this road
**H** have no telephone.
**J** *No mistakes.*

**50.** **A** They're treating us
**B** just like we were
**C** their friends.
**D** *No mistakes.*

Name ______________________ Date ______________

# Assessment for Chapter 22: Using Verbs

**Part 1: Identifying Principal Parts of Verbs**
Write the verb or verb phrase in each sentence. Then, identify the principal part used to form the verb: *present*, *present participle*, *past*, or *past participle*.

1. Last fall my father went to Japan.
   Verb: ______________ Principle Part: ______________
2. Since his return, I have asked him questions about Japan.
   Verb: ______________ Principle Part: ______________
3. Dad is telling me about Japanese schools.
   Verb: ______________ Principle Part: ______________
4. Schools in Japan are very different from American schools.
   Verb: ______________ Principle Part: ______________
5. Students in Japan attend school 240 days a year, with only six weeks of summer vacation.
   Verb: ______________ Principle Part: ______________
6. After school, most students are working hard on three hours' worth of homework.
   Verb: ______________ Principle Part: ______________
7. Dad also learned about Japanese "cram schools."
   Verb: ______________ Principle Part: ______________
8. There, students study for special entrance tests for high school.
   Verb: ______________ Principle Part: ______________
9. Students have known the importance of these tests since kindergarten.
   Verb: ______________ Principle Part: ______________
10. Their success in school has always depended on their test scores.
    Verb: ______________ Principle Part: ______________

**Part 2: Using the Past and Past Participle of Irregular Verbs**
For each sentence, choose the correct verb form in parentheses and write it on the line.

11. My dad (teached, taught) me how to write some words in Japanese.
    ______________________________
12. I had (began, begun) by tracing the Japanese characters with a pencil.
    ______________________________
13. Then I (drew, drawed) the characters with a brush dipped in ink.
    ______________________________
14. I was disappointed when I (saw, seen) what I had (did, done).
    ______________________________
15. I wished I had (took, taken) more time to make the characters better.
    ______________________________

Name ______________________________

16. The brush and the ink had (cost, costed) several dollars.

______________________________

17. I (tore, teared) up my first word and (threw, throwed) it away.

______________________________

18. Since then, I have (wrote, written) the word again, and it has (came, come) out much better. ______________________________

19. I (bringed, brought) my work to school to show the class.

______________________________

20. My teacher (putted, put) my work up on the bulletin board.

______________________________

**Part 3: Identifying the Tense and Form of Verbs**
Write the tense of each underlined verb. If a verb is in the progressive form, don't forget to include the word *progressive* when you write the tense.

21. A man named Tim Berners-Lee dreamed up the idea for the World Wide Web. ______________
22. He was working as an engineer in Switzerland at the time. ______________
23. He had wanted a way to keep track of all his ideas and link them together. ______________
24. He had also been hoping to link his files to those of other scientists and engineers. ______________
25. We use his ideas every time we log on to the Internet. ______________
26. The number of Internet users has grown at an amazing rate. ______________
27. Millions of us are logging on every day. ______________
28. How will the Internet change our lives in years to come? ______________
29. I have been wondering about this question. ______________
30. In a few years, this invention will have linked almost everyone in the world. ______________

**Part 4: Forming Verb Tenses**
Write the verb in parentheses in the tense indicated.

31. I (like—present perfect) to invent things since I was little. ______________
32. Last year I (make—past) an electric hair brush. ______________
33. I (hope—past perfect) to sell it for lots of money. ______________
34. I (dream—past progressive) of becoming rich and famous. ______________
35. Right now I (work—present progressive) on an electric dog walker. ______________
36. I (work—present perfect progressive) on it for six months. ______________
37. By April, I (complete—future perfect) my invention. ______________

Name ____________________

38. I (demonstrate—future) my invention at the school science fair in May. ____________

39. Everyone (enjoy—present) the annual science fair. ____________

40. Maybe I (win—future) a prize this year. ____________

**Part 5: Revising Sentences to Use the Active Voice**
Revise the following sentences, changing the verb from the passive voice to the active voice.

41. Math homework was being done by Amanda.

42. By eight o'clock, her homework had been completed by her.

43. Tomorrow, a report will be written by Brad.

44. His report will be finished on time.

45. His hard work is appreciated by his teacher.

**Part 6: Revising Usage of Troublesome Verbs**
Revise the following sentences, correcting verb usage errors. Write *correct* if the sentence contains no errors.

46. Last night, I seen a movie about the Revolutionary War.

47. The movie learned me a lot about the winter of 1776.

48. The defeated Americans retreated across New Jersey and drug their cannons behind them.

49. Many people thought George Washington should of went up to the British and surrendered.

50. Instead, Washington's army crossed the Delaware and set up camp in Pennsylvania.

51. The British decided to leave the battlefield until spring.

52. Then, Washington done something totally unexpected.

53. He spoke to his troops and says that he ain't ready to surrender.

54. Overnight, Washington's army crossed the river again and attacked Trenton before the sun raised in the sky.

 

Name ______________________________________

55. The victory in Trenton rose the hopes of the Americans, even though many difficult times laid ahead.

______________________________________________________________

**Part 7: Standardized Test Practice**
For each sentence, circle the letter of the line that has an error in usage. If the sentence has no errors, circle the letter for *No mistakes.*

**56.** A After the man had spoke,
B he sat down in his chair
C and wrote some notes.
D *No mistakes.*

**57.** J Can you teach me
K how to set up the pins
L the way that you done it?
M *No mistakes.*

**58.** A I ain't sure
B what time she left
C or what she took with her.
D *No mistakes.*

**59.** J This radio that I bought yesterday
K cost me a hundred dollars,
L but I've already broken it.
M *No mistakes.*

**60.** A Have you found
B the picture that I drawed
C and put on the windowsill?
D *No mistakes.*

Name ______________________ Date ____________

# Assessment for Chapter 23: Using Pronouns

**Part 1: Identifying the Case of Pronouns**
Identify each underlined pronoun as *nominative*, *objective*, or *possessive* case.

1. My favorite childhood game was Duck, Duck, Goose. ____________
2. It is a fun game to play with a large group of children. ____________
3. I taught the game to your little brother's class. ____________
4. Playing with them was lots of fun. ____________
5. The children who enjoyed the game most were Ethan and she. ____________

**Part 2: Using Nominative and Objective Case Pronouns Correctly**
Choose the correct pronoun from the choices in parentheses.

6. Sam and (I, me) like to play Capture the Flag. ____________
7. Caitlin played on a team with (he and I, him and me). ____________
8. Caitlin and I gave (he, him) the flag. ____________
9. It was (he and she, him and her) who planned our attack. ____________
10. The best players on the other team were Matt and (she, her). ____________
11. When they charged, we had a trap ready for (they, them). ____________
12. Sam and Caitlin had told (we, us) the plan. ____________
13. I asked Liz and (she, her) if they wanted to play on our team. ____________
14. I hope that Cody and (he, him) will play on our team next time. ____________
15. With (they, them) on our side, we'll be the fastest team ever. ____________

**Part 3: Using Possessive Case Pronouns Correctly**
Choose the pronoun in parentheses that completes each sentence correctly.

16. Is this basketball (yours, your's)? ____________
17. (Its, It's) not mine. ____________
18. Ask the neighbors if (their's, theirs) is missing. ____________
19. John says that the basketball is (his, his's). ____________
20. He can recognize his ball by (its, it's) green stripe. ____________

**Part 4: Using *Who* and *Whom* Correctly**
Choose the pronoun in parentheses that completes each sentence correctly.

21. (Who, Whom) should we invite to the school carnival? ____________
22. I know (who, whom) has the keys to the gym. ____________
23. (Who, Whom) wants to be in charge of the games? ____________
24. Mrs. Morelli is the teacher to (who, whom) you should speak about prizes. ____________
25. With (who, whom) would you like to work? ____________
26. Michelle is the person (who, whom) asked to work with me. ____________
27. (Who, Whom) knows the rules to this game? ____________

Name ____________________

28. We need to keep track of (who, whom) donates food. ____________

29. In case I have any questions, (who, whom) should I call? ____________

30. To (who, whom) did you give the decorations? ____________

**Part 5: Revising Sentences for Correct Pronoun Usage**
Rewrite the following sentences, correcting errors in pronoun usage. For sentences without errors, write *correct.*

31. Dad is teaching Amanda and I to play chess.

32. Its a hard game to learn.

33. Who knows the names of all the chess pieces and how they can be moved?

34. We need to find some friends with who we can practice.

35. Amanda and me play chess together once a week.

36. I like the knight piece best because its moves are tricky.

37. Whose turn is it now, mine or your's?

38. From whom did you learn the game?

39. Is this chess board ours or theirs?

40. The best chess players in our class are Danielle and him.

**Part 6: Standardized Test Practice**
For each sentence, circle the letter of the line that has an error in pronoun usage. If the sentence has no errors, circle the letter for *No mistakes.*

**41.** **A** Her and I brought
**B** our croquet set. It
**C** has our names on it.
**D** *No mistakes.*

**42.** **F** Maya and I
**G** told them that
**H** the game was our's.
**J** *No mistakes.*

**43.** **A** Bill and she thought
**B** that they would need
**C** it for the tournament.
**D** *No mistakes.*

Name ______________________________

44. F Bill and he tied
G when they played
H there first round.
J *No mistakes.*

45. A Who told you that
B it's too late for
C Brad and me to register?
D *No mistakes.*

46. F The people who you
G should ask about him
H are Haley and she.
J *No mistakes.*

47. A Their father told
B Jessie and she
C who won the game.
D *No mistakes.*

48. F Whom do you think
G can beat him when
H he's playing his best?
J *No mistakes.*

49. A Take your time before
B you and she decide
C who you want to invite.
D *No mistakes.*

50. F Dad will take him
G and I out for ice
H cream when we're done.
J *No mistakes.*

Name ______________________ Date ______________

# Assessment for Chapter 24: Making Words Agree

**Part 1: Choosing the Verb That Agrees With Its Subject**
For each sentence, write the correct verb in parentheses.

1. In every country occupied by the Axis powers, there (was, were) people who fought back. ______________
2. These brave patriots (was, were) known as the Resistance movement. ______________
3. Spying and sabotage (was, were) important techniques used by the Resistance. ______________
4. The leader of the French Resistance forces (was, were) very courageous. ______________
5. Neither threats nor capture by the Nazis (was, were) enough to make him betray the movement. ______________
6. (Here's, Here are) some pictures of Resistance leaders in Norway. ______________
7. Everyone in movements like these (face, faces) constant danger. ______________
8. Many of the Resistance leaders (was, were) caught. ______________
9. Constantly on the alert for any sign of resistance (was, were) Nazi officials stationed in the occupied countries. ______________
10. Neither family nor friends of a resister (is, are) safe in this kind of situation. ______________
11. Either Tanya or Jamahl (is, are) writing a report on the Danish Resistance movement. ______________
12. Each of the Jews rescued by Danish Resistance fighters (was, were) offered a new life. ______________
13. Ways of resisting Nazi oppression (was, were) often very clever. ______________
14. Every small rebellion and resistance (make, makes) a difference in these situations. ______________
15. A brave action (is, are) never forgotten by the people it helps. ______________

**Part 2: Choosing Pronouns That Agree With Their Antecedents**
For each sentence, write the correct pronoun in parentheses.

16. Several of the girls in my class want to get (her, their) college degree in architecture. ______________
17. To become an architect, Cassie knows that (she, you) must complete many years of education and training. ______________
18. Each of the architecture colleges in the United States requires (its, their) students to complete a five-year program for a bachelor's degree. ______________
19. Students who take an additional one or two years of courses can receive (his or her, their) master's degree. ______________

Name ______________________________

20. Each architecture student must plan (his or her, their) high-school and college courses carefully. ____________

21. Art, math, and science are some of the courses that architecture students must have on (his or her, their) schedules. ____________

22. Every school of architecture sets (its, their) own specific requirements. ____________

23. Some prefer students with high grades; others base (its, their) admissions on students' drawings and other artistic work. ____________

24. Once a student gets a degree in architecture (he or she, they) must work as an intern in an architecture firm. ____________

25. After two years as interns, young architects take a state examination to earn (his or her, their) licenses as registered architects. ____________

26. Either Cassie or Elizabeth will do (her, their) next report on careers in architecture. ____________

27. Both girls are seriously considering (her, their) careers. ____________

28. To get her license at last, Elizabeth knows that (she, you) must pass the Architect Registration Exam. ____________

29. Cassie and Elizabeth are working together to plan (her, their) futures. ____________

30. A building must meet high standards of function, appearance, and durability before (it, they) can be considered a successful work of architecture. ____________

**Part 3: Revising to Correct Errors in Agreement**

Rewrite any sentences that contain errors in agreement between subject and verb or between pronoun and antecedent. If a sentence has no errors, write *correct.*

31. Both Ryan and Brady is planning careers in journalism.

______________________________

______________________________

32. Ryan wants to report on technology, because he thinks you can get more work in that field.

______________________________

______________________________

33. Brady likes medical reporting and business, because it's so interesting.

______________________________

______________________________

34. Either Ryan or Brady is going to ask his parents to drive to the Career Night meeting.

______________________________

______________________________

 

Name ____________________

35. At Career Night, students can meet college representatives and learn what he or she needs to study.

____________________

____________________

36. Some of the students are bringing their parents with them to the conference.

____________________

____________________

37. One of the college representatives are setting up their display table now.

____________________

____________________

38. It is very exciting to see all the opportunities that are available at college.

____________________

____________________

39. Here's some catalogs Ryan needs if you want to find out more information.

____________________

____________________

40. If Brady want some catalogs, there are many available.

____________________

____________________

**Part 4: Standardized Test Practice**

For each sentence, circle the letter of the line that contains an error. If the sentence has no errors, circle the letter for *No error.*

41. **A** Most employers in journalism
    **B** requires that employees
    **C** have their college degrees.
    **D** *No error.*

42. **F** One of the best ways
    **G** for students to get started in journalism is
    **H** to write for your school newspaper.
    **J** *No error.*

43. **A** There's many different jobs needed
    **B** that a journalist can choose
    **C** once he or she has the education and experience.
    **D** *No error.*

44. **F** Among the jobs in this field
    **G** are columnist, feature writer,
    **H** editor, and reporter.
    **J** *No error.*

45. **A** Either newspaper reporter or television anchor
    **B** are Sara's first choice
    **C** for the job of her dreams.
    **D** *No error.*

Name ____________________

46. **F** Of course,
**G** if anyone wants to write,
**H** they have a wide range of opportunities.
**J** *No error.*

47. **A** Documentary writing, speech writing, textbook writing,
**B** and book review writing is
**C** just a few of the possibilities.
**D** *No error.*

48. **F** A writer must have both the technical skills to produce good writing
**G** and a good knowledge of the topic
**H** about which they are writing.
**J** *No error.*

49. **A** Anyone who wishes to be a good writer
**B** has a considerable amount of work
**C** in his or her future.
**D** *No error.*

50. **F** However, for anyone
**G** who wishes to do the work,
**H** writing are a satisfying and rewarding career.
**J** *No error.*

Name ______________________________ Date ______________

# Assessment for Chapter 25: Using Modifiers

**Part 1: Forming Degrees of Modifiers**
Complete the chart by writing the missing positive, comparative, and superlative degrees of the modifiers.

| Positive Degree | Comparative Degree | Superlative Degree |
|---|---|---|
| 1. sharp | | |
| 2. | deeper | |
| 3. | | lowest |
| 4. | more talkative | |
| 5. icy | | |
| 6. | | most happily |
| 7. good | | |
| 8. bad | | |
| 9. | | most afraid |
| 10. clumsy | | |
| 11. stoically | | |
| 12. | fewer | |
| 13. | | most evasive |
| 14. | | longest |
| 15. many | | |
| 16. | further | |
| 17. fascinating | | |
| 18. | lovelier | |
| 19. well | | |
| 20. | faster | |

**Part 2: Correcting Errors in Degree**
Rewrite the following sentences that contain errors in degree. If a sentence has no errors, write *correct*.

21. Of those two skaters, Heather is best.

______________________________

______________________________

22. She is more stronger and moves more gracefully.

______________________________

______________________________

23. The bestest skater in our class is Ashley.

______________________________

______________________________

Name ______________________________

24. Katie can skate faster and farther than I can.

25. However, my jumps are more better than hers.

26. My worstest jump is my double axel.

27. I need more practice so that I can do it more skillfully.

28. I can do it better than I could a few weeks ago, but I'm still hoping for further improvement.

29. This jump is more harder than that one.

30. The most youngest skater in our class is Melissa.

**Part 3: Making Logical Comparisons**
Rewrite the following sentences. Correct the illogical comparisons by balancing them or by adding *other* or *else* to make them logical.

31. Heather's spins are better than Katie.

32. Heather can spin faster than anyone.

33. She has better balance than any girl in the class.

34. This year's practice times are later than last year.

35. I arrive earlier than anyone.

Name ______________________________

**Part 4: Correcting Errors Caused by Troublesome Modifiers**

Rewrite the following sentences that contain errors involving troublesome modifiers. If a sentence has no errors, write *correct.*

36. We all felt badly about losing the figure-skating competition.

37. Heather and Ashley were only the ones on our team who received high scores.

38. We did less jumps than the other team did.

39. Katie had a bad fall, and she badly injured her ankle.

40. Heather skated as good as she could.

41. I had a bad cold and didn't feel well that day.

42. We just have two weeks to prepare for the next competition.

43. That is less time than we usually have.

44. We have fewer confidence than we did before the competition.

45. Our coach says we need to just practice a little harder.

Name ______________________________

**Part 5: Standardized Test Practice**
Read the passage and choose the letter of the word or group of words that belongs in each space. Circle the letter of the response you have chosen.

In Minnesota, winters are long and ___(46)___. In January, usually the ___(47)___ month of the year, many cities hold winter carnivals. The ___(48)___ winter carnival of all is held in St. Paul, the state capital. Many ___(49)___ cities, such as Winona, also hold their own winter carnivals. The ___(50)___ event of all is the ice-fishing contest.

**46.** **A** cold
**B** colder
**C** more cold
**D** most coldest

**47.** **F** cold
**G** colder
**H** coldest
**J** most coldest

**48.** **A** spectacular
**B** spectacularest
**C** more spectacular
**D** most spectacular

**49.** **F** more smaller
**G** most smallest
**H** smaller
**J** smallest

**50.** **A** more interesting
**B** most interesting
**C** interestingest
**D** most interestingest

Name ____________________ Date ____________

# Assessment for Chapter 26: Punctuation

**Part 1: Proofreading Sentences for End Marks and Commas**
Copy the sentences on the lines, adding end marks and commas where they are needed.

1. Days in the desert can be very hot so many animals sleep in burrows or under rocks
2. Do desert bats sleep during the day or do they just hide in caves
3. Wow Those amazing bats can find tiny insects in the dark
4. Look at this picture of an owl hunting at night
5. Small owls hunt for insects and spiders and larger owls capture mice and snakes

**Part 2: Proofreading Sentences for Commas**
Copy the sentences on the lines, adding commas where they are needed. If the sentence does not need any commas, write *correct.*

6. Scorpions hunt for insects spiders and other small creatures.
7. The only scorpion that is harmful to people is the sculptured scorpion of Arizona.
8. The mountain lion the largest wild cat in the United States weighs 150 pounds or more.
9. Prowling the desert for rodents foxes may also catch birds or even eat plants.
10. The kit fox is a light-colored big-eared member of the fox family.

Name ______________________________

11. Using sound bats find their prey in the dark.

12. When the bat's squeaks hit an object they echo back to the bat's ears.

13. A creature called the sandfish lives in the sands of the Arabian Desert.

14. The sandfish is actually a lizard however not a fish.

15. Moving its long smooth body from side to side the sandfish appears to be swimming through the sand.

16. The sandfish has a long chisel-shaped nose which helps it push its way through the sand.

17. The amazing green toad defends itself with its poisonous warts.

18. The green toad you know can lay its eggs only after a rainstorm.

19. "On March 15 2001" Brady said "this green toad laid more than 10000 eggs."

20. To find out about endangered animals Nick you can write to the World Wildlife Fund 1250 Twenty-Fourth Street N.W. Washington D.C. 20077.

**Part 3: Proofreading Sentences for Semicolons and Colons**

Determine where semicolons and colons are needed in the following sentences. In some cases, you will need to replace a comma with a semicolon. On the line, write the needed punctuation and the words or numerals on either side of it.

21. Assateague is a large island off the coast of Virginia, it is inhabited by wild ponies.

Name ____________________

22. For most of the year, the ponies roam freely however, during the last week of July, some are rounded up and sold at auction.

23. There are three historic cities in eastern Virginia Williamsburg, Jamestown, and Yorktown.

24. On our vacation, we visited the following historic cities Gettysburg, Pennsylvania, Morristown, New Jersey, and Yorktown, Virginia.

25. Notice The history museum will be closed from 1230 P.M. until 230 P.M.

**Part 4: Proofreading Direct and Indirect Quotations**
On the lines provided, rewrite the direct quotations with the proper punctuation. If the sentence is an indirect quotation, write *correct.*

26. Many important leaders of the American Revolution were Virginians said Jessica.

27. I asked her to name some of them.

28. Jessica said Didn't you know that George Washington, Patrick Henry, and Thomas Jefferson were Virginians?

29. Which famous Virginian said Give me liberty or give me death?

30. I think said Jessica that James Madison and James Monroe were Virginians.

31. Tina recalled that she had really enjoyed her visit to Virginia.

32. We asked her which part of her visit she remembered best.

33. Let's go to Jamestown Landing Day next May said Brandon. It's a super celebration!

Name ______________________________

34. Wouldn't you rather go to Norfolk's Harborfest in June asked Sarah.

35. Their parents asked them to decide which festival they'd rather attend.

**Part 5: Using Underlining and Quotation Marks With Titles**

Write the titles from the following sentences, using underlining and quotation marks.

36. I read the chapter Gold Fever in the book The Great American Gold Rush.

37. Have you read Jack London's famous short story To Build a Fire?

38. Many prospectors read about the gold rush in a newspaper called the Oregon Spectator.

39. Two popular songs during the gold rush were The Gold Digger's Waltz and Oh, Susannah.

40. Many gold seekers traveled west on the steamship California.

**Part 6: Proofreading for Hyphens**

Write the words in the following sentences that need hyphens, adding hyphens where they are needed. If no hyphen is needed in a sentence, write *correct*.

41. Thirty three members voted for the new proposal, passing it by a two thirds majority.

42. Thanks to the new proposal, the club can make some badly needed improvements.

43. The ex president was full of self confidence.

44. Three fifths of the members agreed on the all American festival.

45. My great grandfather was once a much admired member of that club.

**Part 7: Proofreading for Apostrophes**

Write the words in the following sentences that need apostrophes, adding apostrophes where necessary.

46. My familys last name is the same as yours.

47. The womens husbands hadnt met, even though the women were old friends.

Name ______________________________

48. Lets check everyones answers to make sure theyre correct.

______________________________

49. The two students answers were the same.

______________________________

50. Several boys wallets were missing from the mens locker room.

______________________________

**Part 8: Standardized Test Practice**
Choose the best way to write each section so that it is punctuated correctly. If the underlined section needs no change, choose "Correct as is." Circle the letter of the response you have chosen.

[51] My mothers favorite movie is <u>The Miracle Worker</u>. [52] "I watch it every chance I get, she says. And it always makes me cry." [53] The movie tells the true story of Helen Keller and the teacher who taught her to communicate with her hands. [54] This critically-acclaimed movie focuses on the relationship between Helen and her teacher; the film is very inspiring. [55] What a thrill it is when Helen finally learns to spell the word <u>water</u> into her teacher's hand?

**51.** **A** My mothers' favorite movie is <u>The Miracle Worker</u>.
**B** My mothers' favorite movie is "The Miracle Worker."
**C** My mother's favorite movie is <u>The Miracle Worker</u>.
**D** Correct as is.

**52.** **F** "I watch it every chance I get," she says, "and it always makes me cry."
**G** "I watch it every chance I get," she says. "And it always makes me cry."
**H** I watch it every chance I get." she says, "and it always makes me cry."
**J** Correct as is.

**53.** **A** The movie tells the true story of Helen Keller and the teacher, who taught her to communicate with her hands.
**B** The movie tells the true story of Helen Keller, and the teacher who taught her to communicate with her hands.
**C** The movie tells the true story of Helen Keller, and the teacher, who taught her to communicate with her hands.
**D** Correct as is.

**54.** **F** This critically-acclaimed movie focuses on the relationship between Helen and her teacher, the film is very inspiring.
**G** This critically acclaimed movie focuses on the relationship between Helen and her teacher; the film is very inspiring.
**H** This critically-acclaimed movie focuses on the relationship between Helen and her teacher: the film is very inspiring.
**J** Correct as is.

**55.** **A** What a thrill it is when Helen finally learns to spell the word <u>water</u> into her teacher's hand!
**B** What a thrill it is when Helen finally learns to spell the word "water" into her teacher's hand?
**C** What a thrill it is when Helen finally learns to spell the word "water" into her teacher's hand!
**D** Correct as is

Name ______________________________ Date ______________

# Assessment for Chapter 27: Capitalization

**Part 1: Using Capitals for First Words**
Rewrite each of the following sentences, adding capital letters where they are needed.

1. last year I went to England.

___

2. wow! what a great trip that was!

___

3. at the Tower of London, we took a tour.

___

4. "this is the Roman wall," the guide told us. "here is where the Crown Jewels are stored."

___

___

5. "long ago," the guide continued, "political prisoners were held here."

___

___

**Part 2: Using Capitals for Proper Nouns and Adjectives**
On the line following each sentence, write the words that should be capitalized.

6. A few years ago, the art institue of chicago sponsored a trip to italy.

___

7. The goal was to study the art of the italian renaissance.

___

8. The schedule included visiting the cities of rome and florence.

___

9. Statues and paintings by michelangelo and bernini would be featured.

___

10. The trip, which left in late august and returned in early september, was definitely one I wanted to take.

___

11. When we got to florence, which is in the region of tuscany, I found that our hotel, the hotel berchielli, was on the arno river.

___

12. On monday, we visited the great cathedral, called the duomo, and saw giotto's tower and the famous doors created by ghiberti.

___

13. Tuesday took us to the fabulous pitti palace and boboli gardens.

___

14. After four days in florence, we took the train to rome.

___

Name ____________________

15. In rome, we visited vatican city.

16. Of course, the most famous painting in vatican city is michelangelo's amazing work on the ceiling of the sistine chapel.

17. I love the part of the painting where god is reaching out to touch adam's hand.

18. We also toured st. peter's cathedral, which is called san pietro in italian.

19. We strolled along the main thoroughfare of rome, the via veneto.

20. I learned that, according to myth, rome was founded by romulus and remus, twin sons of the roman god mars.

**Part 3: Using Capitals for the Titles of People and Works**

On the line following each sentence, write the words that should be capitalized.

21. Yesterday, mother and I went to the store, and I bought the latest national geographic.

22. Mom bought the C. S. Lewis books out of the silent planet, perelandra, and that hideous strength.

23. We also walked through the music section, and I found a recording of "scotland the brave" played on bagpipes.

24. I looked at a book about queen Elizabeth and prince Charles.

25. I asked, "mom, did you see this picture of the queen talking to the president of the united states?"

26. Since I like stories of adventure, I was interested in a book about captain James Cook, as well as one on sir Frances Drake.

27. The book all cloudless glory is an account of the life of president George Washington, and includes comments from the French generals who served with him.

28. After an hour, the only thing I still needed was a gift for my teacher, miss Ross.

29. Mom needed to find gifts for aunt Ruth, my little sister, and mister Johnson, the principal.

Name ____________________

30. She bought Tolkien's the lord of the rings, a video of Lewis's the lion, the witch, and the wardrobe, and a book by general Patton.

____________________

**Part 4: Applying All the Rules of Capitalization**

Rewrite each of the following sentences, adding capital letters where they are needed. Apply all of the rules of capitalization that you have learned.

31. the largest city in africa is cairo, the capital of egypt.

____________________

____________________

32. the mediterranean sea lies to the north of egypt, and the red sea borders the nation on the east.

____________________

____________________

33. most of the egyptian population follows the religion of islam and its holy book, the koran.

____________________

____________________

34. the official language of the nation is arabic.

____________________

____________________

35. in 1981, president mohammed hosni mubarek took office.

____________________

____________________

36. the people of egypt have always depended on the nile river, which flows through the city of cairo.

____________________

____________________

37. in the desert near cairo, you can see two famous monuments called the great sphinx and the great pyramid at giza.

____________________

____________________

38. egypt's legislature is called the people's assembly, and its highest court is called the supreme constitutional court.

____________________

____________________

39. the nation's largest political party is called the national democratic party.

____________________

____________________

Name ______________________

40. two thirds of egypt is covered by a dry, sandy plateau called the western desert, which is part of the huge sahara desert that stretches across africa.

______________________

______________________

41. my father studied about egypt with professor samuel d. jones at smithtown university.

______________________

______________________

42. "to me, it is the most fascinating country in the world," dad said.

______________________

______________________

43. "my favorite historical period is called the old kingdom," he continued. "that's when the great pyramid at giza was built for king khufu."

______________________

______________________

44. "i can still remember learning about the mythical goddess named isis and her brother, osiris," my father said.

______________________

______________________

45. dad bought me a great book called <u>ancient egyptian gods and goddesses.</u>

______________________

______________________

**Part 5: Standardized Test Preparation**

For each sentence, circle the letter of the line that has a missing capital letter or a capital letter used incorrectly. If the sentence has no error, choose *No errors.*

**46.** **A** The city of Kyoto,
**B** located on the island of Honshu,
**C** was once the Capital of japan.
**D** *No errors.*

**47.** **F** Long ago, Japanese emperors
**G** invited Chinese teachers
**H** to come to Kyoto.
**J** *No errors.*

**48.** **A** The Chinese brought
**B** the Religion called buddhism
**C** to the islands of Japan.
**D** *No errors.*

**49.** **F** The Kamo river flows
**G** through Kyoto, and Mount Daimonji
**H** lies just outside the city.
**J** *No errors.*

**50.** **A** Murasaki Shikibu wrote a famous
**B** book about a Japanese prince;
**C** it is called <u>The tale of Genji.</u>
**D** *No errors.*

Name ______________________ Date ______________

# Grammar, Usage, and Mechanics: Cumulative Mastery Test

**Part 1: Identify Parts of Speech**
On the lines, write the part of speech of each underlined word.

1. Orange trees <u>originated</u> in southern China.

   ______________________

2. <u>Who</u> brought the first oranges to the Americas?

   ______________________

3. <u>Spanish</u> explorer Hernando de Soto planted the first orange trees in Florida.

   ______________________

4. The Seminole Indians <u>really</u> enjoyed orange slices marinated in honey.

   ______________________

5. Arab traders introduced bananas <u>throughout</u> the Near East.

   ______________________

6. <u>When</u> bananas were introduced at Philadelphia's Centennial Exposition in 1876, they were a great curiosity.

   ______________________

7. Bananas were not widely <u>available</u> in the United States until after World War I.

   ______________________

8. The <u>invention</u> of refrigeration allowed these fragile fruits to be shipped long distances.

   ______________________

9. <u>Wow!</u> Can you imagine the first person who tried to eat a pineapple?

   ______________________

10. That person must have been <u>very</u> brave.

    ______________________

**Part 2: Identify Subjects and Verbs**
Identify the simple subject and the verb in each of the following sentences.

11. The domestication of dogs occurred thousands of years ago.

    S: ______________ V: ______________

12. Today, there are more than a hundred different breeds.

    S: ______________ V: ______________

13. Think of the long relationship between people and dogs.

    S: ______________ V: ______________

14. When were dogs first used as herding animals?

    S: ______________ V: ______________

15. Among the earliest breeds of dogs were greyhounds and Afghans.

    S: ______________ V: ______________

 

Name ______________________________

**Part 3: Identify Complements**
Write the complements in the following sentences and label each one *direct object*, *indirect object*, *predicate noun*, or *predicate adjective*.

16. Afghans became popular in Europe after World War I.

17. Collies have a reputation for being gentle and trustworthy.

18. You should always give a border collie useful work to do.

19. Jan's favorite breed of dog is the beagle.

20. Dogs provide us with so much companionship and service.

**Part 4: Identify Phrases and Clauses**
Write all the phrases in the following sentences and label each one *adjective phrase*, *adverb phrase*, *appositive phrase*, *participial phrase*, *gerund phrase*, or *infinitive phrase*. Then, write any subordinate clauses in the sentences and label them *adjective* or *adverb*.

21. William Monroe, America's first pencil-maker, started his business in 1812.

22. Improving the pencil considerably, Hyman Lipman decided to add an eraser at the top of the pencil.

23. After he was granted a patent, Lipman sold his idea to a businessman named Joseph Rechendorfer.

24. Doing math homework must have been difficult before pencils became available.

25. Even since typewriters and computers have been invented, pencils and pens remain tools that no home or business can do without.

**Part 5: Correcting Phrase Fragments, Clause Fragments, Run-ons, and Misplaced Modifiers**
Revise each of the following items, correcting all errors in sentence structure.

26. Using my new tools, the bookcase was made in a few hours.

Name ______________________

27. I made one tall bookcase. Instead of two smaller ones. Because that's what my mother wanted.

28. My father helped me buy the wood and then we took it home and measured it carefully. Before I started sawing.

29. Thinking of starting a small carpentry business of my own.

30. Needing some money to get started, my dad might give me a small loan.

**Part 6: Choosing the Correct Usage**
For each sentence, write the correct form from the pair of words or phrases in parentheses.

31. (Their, There) are many good reasons for getting plenty of exercise.

32. One reason is (because, that) exercise keeps the heart and lungs healthy.

33. Having a strong heart is (kind of, quite) important to living a long, healthy life.

34. (Beside, Besides) keeping you healthy, exercise can help you lose weight (to, two, too).

35. Allie didn't tell (anybody, nobody) that she was learning karate.

36. The exercise and discipline of the sport have had a good (affect, effect) on her.

37. Allie says that karate is different (than, from) other types of martial arts.

38. She now has a green belt and hopes to make (farther, further) progress.

39. I like watching most sports, (accept, except) for golf.

40. I hardly (ever, never) watch golf on television.

 

Name ______________________________

**Part 7: Using Irregular and Troublesome Verbs**
For each sentence, write the correct verb form in parentheses.

41. That player was (took, taken) out of the basketball game last night.

______________________________

42. I (saw, seen) the game on television.

______________________________

43. His behavior may have (cost, costed) his team the championship.

______________________________

44. He (hit, hitted) an opponent with his elbow when he was jumping up for a rebound.

______________________________

45. Then he (spoke, spoken) rudely to the referee.

______________________________

46. I think he (should of, should have) (knew, known) better.

______________________________

47. When he (went, gone) to the bench, he just (sat, set) there with his head down.

______________________________

48. After the game, the player (says, said) that he (did, done) a foolish thing.

______________________________

49. I hope that this incident has (learned, taught) him a lesson.

______________________________

50. A successful future (lies, lays) ahead of him if he can control his temper.

______________________________

**Part 8: Using Pronouns Correctly**
Write the correct pronoun from each pair in parentheses.

51. Jason and (I, me) are going to the movies with Ben and (she, her).

______________________________

52. (Who, Whom) will drive us to the theater?

______________________________

53. Jason wants to see the science fiction movie, but (its, it's) too long.

______________________________

54. (Who, Whom) did you ask to pick us up after the movie?

______________________________

55. My best friends are Maya and (she, her).

______________________________

56. They are the friends with (who, whom) I feel most comfortable.

______________________________

57. Are these seats (ours, our's) or (theirs, their's)?

______________________________

Name ______________________________

58. Jason was sitting between Carrie and (I, me).

______________________________

59. I liked the movie, even though (its, it's) plot was very complicated.

______________________________

60. Liz and (she, her) were sitting two rows behind Hector and (he, him).

______________________________

**Part 9: Making Words Agree**
For each sentence, write the correct verb or pronoun in parentheses.

61. One of the best forms of exercise (is, are) walking.

______________________________

62. (There's, There are) many older people who walk around the mall every morning.

______________________________

63. Some of the girls in my class (is, are) starting (her, their) own walking club.

______________________________

64. Each of the girls (is, are) wearing (her, their) track suit.

______________________________

65. Samantha knows that (she, you) must keep a regular exercise routine to stay fit.

______________________________

66. Joining Samantha at the lake every morning (is, are) her friends Tricia and Whitney.

______________________________

67. Here (comes, come) two skaters behind us.

______________________________

68. Tony and Ian (takes, take) good care of (his, their) skates.

______________________________

69. Neither Tony nor Ian (has, have) forgotten to wear (his, their) helmet.

______________________________

70. Everyone (needs, need) to protect (his or her, their) head from injuries.

______________________________

**Part 10: Using Modifiers Correctly**
Write the correct form of the modifiers in parentheses.

71. This is the (worst, worstest) winter we've ever had.

______________________________

72. The wind feels (colder, more colder) today than it did yesterday.

______________________________

73. Of my two jackets, this one is the (warmer, warmest).

______________________________

74. These boots are (comfortabler, more comfortable) than those.

______________________________

 

Name ______________________________

75. They feel so (good, well) on my feet.

______________________________

76. Jan likes winter more than (any, any other) season.

______________________________

77. She stays outside longer than (anyone, anyone else).

______________________________

78. I stayed outside (only for, for only) fifteen minutes yesterday.

______________________________

79. My fingers were hurting (bad, badly) from the cold.

______________________________

80. I hope we will have (less, fewer) inches of snow next year.

______________________________

**Part 11: Punctuation**

Copy the following sentences, adding commas, semicolons, colons, quotation marks, underlining, hyphens, and apostrophes where they are needed.

81. The Golden Apples of the Sun a book of short stories by Ray Bradbury is a well loved classic.

______________________________

______________________________

82. Among the reasons for the success of Bradburys stories are the following elements vivid settings strange conflicts and ironic climaxes.

______________________________

______________________________

83. Of the twenty two stories in this book the one called The Flying Machine is many peoples favorite.

______________________________

______________________________

84. When a Chinese inventor creates a flying machine the Emperor Yuan orders the invention and its creator to be destroyed.

______________________________

______________________________

85. The emperor admires the beauty of the flying machine but he fears the consequences of such an invention.

______________________________

______________________________

86. The emperor is afraid that such a machine could be used to attack his country he can foresee the use of flying machines as weapons of war.

______________________________

______________________________

Name ______________________________

87. I love that story said Alex because it really made me think about different views of creativity progress and fear.

______________________________

______________________________

88. I like the imagery in his stories, said Dan. He is one of my favorite writers.

______________________________

______________________________

89. What is your favorite Ray Bradbury story? asked Jamie.

______________________________

______________________________

90. Wow said Sarah. Bradbury sounds great. She added I cant wait to read one of his books.

______________________________

______________________________

**Part 12: Capitalization**

Copy each of the following sentences, adding capital letters where they are needed.

91. norway, sweden, and denmark make up the european region known as Scandinavia.

______________________________

______________________________

92. finland is not considered a Scandinavian country because its people originally migrated from asia, not europe.

______________________________

______________________________

93. the finnish language is actually more similar to hungarian than to swedish.

______________________________

______________________________

94. the islands of greenland and iceland were also colonized by Scandinavians.

______________________________

______________________________

95. the Scandinavian explorer leif ericson crossed the atlantic ocean and reached the continent of north america many centuries ago.

______________________________

______________________________

96. one famous person from denmark was hans christian andersen, the writer of stories such as "the emperor's new clothes."

______________________________

______________________________

97. the city of copenhagen is known for a famous amusement park called tivoli gardens and for the christianborg palace.

______________________________

______________________________

 

**Name** ______________________________

98. many people of Scandinavian ancestry are protestants who belong to a lutheran denomination.

______________________________

______________________________

99. my grandfather, dr. thomas nansen, immigrated to the united states from norway.

______________________________

______________________________

100. "sometimes," grandfather says, "i still miss the north sea and the city of oslo."

______________________________

______________________________

# Part 3: Academic and Workplace Skills

Name ______________________ Date ____________

# Assessment for Chapter 28: Speaking, Listening, Viewing, and Representing

1. Which of the following is *not* an example of sound preparation for communicating effectively in a group discussion? On the line, explain your answer.
   a. Do the required homework and reading.
   b. Speak honestly and forcefully, even if you risk offending someone in the group.
   c. Volunteer to contribute your ideas.
   d. Plan the points you want to make before the discussion begins.

   ______________________

2. Imagine that you need to tell a friend how to get to your house. What are two strategies for giving clear and accurate directions?

   ______________________

   ______________________

3. Tell whether each type of speech described below is explanatory, persuasive, or entertaining.
   a. a speech at a friend's graduation party ____________
   b. a speech in which you announce that you are running for class president ____________
   c. a speech describing the events leading to the Persian Gulf War ____________

Read the following scenario. Then, respond to questions 4–6, which ask you to prepare a speech about the situation described.

> Many students have begun riding bicycles to school in an effort to support environmental causes. There are not enough bike racks available on campus, however, and students are not allowed to chain their bikes to any other structures. Prepare a speech in which you try to persuade the school administration to install more bike racks.

4. a. Describe your audience and tell how you can address this group of people.

   ______________________

   ______________________

   b. Explain what information you might include in your speech. Tell how you will gather this information.

   ______________________

   ______________________

   ______________________

   c. Write an outline of your speech on the following lines. Your outline should include your main points and supporting details.

   ______________________

   ______________________

   ______________________

   ______________________

   ______________________

   ______________________

Name ______________________________

5. List three strategies that can help you as you deliver your speech.

______________________________

______________________________

______________________________

6. Give an example of a question you can ask to help you evaluate another person's speech.

______________________________

______________________________

7. If you wanted to listen effectively to a speech, would you use complete sentences to write down every detail while taking notes? Explain your answer.

______________________________

______________________________

8. Determine your purpose for listening in each of the following situations.

   a. Your history teacher describes the founding of your community. ______________

   b. A professional storyteller performs. ______________________________

9. Name one thing you can do to eliminate distractions in order to listen effectively to a speaker in your classroom.

______________________________

10. Imagine you are watching a political speech or debate on television.

   a. Explain how recognizing fact and opinion can help you to be a critical listener.

   ______________________________

   ______________________________

   b. Explain how analyzing persuasive language can help you to be a critical listener.

   ______________________________

   ______________________________

11. Give two examples each of verbal and nonverbal signals that may help you interpret a speaker's message.

   Verbal signals: ______________________________

   Nonverbal signals: ______________________________

12. Describe two ways in which you can evaluate and improve your listening comprehension skills.

______________________________

______________________________

______________________________

______________________________

13. Which of the following describes information that would most likely be conveyed by a historical map? Explain your answer on the line provided.

   a. a country's major highways
   b. the battles that have taken place during a particular war
   c. a country's climate
   d. the current population of a particular city

______________________________

**Name** ______________________

Study the following map.

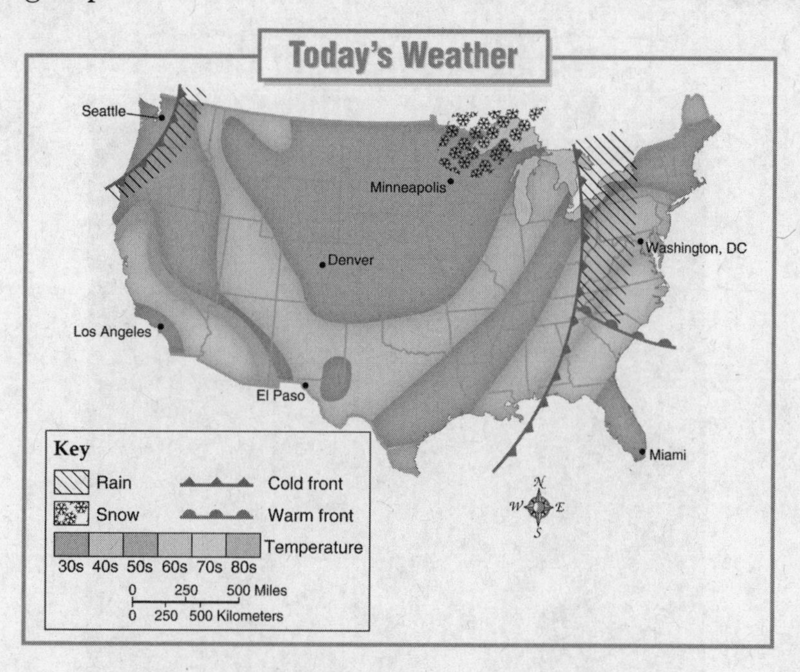


14. What is the purpose of this map?

______________________

15. How do the symbols in the key help you understand the map?

______________________

______________________

16. Based on the title, where would you expect to find this map?

______________________

17. Explain the purpose of each type of graph.

a. pie graph ______________________

b. bar graph ______________________

c. line graph ______________________

Name ________________________________

Study the following graph.

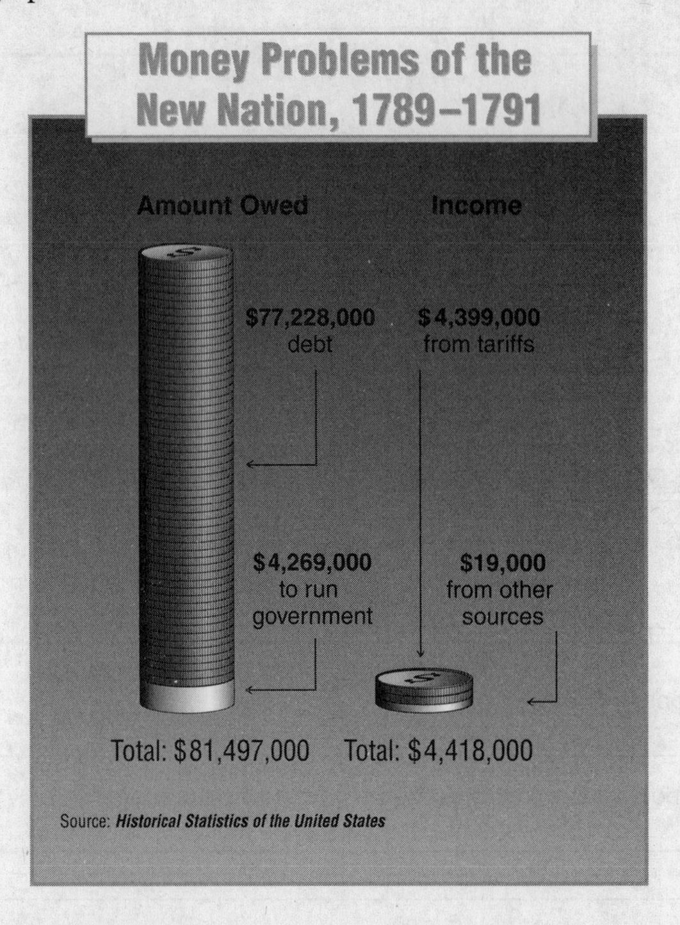


18. a. What kind of graph is this? ________________________________

 b. Why does this graph use coins in the visual representation?

 ________________________________

19. Based on the graph, if the new nation were not in debt, would it then have enough money to run the government? Explain your response.

________________________________

________________________________

Name ___________________________________

Study the following graph.

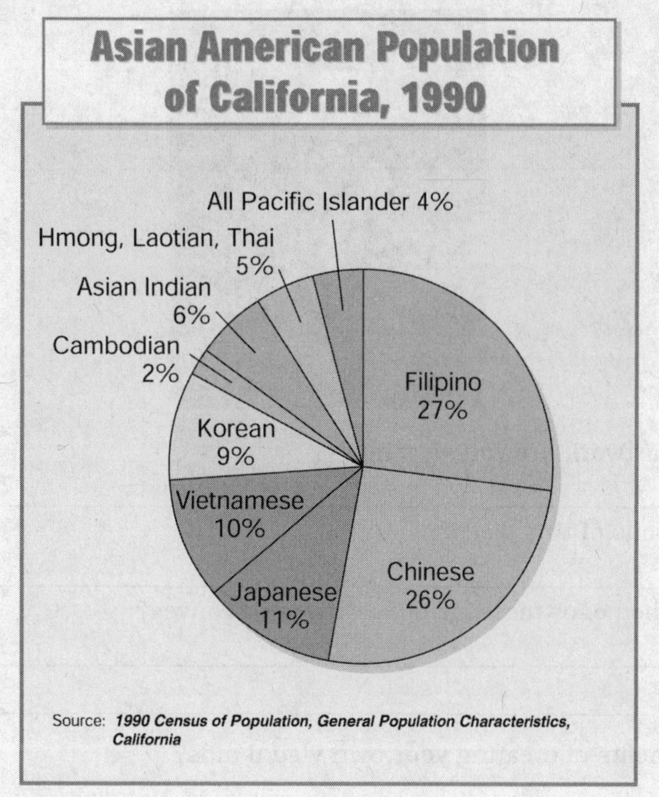


20. Explain what information you learn from this graph.

_______________________________________________

_______________________________________________

21. Which nationality is the most represented in the Asian American population in California in 1990? Which is the least represented?

_______________________________________________

22. Why do you think this information is presented as a pie graph, as opposed to a different type of graph?

_______________________________________________

_______________________________________________

23. a. Give one reason for evaluating persuasive techniques used by the media in presenting information.

_______________________________________________

_______________________________________________

b. List two questions you can ask to evaluate information from the television media.

_______________________________________________

_______________________________________________

_______________________________________________

_______________________________________________

Name ______________________________

Study this piece of art.

24. a. What kind of artwork are you viewing?

b. What is the focus of this piece?

c. What mood, theme, or message does this work convey?

25. What are two benefits of creating your own visual aids?

Read the following information and then answer question 26.

In the late 1800's, Americans invented so many new devices that the United States became know as "the land of invention." Alexander Graham Bell invented the telephone in 1876. The next year, Thomas Edison invented the phonograph. In 1884, Lewis E. Waterman came up with the fountain pen. Granville T. Woods invented an automatic air brake for railroad trains in 1887. Working together, Charles and J. Frank Duryea developed the gasoline-powered automobile in 1893.

26. Use the following grid to show how you could arrange the above information visually. Give the table a title, fill in the three column headings, and then insert the appropriate information in each row.

Title: ______________________________

| | | |
|---|---|---|
| | | |
| | | |
| | | |
| | | |
| | | |

Name ______________________

27. How would the following formatting features, found on word-processing programs, help you visually enhance your written texts?

    a. Numbered or Bulleted Lists ______________________

    b. Boldface or Italics ______________________

28. Imagine that you are giving a multimedia presentation on the civil rights movement of the 1960's. Name two examples of media you might use, and tell what equipment you would need.

    ______________________

    ______________________

29. Explain the purposes of the following steps in creating a video.

    a. writing a shooting script ______________________

    ______________________

    b. creating an outline of scenes ______________________

    ______________________

30. Imagine you are going to perform a speech or monologue from a play by Shakespeare. Based on the topic of the speech, identify the mood you would try to establish. Next, describe the lighting and music you might use. Finally, explain how you would use your voice and movement to help you convey the appropriate mood.

    ______________________

    ______________________

    ______________________

Name ______________________ Date ______________

# 29 Assessment for Chapter 29: Vocabulary and Spelling

1. a. How can participating in conversations help you improve your vocabulary?

   b. How can listening to recorded books help you develop your vocabulary?

2. a. What is a word's context? How can context help the reader understand a word's meaning?

   b. List two steps you can use to determine a word's meaning from its context.

3. Read the following passage. Try to determine the meaning of the underlined words by looking for context clues. Then, on the lines that follow, write the meaning of each word as it is used in the passage.

   Saturday afternoon, I was (a) <u>diligently</u> studying my vocabulary list. I was working hard when my parents asked me to watch my little sister while they went to the mall. My young (b) <u>sibling</u> looks harmless, but looks can be (c) <u>deceiving</u>. Don't ever believe an eight-year-old girl is harmless. While I was studying, she was quietly trying a chemistry experiment in the kitchen. When I heard the explosion, I thought a bomb had (d) <u>detonated</u>. I ran in and found her covered in baking soda and vinegar. "What a (e) <u>fiasco</u>!" I cried. "It's not a failure," my sister replied happily. "It was supposed to explode."

   a. diligently: ______

   b. sibling: ______

   c. deceiving: ______

   d. detonated: ______

   e. fiasco: ______

4. You are reading a magazine and come across this sentence:

   A *hermeneutic* study of Aristotle's ideas, Professor Vitanza's book takes several interpretive approaches.

   Explain how you would try to figure out the meaning of the word "hermeneutic" by using the five steps of the possible-sentences strategy.

Name ______________________________

5. You are reading in your social studies textbook and find the word "vizier."
   a. Where could you look up this unfamiliar word? ______________________
   b. Where could you record this word and its definition?

   ______________________________________________

Read the dictionary entry below. Then answer items 6 and 7.

> **nul · li · fy** (nul′ ə fī) *vt.* **-fied′, -fy′ing** [LL(Ec) *nullificare*, to despise <L *nullus*, none (see NULL) + *facere*, to make, DO[1]] **1** to make legally null; make void; annul **2** to make valueless or useless; bring to nothing **3** to cancel out—**nul′ li fi′ er** *n.*

6. Show how you could record this word on a page in your vocabulary notebook.

   Word: ______________________

   Bridge Word: ______________________

   Definition: ______________________

7. Write a sentence using "nullify," and reinforce the meaning by using its definition in the sentence.

   ______________________________________________

   ______________________________________________

8. Name one other way to study new words besides keeping a vocabulary notebook or writing sentences with new vocabulary words.

   ______________________________________________

9. Which of the following is something that you will *not* necessarily learn about a word in a dictionary? Explain your answer on the line.
   a. its origin
   b. its pronunciation
   c. a synonym
   d. its use as different parts of speech

   ______________________________________________

10. What can you learn about a word in a thesaurus?

    ______________________________________________

11. How can learning the roots of words help you learn the meanings of words?

    ______________________________________________

12. Identify the root shared by the pairs of words. Then, write the meaning of each root.

| | ROOT | MEANING |
|---|---|---|
| a. antonym; synonym | ________ | ________ |
| b. inspect; spectator | ________ | ________ |
| c. dynasty; dynamite | ________ | ________ |

13. Identify the prefix in each word. Then write the definition of the word.

| | PREFIX | DEFINITION |
|---|---|---|
| a. export | ________ | ________ |
| b. review | ________ | ________ |
| c. unknown | ________ | ________ |

Name ______________________________

14. Write a word using each suffix. Then, identify the word's part of speech.

| | WORD | PART OF SPEECH |
|---|---|---|
| a. -able | ____________ | ____________ |
| b. -ance (or -ence) | ____________ | ____________ |
| c. -cy | ____________ | ____________ |
| d. -less | ____________ | ____________ |
| e. -ly | ____________ | ____________ |

15. Write the prefix, root, and suffix for each word. If a word lacks one of these parts, write "none" in the space. Then, write a definition of the whole word.

| Word | Prefix | Root | Suffix | Definition |
|---|---|---|---|---|
| respectable | | | | |
| postponement | | | | |
| synonym | | | | |

16. What historical event brought words such as "reign," "court," and "glory" into the English language?

______________________________

17. Read the following dictionary entry. Then, answer the question that follows.

**me · tab · o · lism** (mə tab′ ə liz′əm) **n.** [< Gr *metabolè*, change < *meta*, beyond (SEE META-) + *ballein*, to throw (SEE BALL²) + -ISM] the chemical and physical processes continuously going on in living organisms and cells, consisting of anabolism and catabolism

What is the language of origin for metabolism? ____________

18. Read the following dictionary entry.

**psy · chol · o · gy** (sī käl′ ə jē) *n., pl.* **-gies** [ModL *psychologia*: see PSYCHO- & -LOGY] **1** *a)* the science dealing with the mind and with mental and emotional processes *b)* the science of human and animal behavior **2** the sum of the actions, traits, attitudes, thoughts, mental states, etc. of a person or group [the *psychology* of the adolescent] **3** a particular system of psychology

Now enter *psychology* into this "Frequently Misspelled Words" chart.

| Word | Pronunciation | Definition | Sentence / Memory Aid |
|---|---|---|---|
| | | | |

19. List two of the steps for reviewing spelling words.

______________________________

______________________________

Name ______________________________

20. Correct the spelling of each of the following words. If the word is correct, write "correct" on the line.

a. neice ____________

b. weigh ____________

c. percieve ____________

d. shield ____________

21. Add the suffix to each of the following words. Then, write the correct spelling of the new word.

a. try + -ing ____________

b. beauty +-ful ____________

c. gay +-ly ____________

d. annoy +-ance ____________

22. Correct each misspelled word. If the word is correct, write "correct" on the line.

a. moveable ____________

b. courageous ____________

c. tracable ____________

d. judgement ____________

23. Find the misspelled word in each sentence and write it correctly. If there are no misspelled words, write "correct" on the line.

a. A dictionary and a thesaurus are referrence books. ____________

b. An eclipse is an unusual occurrence. ____________

c. Have you submited your essay for the contest yet? ____________

24. Add the prefix to the following words. Then, write the correct spelling of the new word.

a. dis- + satisfied ____________

b. un- + necessary ____________

c. de- + emphasize ____________

25. Write the plural form of the following words.

a. tax ____________

b. wish ____________

c. circus ____________

d. bench ____________

e. dress ____________

26. Write the plural form of the following words.

a. piano ____________

b. echo ____________

c. patio ____________

Name ____________________

27. Change the underlined word in each sentence to its plural form.
    a. My favorite city in Europe are Paris and Prague. ____________________
    b. I lost the key to the car. ____________________
    c. A sushi cook uses many different knife. ____________________
    d. The leaf of the ancient book are fragile. ____________________

28. Write the plural form of each word.
    a. child ____________________
    b. emphasis ____________________
    c. curriculum ____________________
    d. sheep ____________________

29. Underline the correct word from each pair in parentheses.
    a. (They're, Their) trip to the mountains was postponed.
    b. She looked (through, threw) the window to watch the rain.
    c. (Whose, Who's) house is this?
    d. We are coming, (to, too).

30. Proofread the following passage and underline the six misspelled words. Then, write them correctly on the lines below.

    My brother and I share a room, so we often have arguements over who's things go where. Yesterday he got mad because my mudy shoes were on his bookshelfs. He definitly has no since of humor when it comes to my stuff.

    ____________________
    ____________________
    ____________________

Name ______________________ Date ____________

# 30 Assessment for Chapter 30: Reading Skills

1. Write the letter of the correct definition in the space next to the textbook section it describes.

| | |
|---|---|
| ____ Table of Contents | a. lists subjects with page numbers in back of book |
| ____ Appendix | b. charts, documents, or other material in back of book |
| ____ Index | c. lists books and other sources in back of book |
| ____ Glossary | d. shows how the book is organized |
| ____ Bibliography | e. lists terms and definitions in back of book |

2. Write the name of each special section of a textbook in which you would find the following information.

   a. the page number for the beginning of Chapter 11 ____________

   b. the page numbers on which prisms are discussed ____________

   c. a timeline of events during the Peloponnesian War ____________

   d. a discussion or summary of a chapter's text ____________

   e. a definition of "matrilineal" ____________

3. a. Explain how titles, headings, and subheadings can help you read and study a chapter in a textbook.

   ____________

   b. Explain how the questions and exercises at the end of a textbook chapter can help you study.

   ____________

   c. How can pictures and captions help you as you read a textbook chapter?

   ____________

4. Identify the situation in which you would use each reading style: skimming, scanning, or close reading.

   a. You want to get a general idea of what Chapter 11 is about before beginning to read it.

   ____________

   b. You want to find an explanation of photosynthesis in a chapter on plants in a biology textbook.

   ____________

   c. You are studying a social studies chapter on labor unions for a test tomorrow.

   ____________

5. Learning Question-Answer Relationships (QARs) can help you answer questions about a text. Match the definition with the QAR it describes.

| | |
|---|---|
| ____ right there | a. The answer, for the most part, is not in the text. |
| ____ think and search | b. The answer is not just in the text. Think about what the author has said, what you already know, and how these fit together. |
| ____ author and you | c. The answer is in the text. |
| ____ on your own | d. The answer is in the text, but you have to think about the answer and look for evidence to support it. |

Name ______________________________

6. Explain the strategies for the SQ4R Method.

   Survey: ______________________________

   Question: ______________________________

   Read: ______________________________

   Record: ______________________________

   Recite: ______________________________

   Review: ______________________________

**Read this passage about an early U.S. labor union. Then, answer questions 7 and 8.**

In 1869, workers formed the Knights of Labor. At first, the union was open to skilled workers only. Members held meetings in secret because employers fired workers who joined unions.

In 1879, the Knights of Labor selected Terence Powderly as their president. Powderly worked to strengthen the union by opening membership to immigrants, blacks, women, and unskilled workers.

Powderly wanted the Knights to make the world a better place for both workers and employers. He did not believe in strikes. Rather, he relied on rallies and meetings to win public support. Goals of the Knights included a shorter workday, an end to child labor, and equal pay for men and women.

In 1885, some Knights of Labor launched a strike that forced the Missouri Pacific Railroad to restore wage cuts. The Knights did not officially support the strike. Still, workers everywhere saw the strike as a victory for the union. Membership soared to 700,000, including 60,000 African Americans.

Name ____________________________________________

7. Fill in the timeline below. Include the unit of time used, the initiating event, two in-between events and their corresponding dates, and the final event.

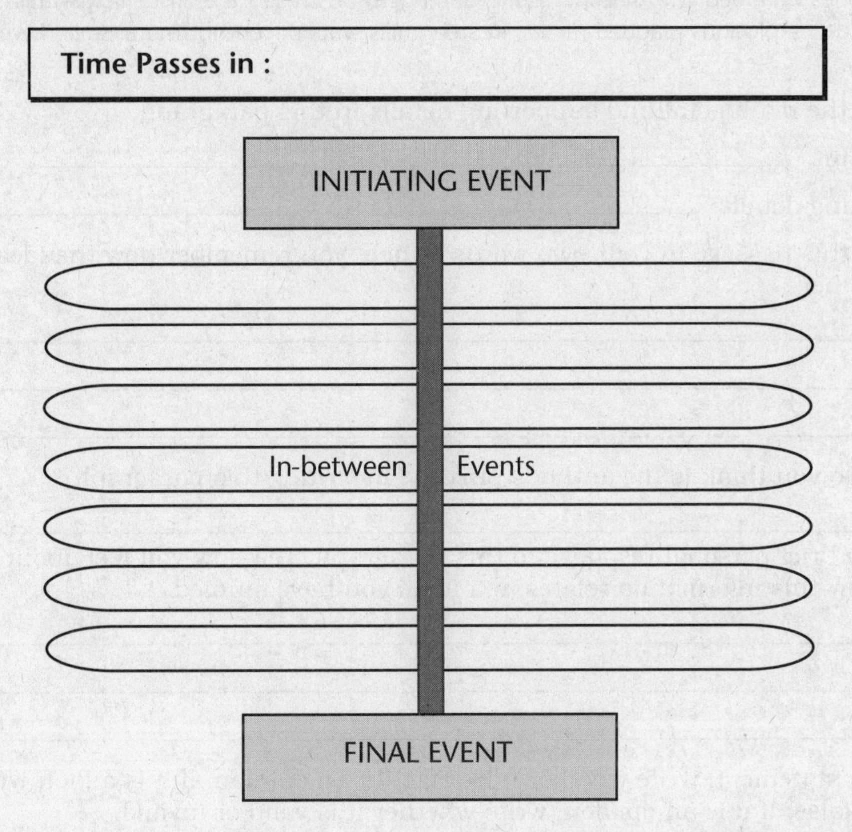


8. Fill in the Question-and-Answer chart with major details from the passage above.

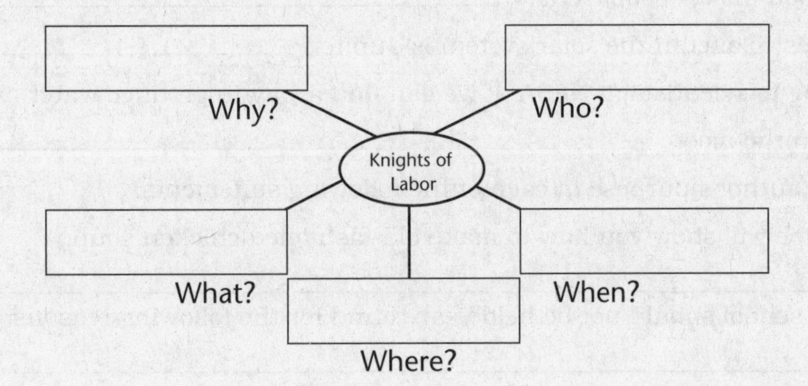

**Name** ______________________________

Read this passage about U.S. factories around 1900. Then, answer questions 9 and 10.

> Factories brimmed with hazards. Lung-damaging dust filled the air of textile mills. Cave-ins and gas explosions plagued mines. In steel mills, vats of red-hot metal spilled without warning.

9. a. Identify the main point and supporting details in this paragraph.

   Main point: ______________________________

   Supporting details: ______________________________

   b. Restate this passage in your own words to help you remember how the ideas relate to one another.

   ______________________________

   ______________________________

   ______________________________

10. a. What do you think is the author's purpose in writing this paragraph?

   ______________________________

   b. Write a brief personal response to this paragraph. Tell how you feel about this topic and how this information relates to a topic you have studied.

   ______________________________

   ______________________________

   ______________________________

11. After each statement, write whether it is a fact or an opinion. If it is a fact, write whether it is true or false. If it is an opinion, write whether it is valid or invalid.

   a. The sun revolves around the Earth. ______________________________

   b. A full moon makes people crazy. ______________________________

   c. The largest planet in the solar system is Jupiter. ______________________________

   d. According to scientists at NASA, if we can find a way to produce water, we can build a colony on the moon. ______________________________

12. Identify the author's purpose in each of the following statements.

   a. This recipe will show you how to make old-fashioned chicken soup.

   ______________________________

   b. I believe school should not be held year-round for the following reasons.

   ______________________________

   c. Here's the car of your dreams, at the price of your dreams.

   ______________________________

   d. Now that she has learned to enjoy camping, my mother likes to recall her first camping trip, complete with pouring rain, mudslides, and water snakes in the tent.

   ______________________________

13. Identify the generalizations in these sentences as *valid* or *invalid.*

   a. More girls than boys in our class earned A's in earth science. Therefore, girls are better in science than boys are. ______________________________

   b. In our class, nine girls and five boys made the honor roll. Therefore, in our class more girls than boys had top grades. ______________________________

Name ______________________________

14. Explain the difference between using words in a denotative way and in a connotative way.

_______________________________________________

_______________________________________________

15. a. What is jargon?

_______________________________________________

b. What is the opposite of jargon?

_______________________________________________

16. An author may organize his or her ideas by showing cause and effect.

a. What is a cause? ____________________

b. What is an effect? ____________________

c. List two words or phrases that give clues that the author is using a cause-and-effect structure. ____________________

17. a. Why would an author use a comparison-and-contrast structure?

_______________________________________________

b. List three words or phrases that signal comparison.

_______________________________________________

c. List three words or phrases that signal contrast.

_______________________________________________

18. a. Why would an author use chronological order?

_______________________________________________

b. List three words or phrases that signal chronological order.

_______________________________________________

19. Which of the following is *not* a type of literary writing?
a. fiction
b. journalism
c. poetry
d. drama

20. Identify the point of view for each of the following types of narrators.

a. The narrator is a character in the story, referring to himself or herself as *I*.

_______________________________________________

b. The narrator knows what all the characters think and feel.

_______________________________________________

c. The narrator knows the thoughts and feelings of only one character, and everything is seen from this person's point of view.

_______________________________________________

21. Name the two types of conflict found in fiction. Explain each one.

_______________________________________________

22. When reading fiction, try to create mental pictures of the action, setting, and characters. Name two of the three kinds of words that can help you do this.

_______________________________________________

_______________________________________________

Name ____________________

23. Why is it a good idea to read the cast of characters before you begin reading a play?

24. Why should you note the stage directions carefully when reading a play?

25. List two questions you might ask yourself about the characters and events as you are reading a play.

26. a. When reading poetry, should you pause at the end of each line or only at punctuation marks? ____________________

b. When you read a poem, why should you paraphrase each stanza or group of lines?

27. Who is the speaker of a poem?

28. Identify the types of figurative language in the following sentences.

a. Her heart beats like the wings of a sparrow. ____________________

b. Her heart is a frightened sparrow. ____________________

c. Fear entered her heart and shut the door. ____________________

29. List one way you can better understand a folk tale, legend, or myth.

30. Tell why you might read each of the following sources.

a. newspapers

b. anthologies

c. electronic texts (Web pages)

Name ______________________ Date ____________

# Assessment for Chapter 31: Study, Reference, and Test-Taking Skills

1. Which of the following is *not* a suitable study area? Explain your answer on the line provided.
   a. an area with a television set
   b. an organized area
   c. a well-lit area
   d. a comfortable area

   ______________________________

2. List two important details about assignments that you should record in your assignment book.

   ______________________________

3. Identify two tips for taking notes.

   ______________________________

   ______________________________

Read the following passage. Then, answer questions 4 and 5.

> Alexander Hamilton and Thomas Jefferson disagreed about economic policy. Hamilton felt the government should encourage manufacturing and trade. He also favored the growth of cities and the merchant class who helped make cities prosperous.
>
> Jefferson believed that farmers, rather than merchants, were the backbone of the new nation. "Cultivators of the earth," he wrote, "are the most valuable citizens." He feared that a manufacturing economy would corrupt the United States by concentrating power in the hands of a small group of wealthy Americans.

4. Write a modified outline of this passage.

   ______________________________

5. Using your own words, write a summary of the main ideas and major details of this passage.

   ______________________________

6. Library resources use word-by-word alphabetizing. Arrange the following listings in word-by-word alphabetizing order. Write the letters in the correct order on the line below.
   a. Northern Hemisphere
   b. The North Pole
   c. North Dakota
   d. North Carolina

   ______________________

7. List two of the three forms of the library catalog in which you can find information about library resources.

   ______________________

8. In the library, in what order would you find these novels by James Fenimore Cooper? List the order of titles by writing their corresponding letters on the line below.
   a. *The Deerslayer*
   b. *The Prairie*
   c. *The Last of the Mohicans*
   d. *The Pathfinder*

   ______________________

9. Name the steps you would take to locate a nonfiction book on American explorers in your library.

   ______________________

   ______________________

   ______________________

10. Where would you look for a biography of James Fenimore Cooper in your library?

   ______________________

11. a. What are periodicals?

   ______________________

   b. What kind of information is found in periodicals?

   ______________________

   c. What library resource will you use to find articles on a specific topic?

   ______________________

12. List two steps you would take to find a periodical article on earthquakes.

   ______________________

   ______________________

13. Where in the library would you find a pamphlet on your local government?

   ______________________

14. Which of the following information is *not* usually found in a dictionary?
   a. the pronunciation of a word
   b. the history of a word
   c. antonyms for a word
   d. how a word is used in a sentence

15. a. On the line, list three different spellings of the sound *a*, as in *lane*.

   ______________________

   b. Give examples of words with each of the above spellings.

   ______________________

Name ______________________

16. List any two of the three steps for looking up the word *jurisdiction* in the dictionary.

______________________

______________________

______________________

Read this dictionary entry. Then, answer questions 17–19.

> **om · nis · cient** (äm · nish′ · ənt; *Brit & Cdn.* -nis′ē ənt) ***adj.*** [ML *omnisciens* < L *omnis*, all + *sciens*, knowing: see SCIENCE] having infinite knowledge; knowing all things **-the Omniscient** God om · niś · cient · ly ***adv***.

17. a. How many syllables does *omniscient* have? ______________

    b. Which syllable is most heavily stressed when you pronounce the word? ______________

18. What part of speech is *omniscient*? ______________

19. a. What is the language of origin of *omniscient*? ______________

    b. What is a word derived from *omniscient*, and what is its part of speech?

    ______________________

20. Give one tip for using a print encyclopedia.

______________________

______________________

21. In what reference works would you look for the following information?

    a. a physical map of your area ______________

    b. a list of former presidents of the U.S. ______________

    c. a brief biography of former Supreme Court Justice Thurgood Marshall ______________

22. List two ways to judge the reliability of a Web site.

______________________

______________________

23. Why is it important to proofread your answers when taking a test?

______________________

______________________

______________________

24. On a multiple-choice test, why should you read all of the choices before answering?

______________________

______________________

______________________

25. List two strategies for answering matching questions on a test.

______________________

______________________

______________________

______________________

Name ____________________

26. List two tips for determining the answers to true/false questions on a test.

____________________

____________________

27. Write examples of each of the following common analogy relationships.

a. function: ____________________

b. part to whole: ____________________

c. cause-effect: ____________________

d. type: ____________________

28. List one strategy for answering analogy questions on a test.

____________________

____________________

29. On the line, identify the relationship between the first pair of words. Then, circle the letter of the word that completes the second pair.
EAR: HEARING::Eye:

____________________

a. look
b. seeing
c. listen
d. smell

30. List two strategies for answering short-answer and essay questions on a test.

____________________

____________________

 

# Answers

## Key to Ability Levels: E = Easy; A = Average; C = Challenging

**Chapter 1: The Writer in You (p. 3)**

1. E *Samples:* e-mail, phone messages, journal entries, stories, notes, invitations, reports.
2. A *Sample:* Writing provides a permanent record of ideas.
3. A *Sample:* You can collect and focus your throughts before you share them with others.
4. A *Sample:* Organization helps readers follow the ideas in your writing. Word choice helps readers understand exactly what you mean. Sentence fluency creates a flow that sounds smooth and polished. Conventions make it possible to communicate effectively.
5. A *Sample:* A distinctive voice shows a writer's personality.
6. A *Sample:* I might keep the notebook with me at all times so that when I see something interesting, I can jot it down. This way, I can get writing ideas everywhere—outside, in a restaurant, watching TV, or studying in the library.
7. C *Sample:* I might include quotes, interesting facts, or ideas triggered by an article or news story. It might help with my writing and supplying topics or by helping me locate information later.
8. A *Sample:* A writing portfolio is used to monitor writing progress. I might keep my favorite stories or the latest version of everything I've written. I might also include earlier drafts so that I could track my progress.
9. A d. *Sample:* Reading can prompt inspiration and ideas, but it's not a substitute for learning grammar or practicing your own writing. Also, writers often cover the same topics; what makes each work different is the writer's unique ideas and insights.
10. A *Sample:* The writing environment is a time and place for writing. It is important because it encourages creativity and supports both the mental and physical aspects of the process.
11. E You must choose the right spot, prepare your materials, and budget your time.
12. C *Sample:* It's good to leave revising until the end so you won't interrupt the flow of creative thoughts.
13. A *Sample:* Different things work for different people, and by trying different things, you can discover what works best for you.
14. C *Sample:* Group brainstorming is a good way to generate a wide variety of ideas.
15. C *Sample:* Collaborative or cooperative writing works when you have a task that can be broken down into specific tasks and shared.
16. C *Sample:* Peer reviewers help point out strengths and weaknesses in your writing that you may not see yourself.
17. E d.
    *Sample:* Even people who don't write for a living perform important writing tasks as part of their jobs. For example, a doctor might have to write up summaries and diagnoses and a politician might have to write speeches.
18. E *Sample:* My best writing was a short story I wrote last year. I think the ideas were interesting and my word choice was varied and precise.
19. E *Sample:* I would like to be better at organizing ideas.
20. A *Sample:* Publishing would give me a way to share my thoughts with others.

**Chapter 2: A Walk Through the Writing Process (p. 5)**

1. E a. extensive
   b. reflexive
   c. extensive
2. A *Sample:* During prewriting, writers explore ideas and gather details.
3. A *Sample:* During revising, writers correct errors and make improvements in form and content. In the editing and proofreading stage, writers fix errors in grammar, spelling, and mechanics.
4. A c.
   *Sample:* The time to check for punctuation is during editing and proofreading. Writing your ideas freely, from beginning to end, occurs during the drafting stage, and reorganizing paragraphs occurs during revising.
5. E *Sample:* Entertainment: sports, movies, games
6. A *Samples:* sports: in-line skating, baseball
   movies: horror, adventure
   games: board games, video games
7. C *Sample:* If I were writing an essay for teenagers, I might use a casual voice and relate my own experiences as if they were familiar to the audience. For business executives, I might be more formal and give more explanation.
8. E To inform: c.
   To reflect: b.
   To persuade: a.
9. C *Samples:*
   Purpose: to inform
   Audience: general, mostly adults
   Title: In-line Skaters Need Space
   a. What in-line skating is
   b. Who skates, where people skate, need for space
   c. Accidents, responsibility of skaters
10. C *Samples:*
    nouns: skates, pathways, accidents
    verbs: glide, tumble, spin
    adjectives: speedy, fearful, protected
    adverbs: swiftly, expertly, loudly

11. A *Samples:*
a. motion
b. lots of kids, but really anyone
c. It makes you happy and gives you exercise.
d. It can be expensive to get good equipment. It's hard to find uncrowded space.
e. sidewalks, driveways, bike paths
f. skates, pads, helmet, maybe lessons

12. A *Sample:* vivid description, compelling quotation

13. C *Sample:* There he zooms, weaving in and around plodding joggers and spinning cyclists, sometimes veering so close that a fall appears certain.

14. E a. extension
b. elaboration
c. statement

15. A c.
*Sample:* The writer who doesn't link ideas by using transitions jumps from one place to another.

16. E *Sample:* "Actually, my little sister once complained about this."
"My favorite helmet is neon blue and comes to a point in the back."

17. A *Samples:* is: blows
are: sing
is: smiles
are: swing

18. A *Sample:* spelling, capitalization, punctuation, grammar, and usage.

19. A *Sample:* "One drawback to in-line skating is this: It's often hard to find a good place to skate. Like bikers, in-line skaters find city streets too busy to travel on safely. Sidewalks can be too crowded with pedestrians, strollers, and joggers. In-line skaters have joined forces with bikers in working to establish special pathways."

20. A *Sample:* A writing portfolio enables writers to look back at their work and see how they've progressed. It can help students reflect on the writing process and come up with new ideas.

**Chapter 3: Paragraphs and Compositions (p. 9)**

1. E c.
*Sample:*
a. A description can be shorter or longer than a paragraph.
b. Paragraphs are used in many types of writing.
d. Suggestions, directions, or instructions may run longer than a paragraph.

2. A *Sample:* A composition is any group of paragraphs that are logically arranged to develop and support a single main idea, such as a research report, an essay, or a short story.

3. E *Sample:*
a. main idea
b. implied main idea
c. stated main idea

4. C *Sample:*
topic sentence: "To Julia, Luna the golden retriever was the most reliable member of the family."
main idea: Luna is important to Julia.

5. A *Sample:* Today's soccer game was a rough one for Jack.

6. E supporting fact: d.
supporting statistic: a.
illustration: b.
detail: c.

7. A *Sample:*
Fact 1: A farm contains land and open space.
Fact 2: Farm chores involve crops or animals.

8. A *Sample:*
Detail 1: Junk food includes sugary items, such as candy and soda pop.
Detail 2: Many television commercials boost products such as chips and cookies.

9. C *Sample:*
topic sentence: Fruit tastes great and can give you energy.
restatement: When you're tired and thirsty, fruits such as mangoes, pears, and grapes come in handy.
illustration: After today's dance class, I was hot and tired. An orange I'd forgotten in my backpack was enough to rejuvenate me.

10. E *Sample:* a.
A thesis statement is another name for a main idea.

11. A *Sample:*
thesis statement: "Performing onstage requires many different types of skills."
sentence that doesn't fit: "Watching a play can be fun."
explanation: This sentence doesn't offer information about the types of skills needed by an actor.

12. A *Sample:* Coherence in a piece of writing means that the ideas are logically connected and the reader can see how one idea is related to another. To establish coherence, a writer should maintain a logical organization and connect ideas with transitional words and phrases.

13. E *Samples:*
a. later, meanwhile
b. however, similarly
c. therefore, as a result
d. outside, above

14. A *Sample:*
a. indicate focus
b. develop the thesis statement
c. close, or "wrap up," the composition

15. E *Sample:* "Computers play an essential role in today's society."

16. C *Sample:* A topical paragraph contains one main idea and several sentences that support or illustrate that main idea. "Computers play an essential role in today's society. Almost every aspect of daily life is now organized or regulated by computers. Business at banks, libraries, hospitals—even fast food restaurants—would roll to a halt if their computers stopped working."

17. A *Sample:*
purpose: to indicate dialogue
A functional paragraph can also serve to make a transition or to create emphasis.

18. C *Sample:* "Springtime is refreshing. Finally the flowers bloom. Although it rains, the sun welcomes back the robins and geese, melts winter coats into light, pastel jackets, and livens up everyone's mood."

19. C *Sample:*
walked: trudged
color: gray
said: whispered
expression: scowl
"With a scowl, Kevin trudged under a gray sky that whispered bleak predictions for the day ahead."

20. C Formal English observes the conventions of standard language, and might be used for school assignments such as reports. Informal English is the language of everyday speech. It might be used when writing dialogue or a letter to a friend.

**Chapter 4: Narration: Autobiographical Writing**
**Test 1 (p. 12)**

1. E Students' topics should focus on a surprising event and should be narrow enough to cover in three or four paragraphs.
2. E Students should choose an audience that would find the topic interesting. They should provide them with information they may not already know. Students' purposes should relate to the nature of their topics.
3. E Students' answers should specify the time, location, people, and events related to their topic.
4. E Students' answers should address the elements to be included in the lead, the order in which the student will write about the events, and the way in which the surprise will be described.
5. E Students' drafts should fulfill the assignment and contain details from their prewriting and drafting activities.
6. E Revisions should enhance tension or interest in the narratives.
7. E Students should circle two vague nouns and replace them with more precise nouns. These vague and precise nouns should also be written on the lines provided.
8. E *Samples:* Before I went outside,
Hearing that it might rain,
Students' own introductory phrases or clauses should be separated by commas.
9. E Students' answers should reflect an understanding of the rubric.
10. E Students' illustration choices should be appropriate for their essay topics. Students' explanations should demonstrate an understanding of how these illustrations will enhance their autobiographical writing.

**Chapter 4: Narration: Autobiographical Writing**
**Test 2 (p. 14)**

1. A Students should indicate a time when a life event triggered a strong emotion, and they should explain specific reasons for feeling this way.
2. A Students should choose a purpose that relates to the nature of their topic. Then, they should explain how they plan to accomplish their purpose.
3. A Students should identify a topic and provide details called for, including time, place, events, conflicts, dialogue, and people.
4. A Students should identify who or what is involved in the central conflict.
5. A Students' drafts should fulfill the assignment and contain details from their prewriting and drafting activities.
6. A Students should revise their leads to "hook" the reader and explain how their revised leads are more effective.
7. A Students should circle two vague nouns and replace them with more precise nouns. These vague and precise nouns should also be written on the lines provided.
8. A *Sample:* When I got to the basement,
Digging in my pocket,
Terrified,
Students' own introductory phrases or clauses should be separated by commas.
9. A Students' answers should reflect an understanding of the rubric.
10. A Students' suggestions for sharing their writing should be appropriate for an autobiographical narrative, and should indicate how they think they will reach their intended audience.

**Chapter 4: Narration: Autobiographical Writing**
**Test 3 (p. 16)**

1. C Students should state what they discovered about themselves, when they discovered it, and the event(s) that facilitated this new self-knowledge.
2. C Students should specify details about the event and about themselves before and after the event.
3. C The main conflict should be consistent with earlier notes.
4. C Students should explain how tension will be incorporated into narrative and why they think this method will be effective. *Sample:* I will show how my sad mood makes me sluggish and reluctant to go to camp. This will create tension because there is a deadline: I have to go to camp and my refusal creates a problem.

5. C Students' drafts should fulfill the assignment and contain details from their prewriting and drafting activities.
6. C Students should identify the climax and either explain why it represents the point of greatest tension or rewrite it so that it effectively represents the point of greatest tension.
*Sample:* Climax: I looked at the catalogue that I'd just thrown on the floor. It was opened to a page labeled "Fine Arts Programs." Suddenly, I knew how I would solve my problem.
This is a good climax because it shows the turning point.
7. C Students should give a brief summary of the main idea of each paragraph. They should use these summaries as they check their work for coherence.
8. C Students should identify a sentence from their work that has an introductory phrase or clause, or should create such a sentence and punctuate it correctly.
9. C Students' answers should reflect an understanding of the rubric.
10. C Students' suggestions for outlets for their writing should be appropriate for an autobiographical narrative.

**Chapter 5: Narration: Short Story**
**Test 1 (p. 18)**

1. E Students should note vivid details they associate with a hike in the woods and should define the story's central conflict.
2. E Students should list specific details about their story's main character.
3. E Students should describe the main character's response to the conflict and the personal qualities that govern the character's response.
4. E Students' answers should contain specific events with active verbs.
5. E Students' drafts should fulfill the assignment and contain details from their prewriting activities.
6. E Students' answers should combine short, choppy sentences to reflect accurate and clear connections.
7. E Students should replace two colorless verbs with more vivid verbs.
*Samples:* went / trekked; was / towered
8. E "I think we're lost," said Gina. She looked around at the landscape. Then she added, "I don't recognize anything here."
Students' edits should reflect an understanding of correct dialogue punctuation.
9. E Students' answers should reflect an understanding of the rubric.
10. E Students' illustration choices should be appropriate for their story topic.
Students' answers should contain specific references to what they learned about writing a short story.

**Chapter 5: Narration: Short Story**
**Test 2 (p. 20)**

1. A Students should list specific details about the specified story elements.
2. A Students' answers should address the questions posed and list specific details about the story's main character.
3. A Students should identify the story's intended audience and purpose.
*Sample:* audience: other teenagers; purpose: to entertain
4. A Students' answers should describe specific events using active verbs.
5. A Students' drafts should fulfill the assignment and contain details from their prewriting activities.
6. A Students' answers should include two clues that hint at the story's climax or resolution.
*Sample:* description of rickety fence; description of kids playing around or near fence
7. A Students should replace two colorless verbs with more vivid verbs.
*Sample:* gave / tossed; was / loomed
8. A Then Teri cried, "Don't go in there!" Sandy took a deep breath. "I have to," he said. "My sister might be inside."
Students' edits should reflect an understanding of correct dialogue punctuation.
9. A Students' answers should reflect an understanding of the rubric.
10. A *Sample:* I could publish this story in a magazine for young readers, such as *3-2-1 Contact*.
Students should reflect on the writing process and choose an area in which they would like to improve.

**Chapter 5: Narration: Short Story**
**Test 3 (p. 22)**

1. C Students should list specific details about the specified story elements.
2. C Students should address the questions posed and list specific details about the story's main character.
3. C Students should clearly express a conflict and its effect upon the main character.
4. C Students' answers should describe specific events using active verbs.
Students should also identify the "setup" (the point at which facts are offered that make the resolution possible) and the "payoff" (the point at which the connection between the setup and the resolution becomes clear).
5. C Students' drafts should fulfill the assignment and contain details from their prewriting activities.
6. C Students' answers should offer extra details to flesh out their characters' reactions to an event.
7. C Students should replace two colorless verbs with more vivid verbs.
*Sample:* walked / ambled; ate / nibbled

8. C Students' edits should reflect an understanding of correct dialogue punctuation.
*Sample:* "I'm not asking you," said Carla. "I'm telling you."
9. C Students' answers should reflect an understanding of the rubric.
10. C Students' descriptions should be appropriate for the magazine and its readership.
Students' answers should address something specific they learned about one stage of the writing process.

**Chapter 6: Description**

**Test 1 (p. 25)**

1. E Students should list three specific places and a descriptive detail for each; one place should be circled.
2. E Students' answers should focus on the place they will describe and indicate their strongest impression of it.
3. E Students' answers should indicate what details each audience would find most interesting. They should specify the perspective from which the student will write the description.
4. E Students should choose a method of organization and tell how they will begin their descriptions, what will follow, and how they will conclude.
*Sample:* chronological order: begin with background events, focus on events that lead to the most significant event, and conclude with the most important event
5. E Students' drafts should fulfill the assignment and contain details from their notes and prewriting activities.
6. E Students' answers should include two revised sentences with added descriptive words circled.
*Sample:* Henry first thought that the spiral-shaped shells were boring.
7. E *Samples:* big/massive; loudly/forcefully
8. E The first things that Julia noticed were the large, shiny buildings. Suddenly a whirl of honking, screeching sounds assaulted her ears.
Students' corrections should reflect an understanding of the correct use of commas with adjectives.
9. E Students' answers should reflect an understanding of the rubric.
10. E Students should explain why their images are appropriate for their description.
*Sample:* I would use photographs to highlight the colorful beauty of the place.

**Chapter 6: Description**

**Test 2 (p. 27)**

1. A Students should list three specific places and a descriptive detail for each; one place should be circled.
2. A Students' answers should indicate what details each audience would find most interesting. They should specify the perspective from which the student will write the description.
3. A Students' answers should demonstrate an understanding of "cubing" as a detail-gathering strategy and should provide appropriate details.
4. A Students should choose a method of organization and tell how they will begin their descriptions, what will follow, and how they will conclude.
5. A Students' drafts should fulfill the assignment and contain details from their notes and prewriting activities.
6. A Students' rewrites should include more relevant details.
7. A *Sample:* good/unique; slowly/deliberately
8. A As Jesse stepped into the woods, a loud crackling sound filled her ears. Immediately, she sensed a large, dangerous presence. Was it just her imagination, or was a big, hungry bear lurking here?
Students' corrections should reflect an understanding of correct use of commas with adjectives.
9. A Students' answers should reflect an understanding of the rubric.
10. A *Sample:* I could conduct a search for on-line publications for young adults.
Students' answers should contain specific and thoughtful references to what they learned as they revised.

**Chapter 6: Description**

**Test 3 (p. 30)**

1. C Students should list three people and corresponding details that each calls to mind. They should then specify which person they will write about.
2. C Students should specify their purpose for writing, their intended audience, and the ways in which their audience and purpose will affect their description.
3. C Students' answers should demonstrate an understanding of "cubing" as a detail-gathering strategy and should provide appropriate details.
4. C Students will probably choose order of importance or chronological order.
*Sample:* order of importance: Begin with physical description, describe strengths and weaknesses, and conclude with what this person means to student.
5. C Students' drafts should fulfill the assignment and contain details from their notes and prewriting activities.
6. C Students' rewrites should include more relevant details.
7. C Students' answers should demonstrate an understanding of the uses of functional paragraphs.
*Sample:* When I was younger, I was embarrassed by my father's old-fashioned ideas. Then something happened that changed my perspective forever. (Provides a transition.)

8. C Students should identify and correct a sentence with faulty parallels.
*Sample:* He chose a wood with a dark grain and that looked sturdy. Revision: He chose a wood with a dark grain and a sturdy look.
9. C Students' answers should reflect an understanding of the rubric.
10. C Students' answers should be one-sentence blurbs suitable for a magazine cover. They should highlight the most intriguing part of their descriptions.
Students' answers should contain specific, thoughtful references to the insights that they gained.

**Chapter 7: Persuasive Essay**

**Test 1 (p. 32)**

1. E Students should indicate at least one issue related to each specified environmental topic; they should identify the issue they have chosen to write about and explain their position on it.
2. E Students' responses should indicate an understanding of the use of reporter's questions for narrowing their topic.
3. E Arguments should support or refute students' positions on their topics.
4. E Students should identify their thesis statement, circle two persuasive techniques from the list provided, and write an issue-related persuasive sentence using each of the techniques circled.
5. E Students' drafts should fulfill the assignment and contain details from their prewriting activities and notes.
6. E Students should write a sentence that provides further support for a main point, as needed.
7. E A complex sentence includes one independent clause and one or more subordinate clauses. Students' answers should reflect the accurate and clear combination of two short sentences from their drafts.
8. E *Sample:* On the whale watch, I saw two types: humpbacks and finbacks. I also saw this occur: A dolphin became trapped in a fishing net.
Students' edits should reflect an understanding of the correct use of colons and dashes.
9. E Students should use the rubric to identify and address weaknesses in their drafts.
10. E Students' illustration instructions should be appropriate for their topic.
Students should reflect on their new understanding of their topic.

**Chapter 7: Persuasive Essay**

**Test 2 (p. 35)**

1. A Students should indicate at least one issue related to each specified school topic; they should identify the issue they have chosen to write about and explain their position on it.
2. A Students' responses should indicate an understanding of the use of reporter's questions for narrowing their topic.
3. A Arguments should support or refute students' positions on their topics.
4. A Students should identify their thesis statement, circle two persuasive techniques from the list provided, and write an issue-related persuasive sentence using each of the techniques circled.
5. A Students' drafts should fulfill the assignment and contain details from their prewriting activities and notes.
6. A Students' answers should include a transition sentence and demonstrate an understanding of how to create clear connections between paragraphs.
7. A A complex sentence includes one independent clause and one or more subordinate clauses. Students' answers should reflect an accurate and clear combination of two short sentences from their drafts.
8. A *Sample:* Two things upset me above all else: exclusiveness and snobbery. I also hate when this happens: A girl decides to drop her best friend to fit into a clique. What if this happened to you—wouldn't you feel hurt?
Students' edits should reflect an understanding of correct use of colons and dashes.
9. A Students should use the rubric to identify and address weaknesses in their drafts.
10. A Students' suggestions for where to submit their essays for publication should be appropriate for their topic.
*Sample:* school newspapers and talk radio stations
Students' suggestions for strengthening their persuasive essays should be specific and relevant to their issue.

**Chapter 7: Persuasive Essay**

**Test 3 (p. 38)**

1. C Students should indicate at least one issue related to each specified news topic; they should identify the issue they have chosen to write about and explain their position on it.
2. C Students should specify their intended audience and the knowledge, biases, and concerns of this population.
3. C Students should identify their own position and offer a relevant argument for each of the four types of support listed.
4. C Students should identify their thesis statement, circle two persuasive techniques from the list provided, and write an issue-related persuasive sentence using each of the techniques circled.
5. C Students' drafts should fulfill the assignment and contain details from their prewriting activities and notes.
6. C Students should add a compelling image or dramatic anecdote to support a main point.

7. C Students should demonstrate an understanding of parallel sentence structure.
8. C Students' examples should reflect an understanding of the correct use of colons and dashes.
9. C Students should use the rubric to identify and address weaknesses in their drafts.
10. C Students' cover letters should be appropriate for the newspaper in which they are requesting publication.
*Sample:* I'm a student who has grown up around dogs. I'm concerned about the recent crackdown on responsible owners who let their dogs run off leash in city parks. In this essay, I argue that the city should set aside certain areas where dogs can be allowed to run free.
Students' suggestions for strengthening their persuasive essays should be specific and relevant to their issues.

**Chapter 8: Exposition: Comparison-and-Contrast Essay**

**Test 1 (p. 41)**

1. E Students' responses should include two types of animals for each category specified.
*Samples:*
cats: tabbies, Persians
dogs: beagles, Labradors
snakes and amphibians: grass snakes, frogs
birds: canaries, parakeets
fish: goldfish, tropical fish
Students' choices for comparison and contrast will vary.
*Sample:* I will write a comparison-and-contrast essay about <u>beagles</u> and <u>Labradors</u>.
2. E Answers should indicate similarities and differences in the appropriate spaces.
*Samples:*
beagle: hound, small, tracks
Labrador: retriever, large, fetches
overlap: dogs, friendly, used for hunting, like kids
3. E Students should select and illustrate an organizational method appropriate for their topic.
4. E *Samples:* Point 1: These dogs are good with children.
Elaboration: friendly dogs, not easily hurt, our beagle loves to play ball with us
5. E Students' drafts should fulfill the assignment and contain details from their prewriting activities.
6. E *Samples:*
nice—interesting, fun
like—enjoy, appreciate
7. E Students should include a sentence with an indefinite pronoun. The indefinite pronoun, its antecedent, and the verb should be underlined. *Sample:* <u>Beagles</u> and <u>Labs</u> are great dogs. <u>Both</u> <u>are</u> friendly.
8. E *Samples:*
incorrect—she; correct—they
incorrect—they; correct—he or she
Students' edits should reflect an understanding of correct pronoun-antecedent agreement.
9. E Students should demonstrate an understanding of the rubric.
10. E Students' suggestions for possible publications should be appropriate for their subject.
*Sample:* Possible publication—a dog owners' magazine
Students' answers should identify a specific writing strategy.
*Sample:* I found identifying repeated words helpful because it made my writing more lively and interesting.

**Chapter 8: Exposition: Comparison-and-Contrast Essay**

**Test 2 (p. 44)**

1. A *Samples:* Students' responses should include two activities for each of the activity categories specified.
*Samples:* restful: TV, reading
active: baseball, swimming
solitary: drawing, writing letters
group: cards, sports
Students' choices for comparison and contrast will vary.
*Sample:* I will compare and contrast <u>watching TV</u> and <u>playing cards.</u>
2. A Answers should indicate similarities and differences in the appropriate spaces.
*Samples:*
TV: passive, contains stories, requires electronic equipment
cards: interactive, requires strategy and rules, materials are inexpensive
overlap: relaxing, can be done at home
3. A Students should identify audience, purpose, and style.
*Sample:*
Audience: teens
Purpose: to entertain
Style: informal
4. A Students should identify the theme, or main idea, of their comparison-and-contrast essay and should select and illustrate an organizational method.
*Samples:*
Theme: Old-fashioned activities are sometimes the best.
Block Method:
TV, then cards
5. A Students' drafts should fulfill the assignment and contain details from their prewriting activities.
6. A Students' responses should provide a sentence conveying their theme and a note on how they sharpened their theme.
*Sample:*
Statement that conveys theme: "If more kids were aware of old-fashioned pastimes, they might be less bored."
Comment: I deleted an unfocused detail and added a relevant example.

7. A Students' answers should reflect an understanding of the TRI elements.
*Sample:*
T: "There are many different kinds of card games."
R: "One of the most popular games is called hearts."
I: "I first learned how to play hearts at my cousin's house."

8. A *Sample:*
incorrect—his or her; correct—their
incorrect—their; correct—his or her
Students' edits should reflect an understanding of correct pronoun-antecedent agreement.

9. A Students' answers should reflect an understanding of the rubric.
*Sample:* Address audience more clearly. Use point-by-point method of organization.

10. A Students' suggestions for possible collection titles should be appropriate for their subject.
*Sample:* Title: "Twenty-Five Fun Things To Do"
Students' answers should contain a specific reference to one thing they learned about the drafting process.
*Sample:* I learned that the way you organize an essay can affect how clearly your theme comes across.

**Chapter 8: Exposition: Comparison-and-Contrast Essay**

**Test 3 (p. 47)**

1. C Students' responses should include two careers for each of the career categories specified.
*Samples:*
athletic: gym teacher, basketball player
artistic: sculptor, graphic designer
technological: computer programmer, software developer
business: secretary, ad salesman
Students' choices for comparison and contrast will vary.
*Sample:* I have chosen to write a comparison-and-contrast essay about <u>a sculptor</u> and <u>a software developer.</u>

2. C Answers should indicate similarities and differences in the appropriate spaces.
*Samples:*
sculptor: needs a studio, requires art training, gets hands dirty, works to express himself or herself
software: needs tech training, works for a business, materials are clean
overlap: creative, innovative, specialized knowledge

3. C Students should identify the theme, or main idea, of their comparison-and-contrast essay and should select and illustrate an organizational method.
*Sample:*
<u>theme</u>: Sculptors and software developers are more alike than people may think.
Point-by-Point Method: First discuss tasks, then goals, then creativity.

4. C Students should demonstrate an understanding of the SEE method.
*Samples:*
State: "Both of these professions require creativity."
Extend: "However, a software developer's creativity may not seem obvious."
Elaborate: "Some of the new software involves creative thinking to meet a need—such as software that replaces drab desktop folders with decorative icons."

5. C Students' drafts should fulfill the assignment and contain details from their prewriting activities.

6. C Students should provide a sentence conveying their theme and a note on how they sharpened their theme.
*Sample:*
Conveys theme: "It is obvious that sculptors are highly creative, but a software developer's innovative spirit is often a subtle trait."
Comment: I deleted an extraneous detail and added more support to my second point.

7. C Students might use indefinite pronouns to eliminate repetitive sentence patterns.
*Sample:*
repetition: "Sculptors need specialized training. Software developers also need specialized training."
improvement: "Both require specialized training."

8. C Students' examples and edits should reflect an understanding of correct pronoun-antecedent agreement.
*Sample:*
incorrect: "An artistic person longs to express their feelings."
revised: "An artistic person longs to express his or her feelings."

9. C Students' answers should reflect an understanding of the rubric.
*Sample:*
Make organization consistent.
Vary sentence length.

10. C Students' suggestions for ways to publish their essays should be appropriate for reaching fellow students.
*Sample:* publication: school newspaper or bulletin board
Students' responses on how writing this essay differed from other kinds of writing should offer specific examples.
*Sample:* I had never used the point-by-point organization method before; this taught me a new way to present ideas.

**Chapter 9: Exposition: Cause-and-Effect Essay**

**Test 1 (p. 50)**

1. A Topics should address a time when students felt nervous, anxious, or excited. The language students use should be appropriate for the stated audience.

2. E Intended purposes should be realistic and should relate to students' essay topics.

3. E Students' answers should complete the elements of the appropriate graphic organizer.
*Samples:*
Chain of causes and effects: nervous about the game; lack of sleep; tired and distracted the next day; weak and unfocused during the game
4. E Answers should provide elaboration on causal connections.
*Sample:*
Nervousness and not sleeping are connected because it's hard to fall asleep when your mind isn't relaxed.
"I tried many techniques to quiet my mind, but images of the next day's game kept playing in my head."
5. E Students' drafts should fulfill the assignment and contain information from their notes.
6. E Answers should identify a topical paragraph's topic sentence, a sentence that does not relate to the topic sentence, and a revised sentence.
*Sample:*
topic sentence: "By the time bedtime rolled around, I was anything but tired."
unrelated sentence: "And the next day, I wasn't even hungry."
revised sentence: "I tried to relax by thinking about ideas for tomorrow morning's breakfast."
7. E Sentences should include the perfect tense and should logically express a sequence of events. Incorrect tenses should be revised.
*Sample:*
sentence: "I hadn't eaten that morning, so my legs are shaking."
revision: "I hadn't eaten that morning, so my legs were shaking."
8. E <u>in the churning waves</u> (*Churning* should be circled.)
9. E Students should use the rubric to identify and address weaknesses in their drafts.
10. E Reflections on challenges and resolutions should be relevant to cause-and-effect essay writing.
*Sample:* The biggest challenge was linking two events. I learned to write sentences that elaborate on the connections between events.

**Chapter 9: Exposition: Cause-and-Effect Essay Test 2 (p. 52)**

1. A Topics should address a time when students felt happy or received praise.
*Sample:* I will write a cause-and-effect essay about the time I climbed Mt. Cardigan.
Intended audiences should have a potential interest in the topic. Language should be appropriate for the stated audience.
*Sample:* classmates
2. A Intended purposes should be realistic and should relate to students' essay topics.
3. A Students' answers should complete the elements of the appropriate graphic organizer.
*Sample:*
causes: felt tired of winter; made friends with new student who hikes; climbed the mountain
effect: felt proud of myself
4. A Answers should provide elaboration on causal connections.
*Samples:*
Meeting Kim and feeling great about myself are connected because it was Kim who took me hiking.
"I never knew making a new friend could lead me to embark on such a great adventure."
5. A Students' drafts should fulfill the assignment and contain information from their notes.
6. A Answers should identify a topical paragraph's topic sentence, a sentence that does not relate to the topic sentence, and a revised sentence.
*Sample:*
topic sentence: "The long weeks of cold, gray days had turned me into a negative person."
unrelated sentence: "I knew the mountain was nearby, but I'd never thought of climbing it."
revised sentence: "Gray days ensured dull indoor activities and a drab mood."
7. A Sentences should include the perfect tense and should logically express a sequence of events. Incorrect tenses should be revised.
*Sample:*
sentence: "We had hiked at a fast pace, so by afternoon we are tired."
revision: "We had hiked at a fast pace, so by afternoon we were tired."
8. A <u>across the shimmering lake</u> (*Shimmering* should be circled.)
9. A Students should use the rubric to identify and address weaknesses in their drafts.
10. A Answers should be appropriate for the topic and intended audience.
*Sample:* Web sites about sports and outdoor activities would attract people interested in mountain climbing.
*Sample:* I learned that you need to use precise details to explain relationships between events.

**Chapter 9: Exposition: Cause-and-Effect Essay**

**Test 3 (p. 55)**

1. C Topics should address a time that students consider a turning point in their lives.
*Sample:* getting pneumonia due to not taking care of myself
Students should demonstrate an understanding of how the Classical Invention questioning strategy is used to analyze and refine a topic.
*Sample:*
a. personal events
b. being involved in many activities; not taking care of myself
c. becoming ill; going into the hospital
d. going to sleepover camp
e. the start of new school year
2. C Intended audiences should have a potential interest in the topic. Language and details should be appropriate for the stated audience.
3. C Students' answers should complete the elements of the appropriate graphic organizer.
*Sample:*
causes: overnight camp; not sleeping; lots of physical activity; catching a cold
effect: pneumonia; new appreciation for everyday things
4. C Answers should provide elaboration on causal connections.
*Samples:*
Too much activity and getting pneumonia are connected because if you get sick and don't take care of yourself, you might end up becoming seriously ill.
5. C Students' drafts should fulfill the assignment and contain information from their notes.
6. C Answers should identify a topical paragraph's topic sentence, a sentence that does not relate to the topic sentence, and a revised sentence.
*Sample:*
topic sentence: "This camp provided a wealth of great activities."
unrelated sentence: "My sister had never been to overnight camp."
revised sentence: "Swimming and hiking topped my list of favorites."
7. C Sentences should include perfect tense and should logically express a sequence of events. Incorrect tenses should be revised.
*Sample:*
sentence: "I had taken my temperature, so I know I was ill."
revision: I had taken my temperature, so I knew I was ill.
8. C <u>in the sleepy village</u> (*Sleepy* should be circled.)
9. C Students should use the rubric to identify and address weakness in their drafts.
10. C Answers should be appropriate for the essay topic and intended audience.
*Sample:* "In this anthology, writers describe the events that led them to appreciate the little details of everyday life."
Reflections on what was learned should be relevant to cause-and-effect essay writing.
*Sample:* I learned to describe events in detail in order to show causal connections.

**Chapter 10: Exposition: How-to Essay**

**Test 1 (p. 58)**

1. E Students should provide one or two details for each of the web categories specified.
*Sample:*
where: kitchen at home
what: scrambled eggs
when: anytime
how: need eggs, milk, utensils, and non-stick spray
Students should define their how-to essay topic. *Sample:* making scrambled eggs
2. E Students should respond appropriately to the audience profile questions presented.
*Samples:*
age: eighth graders
what they know: Some may know how to make scrambled eggs; almost everyone has eaten them.
skills: Everyone my age has probably prepared some food.
3. E Students should describe an appropriate visual aid. *Sample:* I will show pictures of the best kind of spatula, whisk, and pan to use.
4. E In addition to listing equipment and ingredients, students should demonstrate an ability to list steps in chronological order.
*Samples:*
Equipment: pan, bowl, fork
Ingredients: eggs, oil, milk, salt, pepper
Steps: collect equipment, get out ingredients, break eggs, beat eggs, season, pour in pan, cook, enjoy
5. E Students' drafts should fulfill the assignment and contain details from their prewriting activities.
6. E Students should demonstrate that they understand how to make steps clearer.
*Sample:* I will make the items in the first paragraph into a list.
7. E Students should offer either a revised sentence or a sentence from their draft that shows how an adverb phrase or clause clarifies a step.
*Sample:* Add the milk slowly to the eggs, beating them continuously.
8. E *brownies, scrambled eggs, and pasta*
9. E Students' answers should reflect an understanding of the rubric.
*Sample:* Use a better ordered chronology. Provide more details.

10. E Students' answers should reflect an understanding of appropriate ways to share their how-to essays.
*Sample:* Put together a class recipe book.
Students' reflections about what they learned should be related to how-to essay writing. *Sample:* I learned that a how-to essay requires a certain kind of format to make it easy to follow.

**Chapter 10: Exposition: How-to Essay**
**Test 2 (p. 61)**

1. A Students should provide one or two details for each of the web categories specified.
*Samples:*
where: workroom, outside, garage
what: painting a chair
when: vacation, weekends
how: using acrylics
Students should define their how-to essay topic. *Sample:* painting a wooden chair
Students should tell how they will focus their essay.
*Sample:* materials needed and instructions
2. A Students should respond to the audience profile questions presented.
*Sample:*
age: classmates
what they know: have seen painted chairs in stores or pictures
skills: most kids have painted something
3. A Students should describe and label an appropriate visual aid. *Sample:* I will need to include a series of step-by-step photos. Each will include a short label, such as "sanding," "priming," or "finishing."
4. A Students should explain or identify their organization and format.
*Samples:*
describing a finished piece
a numbered list
what else these skills can be used for
photos of unfamiliar materials
5. A Students' drafts should fulfill the assignment and contain details from their prewriting activities.
6. A Students should revise sentences that will make steps clearer.
*Sample:*
"Apply the primer. Let it dry. Paint on the base coat."
Revision: "First, apply the primer. Then, let it dry. Finally, paint on the base coat."
7. A Students should offer either a revised sentence or an example from their draft that shows how an adverb phrase or adverb clause clarifies a step.
*Sample:* "As you work, refer to your nearby sketch."
8. A "Some kinds of finishes are wax, shellac, and polyurethane. Spray finishes are best for such small pieces as pencil cups, jewelry boxes, and doll furniture."
Students' edits should reflect an understanding of correct usage of commas in a series.
9. A Students' answers should reflect an understanding of the rubric.
*Samples:* Give more specific detail.
Write a more focused conclusion.
10. A Suggested group might be a class, friends, or club. Note might suggest that a demonstration can be a learning experience for the demonstrator, too.
*Sample:* Questions asked would help me clarify steps.

**Chapter 10: Exposition: How-to Essay**
**Test 3 (p. 64)**

1. C Students should provide one or more details for each of the web categories specified.
*Samples:*
where: in the neighborhood
what: dog walking
when: after school, on weekends
how: need practice, patience
Students should define their how-to essay topic. *Sample:* walking people's dogs
Students should tell how they will focus their essay. *Sample:* what it takes; detailed examples
2. C Students should respond to the audience profile questions presented.
*Sample:*
age: classmates
what they know: Some have their own dogs.
skills: Kids may have other pets.
focus: Need to address kids who don't know how to relate to dogs.
3. C *Sample:*
I plan to show a picture of a dog at heel.
caption: "The proper position for a dog is at the walker's left, just slightly behind his or her heel."
4. C Students should explain or identify their organization and format.
*Sample:*
why dog-walking can be fun and lucrative
bulleted list
summarize the most important skills
sidebar on dangers to watch for
5. C Students' drafts should fulfill the assignment and contain details from their prewriting activities.
6. C Students should revise a sentence to avoid unnecessary repetition.
*Sample:*
repeated word: dog
revised sentence: "Make sure you know the animal before you take it out alone."
7. C Students should offer either a revised sentence or an example from their draft that shows how an adverb phrase or adverb clause clarifies a step or description.
*Sample:*
"As you walk, keep an eye out for squirrels or other small animals that can make the dog bolt."

8. C Students' edits should reflect an understanding of correct usage of commas and semicolons.
*Sample:*
old sentence: "Make sure the owner provides a collar, leash and any special instructions."
revision: "Make sure the owner provides a collar, leash, and any special instructions."
9. C Students' answers should reflect an understanding of the rubric.
*Sample:* Make introduction more focused and interesting. Use more bullets to highlight points.
10. C The suggested multimedia display should enhance each of the steps in the essay. Comments on organization should reflect an understanding of both similarities and differences between a written work and a multimedia presentation.

**Chapter 11: Research Report**
**Test 1 (p. 67)**

1. E Note Card #2; it includes quotation marks.
2. E Marc forgot to include the page number on Note Card #4.
3. E Note Card #3 comes from a source on the Internet.
4. E *Sample:* b) Jupiter is surrounded by sixteen natural satellites, or moons. This sentence is the best because, unlike answers a) and c), it focuses on Marc's complete topic. Answer d) is unnecessary.
5. E *Sample:* Ordering by Type. This is the best method because the topic, the thesis statement, and the notes on the cards don't focus on time order.
6. E Section II
7. E Section IV
8. E Section IV
9. E *Sample:* <u>The second thing we notice</u> is that these objects are not traveling together.
10. E *Sample:* For sentence variety, Marc could combine the second and third sentences in this way: "After we shut down the warp drive, we slide into orbit around the planet."
11. E *Sample:* This is a citation that refers to the source and page number where Marc found the preceding information.
12. E Beasant, Simon
13. E <u>1000 Facts About Space.</u> (Needs underline.)
Needs copyright date.
14. E *Sample:* Marc might send it to *3-2-1 Contact Magazine.*
15. E Students' answers should contain specific references to visual aids appropriate for Marc's research paper. *Sample:* a drawing that shows and labels Jupiter and its moons.

**Chapter 11: Research Report**
**Test 2 (p. 70)**

1. A Students should name a "Classical Invention" question. *Sample:* "In what general category does my topic belong?"
2. A Students should name a "Classical Invention" question. *Sample:* "Into what other topics can my topic be divided?"
3. A Students should name a "Classical Invention" question. *Sample:* "What causes and effects does my topic involve?"
4. A Note Card #2; it includes quotation marks, and is attributed to a speaker.
5. A Katy forgot to include the page number.
6. A *Samples:* The note cards do reflect variety because they cite three different books and a Web site. A variety of sources enhances a writer's credibility.
7. A *Sample:* Answer c) is best because it states the focus of Katy's topic. The other answers simply state details.
8. A *Sample:* Note Card #1 supports Section III.
9. A *Sample:* Note Card #3 supports Section IV.
10. A *Sample:* Note Card #4 supports Section IV.
11. A Students should refer to the introductory paragraph offered.
*Samples:*
a) focus: Babe Ruth wasn't just a baseball champion, he was also a champion of the spirit.
b) The last sentence contains appropriate details.
c) The detail about going to reform school doesn't belong in this paragraph.
12. A Answers may vary. *Sample:* "Most people remember Babe Ruth, a man who slugged 714 homeruns, as a homerun hero."
13. A Entry b) contains these mistakes: The book title isn't underlined; there is no copyright date listed.
14. A Students should refer to appropriate ways of reaching sports enthusiasts. *Sample:* Katy might send the paper to a sports magazine or to the sports section of a newspaper.
15. A Students should suggest a visual aid Katy could incorporate into her research paper on Babe Ruth. *Sample:* a timeline of important events in Babe Ruth's career

**Chapter 11: Research Report**
**Test 3 (p. 73)**

1. C Students should name a "Classical Invention" question. *Sample:* "In what general category does my topic belong?"
2. C Students should name a "Classical Invention" question. *Sample:* "Into what other topics can my topic be divided?"
3. C Students should name a "Classical Invention" question. *Sample:* "What causes and effects does my topic involve?"
4. C *Sample:* Note Card #2 doesn't support Ashley's focus: it does not discuss the origins of the dog.
5. C Ashley forgot to include page numbers on Note Card #3.

6. C Students' answers should offer examples to support their responses.
*Sample:* The note cards reflect a variety of sources because they contain a book, an encyclopedia article, a magazine article, and an on-line magazine article.
It's important to use a variety of sources when writing a research report in order to gather many details, to make sure information is up to date, and to double-check information.
7. C *Sample:* Answer b is the best because it states Ashley's main idea. Answers a, c, and d simply state details.
8. C *Sample:* Note Card #1 supports Section III.
9. C *Sample:* Note Card #3 supports Section II.
10. C *Sample:* Note Card #4 supports Section IV.
11. C *Samples:*
All of today's dog breeds have a common ancestor: the wolf.
The last sentence contains an appropriate detail for this paragraph's focus.
The third sentence doesn't belong in this paragraph: its details are not appropriate for the focus of the paragraph.
12. C Student' revisions should use a participial phrase to combine the two sentences.
*Sample:* "By studying teeth fossils, scientists have classified the dog as part of the family *Canidae.*"
13. C *Samples:* Entry a) is correct. In entry b), the book title should be underlined. Entry c) needs a page or disk number and the year of publication.
14. C Students should suggest appropriate places to publish in order to reach an audience of dog owners. *Sample:* Send it to an on-line dog owner's magazine.
15. C Students should suggest a visual aid Ashley could incorporate into her research paper on the origins of dogs.
*Sample:* a family tree of the dog that dates back to its wolf origins

**Chapter 12: Response to Literature**

**Test 1 (p. 76)**

1. E *Sample:* Actor: the speaker or poet
Acts: the speaker's desire to ease pain and suffering and to assist those who need help
Scene: in poetry, throughout life, contemplated in the speaker's mind
Agency: acts of kindness, easing others' pain
Purpose: to make one's life meaningful
2. E Answers should be based on pentad details. *Sample:* The most interesting details are the ways in which the speaker feels poetry can help her believe that her life is worthwhile.
Focus: The poem shows that the speaker's sense of worth is intertwined with her ability to help others.
3. E Students should elaborate on the patterns they notice in the poem. *Sample:*
Characters: Main character is the speaker.
Theme: Helping others gives meaning to life.
Images: mentions various kinds of pain and loss (hearts breaking, aching lives, robins who have fallen from the nest) and the desire to aid the suffering
Theme: Poetry may be able to ease pain and suffering.
Words: *breaking, aching, pain,* and *fainting* are juxtaposed with *not live in vain.*
Theme: Poetry may be able to ease some of life's pains, thereby providing a meaningful existence for the poet.
4. E Students' insights should be based on their focus statements. *Sample:*
Insight: By writing in a format that juxtaposes life's pains with the possibility of easing them, the reader sees that the speaker believes poetry might be a vehicle for injecting meaning into the poet's life.
5. E Students' drafts should fulfill the assignment and contain details from their prewriting activities.
6. E Students should identify and examine their essay's strongest point. *Sample:*
Strongest Point: The use of deeply felt and universal images reinforces the poem's message about finding meaning in helping others.
final paragraph
This placement is effective because it restates my focus in a new way.
7. E Students should support two general points with appropriate details.
8. E Moore uses repetition to create a mood of hopelessness, as when she writes, "and the colors lingered, unchanging."
9. E Students' answers should reflect an understanding of the rubric.
*Samples:* Use a more logical ordering sequence. Connect each point to overall focus.
10. E Students' reflections should explain one way in which their writing experience led to a heightened understanding of Dickinson's poem.
*Sample:* Analyzing this poem made me realize how much a poet may be motivated to affect others with his or her poetry.

**Chapter 12: Response to Literature**

**Test 2 (p. 79)**

1. A *Samples:* Actor: the narrator; Act: made important decision; Scene: the woods; Agency: internal debate; Purpose: to continue the journey

2. A Answers should be based on pentad details.
*Sample:*
The most interesting details are the act (the decision) and the scene (the woods).
Focus: The use of the "roads" metaphor makes the internal decision come alive.

3. A Students should specify their intended audience and purpose for writing.
*Sample:* a) middle school students; b) My purpose is to share my viewpoint and to get others to read the poem.

4. A Details should connect to the focus of the response.
*Sample:*
Detail 1: "Two roads diverged in a yellow wood."
Detail 2: Second road is "grassy and wanted wear."
Detail 3: The narrator pauses as he regrets he cannot travel both roads.

5. A Students' drafts should fulfill the assignment and contain details from their prewriting activities.

6. A Students should identify the point they feel is their strongest. *Sample:* Strongest Point: "Frost's metaphor makes his theme more visual and immediate than if he had simply written a prose statement."
second paragraph
This placement is effective because it summarizes my focus.

7. A Answers should cite a general point and a supporting detail. *Sample:* General Point: "In the first stanza, the narrator pauses to consider his way and wishes he didn't have to choose." Supporting Detail: "And sorry I could not travel both"

8. A Heller emphasizes this point when she writes, "The air had even taken on a grayish tinge."

9. A Students' answers should demonstrate an understanding of the rubric. *Sample:* Support every point; eliminate points that don't support my focus.

10. A Students' reflections should relate their writing experience to their understanding of Frost's poem. *Sample:* Since I read the poem very closely several times, I appreciated many words and phrases that I didn't notice before.

**Chapter 12: Response to Literature**

**Test 3 (p. 82)**

1. C *Sample:* Actors: mushrooms; Act: growing; Scenes: woods, pavement; Agencies: poking through soil and cracks; Purpose: to live out cycle of life.
Focus: By noticing and describing small details, Sylvia Plath creates a sense of wonder at the power of nature.

2. C Students should elaborate on the patterns specified.
*Sample:*
Actors: The main "characters" are mushrooms.
Theme: Wonder can be contained in the smallest things.
Images: description of mushrooms' parts and growth
Theme: the poet creates a sense of contrast between the mushrooms' small size and their great strength.
Words: "whitely, discreetly"; "soft fists insist"
Theme: The growth of nature is inevitable.

3. C Students' insights should be based on their focus statements.
*Sample:* Insight: Plath shows that by focusing on details, even seemingly insignificant life forms can seem powerful.

4. C Students' responses should demonstrate an understanding of varying perspectives.
*Sample:* Upside-down perspective: Plath may be using mushrooms as a metaphor for all life forms that often go unnoticed.
I will include this perspective in my draft because it builds on my focus and adds to the insight.

5. C Students' drafts should fulfill the assignment and contain details from their prewriting activities.

6. C Students should identify and examine their essay's strongest point. *Sample:*
Strongest Point: The strength of Plath's poem is in the details.
second paragraph
This placement is effective because it introduces my focus.

7. C Students should use compound or complex sentences to combine two or more sentences with related or contrasting points.
*Sample:* Plath includes details about how the mushroom takes over its habitat.
This creates a big picture of a small life form.
Revision: Plath includes details about how the mushroom takes over its habitat, which creates a big picture of a small life form.

8. C Students' edits should reflect an understanding of the correct way to punctuate and format quotations.

9. C Students' answers should demonstrate an understanding of the rubric.
*Sample:* Present points more forcefully.
Tighten organization.

10. C Students' title suggestions and insights should reflect a thorough understanding of the poem.

**Chapter 13: Writing for Assessment**
**Test 1 (p. 85)**

1. E Students should select one of the topics and explain their choice.
*Samples:*
I would choose the first topic because I'm most comfortable with a persuasive-writing format.
2. E persuasive essay
comparison-and-contrast essay
cause-and-effect essay
3. E Students should offer one way of analyzing a prompt.
*Sample:* Identify the question.
4. E Students should specify their topic and organizational method.
*Sample:* My topic: a
Order: Order of Importance
5. E Students' drafts should fulfill the assignment and contain details from their prewriting activities.
6. E Students should state the main idea and supporting details from one of their paragraphs.
*Sample:*
Main idea: Mental attitude is just as important for athletics as physical ability.
Extraneous detail: "I wish we had an Olympic-sized pool here."
7. E Students' responses and examples should address particulars of their own conclusions.
*Sample:* A conclusion should accurately restate what I said in the essay. My conclusion <u>does not</u> accomplish this purpose.
My revision: "So, if you examine the whole picture—the nature of skills required, the importance of physical activity for a healthy lifestyle, and the recognition of all types of talents—the case for requiring physical education in junior high is a strong one."
8. E *Sample:* "Many health professionals are worried about the lifestyles of today's teenagers. One common worry is that teenagers watch too much TV."
Students' edits should identify and correct comma splices.
*Sample:*
Old version: "I used to think it was unfair to grade physical education, now I see the logic."
New version: "I used to think it was unfair to grade physical education, but now I see the logic."
9. E Students should demonstrate an understanding of the rubric.
*Sample:*
Use better word choices.
Tighten up paragraphs to eliminate details that don't support the main idea.
10. E Students should mention a strategy they found useful for writing for assessment.
*Sample:* I learned that taking some time to organize my writing saved time in the end.

**Chapter 13: Writing for Assessment**
**Test 2 (p. 87)**

1. A Students should select one of the three topics and explain their choice.
*Sample:* I would choose the third topic because I feel comfortable with the compare-and-contrast format.
2. A persuasive essay
cause-and-effect essay
compare-and-contrast essay
3. A Students should offer two ways of analyzing a prompt.
*Sample:* Write a thesis statement. Identify the question.
4. A Students should specify their organizational method and complete the corresponding graphic organizer.
*Sample:*
Order of Importance
I. Introduction
State that sometimes teenagers are treated unfairly.
II. Differences reflect stereotypes of teenagers.
III. By treating teenagers differently, people can make mistakes in judgment. No one likes to be treated with disrespect.
IV. Treatment may actually increase "bad" behavior.
V. Treat teenagers fairly, and treat them as individuals.
5. A Students' drafts should fulfill the assignment and contain details from their prewriting activities.
6. A Students should state the main idea and extraneous detail(s) from one of their paragraphs.
*Sample:*
Main idea: Store clerks sometimes discriminate against young people.
Extraneous detail: Store clerks are paid pretty well.
7. A Students' choices for revision should address particulars of the revision checklist.
*Sample:*
Problem: Paragraph lacks precise and vivid words.
Old version: "messy clothes"
New version: "wrinkled, mud-stained clothing"
8. A *Sample:* "Adults are treated with respect when they enter a store. However, clerks watch teens with suspicion."
Students' edits should identify and correct comma splices.
*Sample:*
"Teenagers eat in a restaurant, waiters assume they won't tip."
"When teenagers eat in a restaurant, waiters assume they won't tip."
9. A Students should demonstrate an understanding of the rubric.
*Sample:*
Elaborate more on ideas.
Make sentences less repetitive.

10. A Students should explain which writing strategy they found most useful in writing for assessment.
*Sample:* I found that leaving time for revision helped me write a better answer.

**Chapter 13: Writing for Assessment**
**Test 3 (p. 90)**

1. C Students should select one of the topics and explain their choice.
*Sample:* I would choose the second topic because I could think of several story conflicts right away.
2. C Students' answers may vary, but should reasonably identify a type of writing appropriate for each response.
*Sample:*
letter
description/cause-and-effect essay
expository writing
3. C Students should offer two ways of analyzing a prompt.
*Sample:* Write a thesis statement.
Think about the audience.
4. C Students should specify their organizational method and complete the corresponding graphic organizer.
*Sample:*
Chronological Order
—Capulets and Montagues feud.
—Violence and hatred results.
—Romeo and Juliet must meet in secret.
—Tybalt taunts Romeo; Mercutio is killed.
—Romeo and Juliet kill themselves.
5. C Students' drafts should fulfill the assignment and contain details from their prewriting activities.
6. C Students should state the main idea and a non-supporting sentence from one of their paragraphs.
*Sample:*
The main idea of the paragraph is that one act of hostility can lead to another.
The following sentence does not fit: "Juliet was upset when she learned that she could not love Romeo."
7. C Students' choices for revision should address particulars of the revision checklist.
*Sample:*
Problem: Sentence lacks precise and vivid words.
Old version: "As a result, Mercutio died."
New version: "As a result, Mercutio, after taking several halting steps, crumbled in an agonized heap."
8. C Students' edits should identify and correct comma splices.
*Sample:*
Old version: "Tybalt was looking for trouble, Romeo wasn't there."
New version: "Tybalt was looking for trouble, but Romeo wasn't there."
9. C Students should demonstrate an understanding of the rubric.
*Sample:* Use details to "show" instead of "tell." Tighten chronological thread.
10. C Students should identify perceived areas of strength and one area that needs improvement in writing for assessment.
*Sample:* I'm usually pretty good at organizing my writing. I'd like to improve my word choices, so that my writing is more vivid.

**Cumulative Diagnostic Test: Grammar, Usage, Mechanics (p. 95)**

The numbers in brackets indicate the chapter and section of the skills being tested.

1. E verb [15.1]
2. C adjective [16.1]
3. A preposition [17]
4. A conjunction [18.1]
5. A adverb [16.2]
6. E pronoun [14.2]
7. E noun [14.1]
8. C interjection [18.2]
9. A pronoun [14.2]
10. E noun [14.1]
11. E subject: games
verb: are [19.1]
12. A subject: we
verb: did get [19.4]
13. C subject: pieces
verb: are [19.4]
14. A subject: you (understood)
verb: Take [19.4]
15. A subject: we
verb: will have [19.1]
16. A season—predicate noun [19.5]
17. A tulips, daffodils—direct objects [19.5]
18. A flowers—direct object
neighbors—indirect object [19.5]
19. E prettiest—predicate adjective [19.5]
20. C pictures—direct object
us—indirect object [19.5]
21. A in this picture—adjective phrase, whom I haven't seen lately—adjective clause [20.1, 20.2]
22. C my closest childhood friend—appositive phrase, to Texas—adverb phrase, when we were twelve—adverb clause [20.1, 20.2]
23. C Sending him e-mail—gerund phrase, of fun—adjective phrase, because it is so inexpensive—adverb clause [20.1, 20.2]
24. A to play on-line computer games together—infinitive phrase [20.1]
25. A Communicating this way—participial phrase, of us—adjective phrase, that interest both of us—adjective clause [20.1, 20.2]
26. A *Sample answer:* Because the car was making a loud grinding noise in the gears, Dad took it to a mechanic. [21.4]
27. A *Sample answer:* The mechanic took a test drive, looked under the hood, and tested all the engine parts. Finally, he told Dad what the problem was. [21.4]
28. C *Sample answer:* Because the repair would be very expensive, Dad was thinking about whether to buy a new car instead. [21.4]
29. E *Sample answer:* The next day, Dad decided to buy a new car. [21.4]

30. A *Sample answer:* Since I will be getting my license next year, I will have fun driving the new car. [21.4]
31. A except [21.4]
32. E ever [21.4]
33. C that [21.4]
34. E Besides [21.4]
35. C somewhat [21.4]
36. A There [21.4]
37. A effect [21.4]
38. C from [21.4]
39. E too [21.4]
40. A further [21.4]
41. E saw [22.3]
42. A did [22.3]
43. C begun [22.1]
44. A cost [22.1]
45. A bought [22.1]
46. E teach [22.3]
47. A said, am not [22.3]
48. A raised [22.1]
49. C should have [22.3]
50. A sit [22.3]
51. E she [23]
52. C whom [23]
53. A It's [23]
54. A him [23]
55. C she [23]
56. E hers [23]
57. A Who [23]
58. E yours [23]
59. A me [23]
60. C Whom [23]
61. A is, her [24.1, 24.2]
62. A are, their [24.1, 24.2]
63. E she [24.2]
64. C Here are [24.1]
65. C are [24.1]
66. A was [24.1]
67. E needs, his [24.1, 24.2]
68. A are, their [24.1, 24.2]
69. A There are [24.1]
70. C are [24.1]
71. A faster [25.1]
72. E best [25.1]
73. C anyone else [25.1]
74. A better [25.1]
75. E most difficult [25.1]
76. E higher [25.1]
77. C any other [25.1]
78. A fewer [25.2]
79. A well, better [25.1, 25.2]
80. C bad, more relaxed [25.1, 25.2]
81. A <u>Johnny Tremain,</u> a novel about the Revolutionary War, was written by Esther Forbes. [26.2, 26.4]
82. E This novel, which you can find in most libraries, won the Newbery Medal when it was first published. [26.2]
83. C Among the characters in the novel are such well-loved historical figures as Samuel Adams, Paul Revere, and John Hancock. [26.2]
84. E In the beginning of the novel, Johnny is the kind of person who cares very little about politics. [26.2]
85. E When some Boston patriots help him out in a time of desperate need, however, he changes his mind, and soon he is participating in the Boston Tea Party. [26.2]
86. A The novel also describes the Battle of Lexington; this was the battle that occurred after Paul Revere warned the colonists that British troops were approaching. [26.3]
87. C In my opinion, a good novel needs three elements: a good plot, interesting characters, and an important message about life. [26.2, 26.3]
88. A Many people's favorite poem is "Paul Revere's Ride." [26.4, 26.5]
89. A "I like that poem," Joanna said, "because it tells a true story in an exciting way." [26.4]
90. C She said, "It's also fun to read this poem aloud, because it has such a great rhythm to it. Would you like to read it with me, Michael?" [26.2, 26.4]
91. A A speaker named Professor Eleni Andropoulos talked to all the classes at Roosevelt Middle School on Friday. [27]
92. A She teaches courses about the history of Greece at Morgan College in Steelton, Pennsylvania. [27]
93. C She talked about Greek history and culture, and she showed slides of places such as Mount Olympus and a famous building called the Parthenon. [27]
94. E Professor Andropoulos explained that Greece is located on a peninsula, surrounded by the Aegean Sea, the Ionian Sea, and the Mediterranean Sea. [27]
95. C Long ago, the Greeks worshiped gods such as Zeus, Apollo, and Athena. [27]
96. A Today, most Greeks follow the Greek Orthodox religion. [27]
97. E Many Greeks understand English and French, as well as their own Greek language. [27]
98. C Greek Independence Day is celebrated every spring on March 25. [27]
99. E When I got home, I told my mom what we had learned about this fascinating country. [27]
100. A "Did your speaker talk about the island called Crete?" Mom asked. "It's one of my favorite places." [27]

**Chapter 14: Nouns and Pronouns (p. 102)**

1. A bravery, intelligence, qualities, astronaut
2. C astronauts, pilots, program (if students identify *jet* and *space* as nouns, point out that those nouns are used as adjectives here.)
3. A unknown, men, health, stress
4. E skills, aptitudes, success
5. C excitement, fear, emotions, program, launch (*space* is a noun used as an adjective)
6. E collective noun
7. A compound noun
8. E collective noun
9. C compound noun, compound noun
10. C compound noun

11. A collective noun
12. C compound noun, compound noun
13. A compound noun
14. A compound noun
15. E collective noun
16. E Soviet Union–P, lead—C, race (or "space race")—C
17. A satellite—C, sputnik—C, Russian—P, traveler (or "fellow traveler")—C
18. C Americans—P, amazement—C, Soviets—P, animals—C, satellites—C
19. A Moscow—P, men—C, cosmonauts—C, space—C
20. A Yuri Gagarin—P, person—C, space—C, hero—C, Russia—P
21. E their—Americans
22. A his, he—President Kennedy
23. A its—television
24. C they—programs and reports
25. E his—Neil Armstrong
26. A their—Americans; he, his—Neil Armstrong
27. A its—space program
28. E her—Sally Ride
29. C their—successes and tragedies; their—Americans
30. C it—when we blast into space
31. E Who—interrogative
32. C This—demonstrative, that—relative
33. A which—relative
34. C Many—indefinite, anyone—indefinite, who—relative
35. A who—relative
36. C That—demonstrative, whose—relative
37. E What—interrogative, who—relative
38. A Those—demonstrative
39. E Some—indefinite
40. C All—indefinite, these—demonstrative, that—relative
41. E My grandparents are rediscovering their favorite old movies, thanks to cable TV and videos.
42. A Last weekend my grandparents rented an old movie. It was one they had last seen before they were married.
43. A Grandpa loved seeing the movie again. He watched it twice.
44. C Grandma watches the TV schedule for her favorite old movies. She doesn't want to miss any of them.
45. C Grandma and I watch old musicals together. We make popcorn and curl up on her couch together.
46. E B
47. C J
48. E A
49. A H
50. A D

**Chapter 15: Verbs (p. 107)**

1. E wrote—transitive
2. E fights—transitive
3. A dreams—intransitive
4. E turns—intransitive, runs—intransitive
5. C conquers—transitive, returns—intransitive
6. C fights—intransitive, has changed—intransitive
7. A writes—intransitive
8. A created—transitive
9. A established—transitive
10. C read—transitive, admire—transitive
11. E was—*links* Civil War, devastating
12. A seemed—*links* It, important
13. A remained—*links* President Lincoln, determined
14. C turned—*links* situation, ugly
15. A became—*links* war, cause
16. E wrote—action verb
17. E is—linking verb
18. A looks—action verb
19. C appears—action verb
20. C looks—linking verb
21. A remains—linking verb
22. C grows—linking verb
23. C feels—linking verb
24. A feels—action verb
25. E shoots—action verb, fall—action verb
26. A learns—action verb
27. A grew—action verb
28. A had become—linking verb
29. C remained—linking verb
30. E was—linking verb
31. A has been studying;
main verb: studying
helping verbs: has been
32. C had received;
main verb: received
helping verb: had
33. A have heard;
main verb: heard
helping verb: have
34. C Did know
main verb: know
helping verb: Did
35. C was trained
main verb: trained
helping verb: was
36. E would bring
main verb: bring
helping verb: would
37. E was nursing
main verb: nursing
helping verb: was
38. C Do recognize
main verb: recognize
helping verb: Do
39. A had opened
main verb: opened
helping verb: had
40. A would be awarded
main verb: awarded
helping verbs: would be
41. E B
42. A F
43. A D
44. C H
45. C A
46. A J
47. A B
48. E F
49. E C
50. C G

**Chapter 16: Adjectives and Adverbs (p. 111)**

1. A a—indefinite article, modifies *document;* well-crafted—compound adjective, modifies *document*

2. E strong—adjective, modifies *government;* central—adjective, modifies *government*
3. E ten—adjective, modifies *amendments*
4. A the—definite article, modifies *freedoms;* American—proper adjective, modifies *people*
5. C fair, reasonable—adjectives, modify *trials, punishments*
6. A British—proper adjective, modifies *laws*
7. E individual—adjective, modifies *states*
8. C State—noun used as adjective, modifies *laws;* sales—noun used as adjective, modifies *taxes*
9. C Minnesota—proper noun used as a proper adjective, modifies *law;* different—adjective, modifies *law*
10. A much-admired—compound adjective, modifies *document*
11. E adjective
12. A pronoun
13. C pronoun
14. E adjective
15. A pronoun
16. E adjective
17. E adjective
18. A pronoun
19. C adjective
20. A pronoun
21. E interrogative
22. A demonstrative
23. C indefinite, possessive
24. C indefinite, demonstrative
25. E possessive
26. A demonstrative
27. E possessive
28. C indefinite, possessive
29. E interrogative
30. A indefinite
31. A *often* modifies *reduce*
32. E *greedily* modifies *absorb*
33. C *then* modifies *release; slowly* modifies *release*
34. A *very* modifies *useful*
35. A *away* modifies *filter*
36. E *vitally* modifies *important*
37. C *early* modifies *melts; quite* modifies *early*
38. A *easily* modifies *grow; there* modifies *grow*
39. E *urgently* modifies *needed*
40. C *ever* modifies *think; hardly* modifies *ever*
41. A adjective
42. E adjective
43. A adverb
44. C adverb
45. E adjective
46. A *Sample answer:* Some animals run fast.
47. A *Sample answer:* This great book vividly describes several wetlands.
48. E *Sample answer:* My best friend works there.
49. C *Sample answer:* The chocolate chip cookies are very good.
50. A *Sample answer:* The clever boy correctly answered the hard question.
51. E B
52. A G
53. E A
54. A J
55. C B

**Chapter 17: Prepositions (p. 115)**

1. E from, to
2. E in
3. C in, of, near, in
4. A among, of
5. A Through, with
6. E about
7. C of, into, across
8. A of, for, in
9. A Within, of
10. C Besides, of, during
11. A In addition to
12. E in front of
13. C in place of, by means of
14. A in spite of, because of
15. A instead of, on top of
16. A In the <u>bottom</u>; of the ninth <u>inning</u>
17. E over the <u>fence</u>
18. A around the <u>bases</u>; to home <u>plate</u>
19. A in the <u>bleachers</u>; to their <u>feet</u>; with a loud <u>cheer</u>
20. C Because of her <u>home run</u> (or <u>run</u>); into extra <u>innings</u>
21. E Between <u>innings</u>; to <u>us</u>
22. C During the next <u>inning</u>; against <u>us</u>; in spite of my great <u>work</u>; at the pitcher's <u>mound</u>
23. A ahead of <u>me</u>
24. E into the <u>outfield</u>
25. C out of the <u>park</u>; on account of our great <u>victory</u>
26. E preposition
27. E adverb
28. C adverb
29. A preposition
30. C adverb
31. A preposition
32. E preposition
33. E adverb
34. C adverb
35. A preposition
36. E *Sample answer:* Devon ran speedily down the court.
37. A *Sample answer:* The ball flew across the field.
38. C *Sample answer:* In spite of our hard work, we lost the game.
38. A *Sample answer:* Someone stole the ball from me.
40. C *Sample answer:* The end of the game was exciting.
41. C *Sample answer:* Historically, sports were played in addition to festivals and carnivals or after victories.
42. E *Sample answer:* Often, games ranged around the town.
43. E *Sample answer:* In Italy, one goal might be set up in front of a town and the other could be miles away.
44. A *Sample answer:* One entire village could play opposite another.
45. A *Sample answer:* Besides sports, there might be feasting, music, and dancing.
46. E C
47. A G
48. E A
49. C J
50. C A

**Chapter 18: Conjunctions and Interjections (p. 119)**

1. E and
2. A but
3. A or
4. C so
5. A nor
6. E (both) and
7. E (either) or
8. C not only (but also)
9. A (Whether) or
10. C neither (nor)
11. E because there is so much variety
12. C as soon as they reach New York
13. A even though it's not the most famous Chinatown in the U.S.
14. A while others explore areas made famous in books and movies
15. A Before you go to New York
16. A *Sample answer:* Although I prefer tennis, I'm better at baseball.
17. D *Sample answer:* After the game, let's go for a snack.
18. C *Sample answer:* I'll be okay as long as I know I can count on my teammates.
19. E *Sample answer:* I'll be outside unless it rains.
20. C *Sample answer:* Wherever you go, always remember I'm thinking of you.
21. E and—coordinating
22. A When—subordinating
23. A Both . . . and—correlative
24. C but—coordinating; as—subordinating
25. C Not only . . .but also—correlative; while—subordinating
26. E Although—subordinating
27. A Because—subordinating; and—coordinating
28. A yet—coordinating; and—coordinating
29. A Neither. . .nor—correlative
30. E when—subordinating
31. A *Sample answer:* When we visited New York City, we saw many famous historic places.
32. E *Sample answer:* We visited Ellis Island and Liberty Island.
33. A *Sample answer:* Both my great-grandfather and my great-uncle immigrated to America from Russia.
34. C *Sample answer:* Neither my great-grandfather nor my great-uncle is alive today.
35. A *Sample answer:* Many Americans visit Ellis Island because they want to see the place that welcomed their ancestors to America.
36. E Yikes
37. A Hey
38. C No way
39. A Well
40. E Wow
41. E *Sample answer:* Wow!
42. A *Sample answer:* Since
43. E *Sample answer:* but
44. C *Sample answer:* Gosh, yet
45. A *Sample answer:* If
46. E B
47. A F
48. C C
49. E J
50. C B

**Chapter 19: Basic Sentence Parts (p. 124)**

1. E Settlers | reached the Oregon Territory in the 1840's.
2. A The search for gold and silver | attracted miners to California in 1849.
3. E Homesteaders | flocked to the Great Plains in the 1870's.
4. E They | made fences out of barbed wire.
5. C Thousands of African American homesteaders | went west.
6. C Many well-known cowboys | were African Americans.
7. A Nat Love | was a cowboy famous for his skills on cattle drives.
8. C Bose Ikard, a former slave, | managed one of the largest ranches in Texas.
9. A People on the frontier | ate simple foods such as bread, beans, and meat.
10. E Homesteading families on the plains | amused themselves at square dances, house-raisings, and corn-husking parties.
11. E compound subject: Scandinavians, Europeans
12. A compound verb: built, opened
13. C compound verb: hunted, drove, enforced
14. E compound subject: Merchants, farmers, soldiers
15. E compound subject: Miners, cowboys
16. A compound verb: grew, prospered
17. E compound subject: Wood, water
18. C compound verb: brought, sold
19. C compound verb: carried, returned
20. A compound subject: Farmers, ranchers
21. A trails
22. A you (understood)
23. C pathway
24. E settlers
25. C Benjamin Bonneville
26. A wagons
27. A you (understood)
28. E we
29. E maps
30. C most
31. E direct object: people<br>object of prep: West
32. C direct object: chance<br>indirect object: passengers<br>object of prep: way
33. E direct object: dangers
34. C direct object: lines
35. A direct object: mail<br>indirect object: people
36. A direct object: story<br>indirect object: us<br>object of prep: rider
37. A direct objects: machinery, explosives<br>object of prep: miners
38. C direct object: Whom<br>objects of prep: protection, outlaws
39. A direct objects: law, order<br>object of prep: Wild West
40. E direct object: settlers<br>object of prep: Texas
41. A story—predicate noun
42. E Bret Harte—predicate noun

43. E popular—predicate adjective
44. C Mark Twain—predicate noun
he—predicate pronoun
45. A humorous—predicate adjective
exaggerated—predicate adjective
46. C *Sample answer: Billy the Kid* and *Rodeo* are two ballads by Aaron Copland.
47. C *Sample answer:* The main characters of the musical *Oklahoma!* are cowboys and farmers on the frontier.
48. E *Sample answer:* Frederic Remington painted and sculpted images of the West.
49. A *Sample answer:* Remington painted cowboys, galloping horses, and stampeding cattle.
50. C *Sample answer: Stagecoach* and *High Noon* are two classic films about the western frontier.
51. E B
52. A J
53. A A
54. E H
55. A D

**Chapter 20: Phrases and Clauses (p. 128)**

1. E through New Mexico—adverb
2. C of wildlife—adjective
3. A in New Mexico—adverb
4. A along New Mexico's roads—adverb
5. E of the desert—adjective
6. E in New Mexico—adverb
7. A of this state—adjective
8. A on location—adverb
in New Mexico—adverb
9. C in the north—adjective
for skiing or hiking—adjective
10. C for its mineral wealth—adverb
11. E called the piñon—participial phrase
12. C seen on the New Mexico flag—participial phrase
13. A the largest group of Native Americans in New Mexico—appositive phrase
14. A a type of sun-dried brick—appositive phrase
15. C Growing chili peppers—gerund phrase
16. A to make spicy foods—infinitive phrase
17. E the state's largest city—appositive phrase
18. C Containing strange and beautiful rock formations—participial phrase
19. E to see the ancient pictographs—infinitive phrase
20. C painting New Mexico's beautiful scenery—gerund phrase
21. A subordinate—adjective
22. E independent
23. E subordinate—adverb
24. E subordinate—adjective
25. A independent
26. A subordinate—adverb
27. C independent
28. A independent
29. E subordinate—adjective
30. C subordinate—adverb
31. C complex
32. A compound
33. E simple
34. C compound-complex
35. A complex
36. A than you (can do).
37. A than (he likes) running.
38. E as Shalonda (is).
39. C as I (arrive).
40. C than Talia (has spent studying).
41. E *Sample answer:* Amman, the capital of Jordan, was once known as Philadelphia.
42. A *Sample answer:* Amman is home to the Jordan Museum of Popular Traditions, which displays exhibits of traditional clothing and jewelry.
43. E *Sample answer:* The city contains an ancient Roman theater built in the second or third century A.D.
44. C *Sample answer:* Because the city of Aqaba has been a trading center for many centuries, archaeologists can find many ancient artifacts there.
45. A *Sample answer:* A scenic route from Amman to Aqaba is the King's Highway, which runs through ancient biblical lands.
46. E B
47. A F
48. C D
49. C H
50. A A

**Chapter 21: Effective Sentences (p. 133)**

1. A states an idea
2. E asks a question
3. A gives an order or a direction
4. A conveys strong emotion
5. C a mild command or direction ends with a period, while a stronger command would end with an exclamation mark
6. A interrogative (ends with question mark)
7. E declarative (ends with period)
8. A imperative (ends with period)
9. E declarative (ends with period)
10. C exclamatory (ends with exclamation mark)
11. E *Sample answer:* Truck drivers often sleep in their cabs, in an area behind the seats.
12. E *Sample answer:* Many cabs have bunks, televisions, and refrigerators.
13. C *Sample answer:* Trucks are an ideal means for transporting goods because they can deliver right to your door.
14. A *Sample answer:* The caravel and the galleon were two types of sailing ships.
15. E *Sample answer:* Small, powerful tugboats push and pull big ships safely into harbors.
16. E *Sample answer:* People in Venice ride gondolas or motorboats to work.
17. A *Sample answer:* Early airships such as zeppelins were filled with hydrogen, but today's blimps use helium instead.
18. A *Sample answer:* Hydrogen, which is flammable, can be very dangerous in large quantities.
19. C *Sample answer:* In 1937, the zeppelin *Hindenberg* burst into flames, killing thirty-six people.
20. C *Sample answer:* Charles Lindbergh made the first nonstop solo flight across the Atlantic Ocean in 1927; the flight took thirty-three hours.

21. A *Sample answer:* Born in Detroit, Lindbergh began his career as an airmail pilot between St. Louis and Chicago.
22. C *Sample answer:* Waiting for Lindbergh's arrival in France were thousands of French citizens.
23. E *Sample answer:* After his historic flight, Lindbergh was awarded the Congressional Medal of Honor. He later pioneered some of the first commercial airline routes.
24. E *Sample answer:* Suddenly, he became a national hero.
25. A *Sample answer:* For his autobiography, *The Spirit of St. Louis*, he was awarded a 1954 Pulitzer Prize.
26. E *Sample answer:* The first woman to fly solo across the Atlantic was Amelia Earhart. In 1932, she flew from Newfoundland to Northern Ireland in about fifteen hours.
27. A *Sample answer:* Five years later, she took off from California, with her navigator, in an attempt to fly around the world.
28. C *Sample answer:* Reaching New Guinea in June, they had completed more than three-quarters of their journey.
29. A *Sample answer:* The next day there were radio messages from Earhart reporting empty fuel tanks.
30. C *Sample answer:* When efforts to make radio contact with the plane failed, a search was begun.
31. C *Sample answer:* After searching and finding no trace of the plane or crew, people decided that the fate of Earhart and her navigator was a mystery that couldn't be solved.
32. E *Sample answer:* Earhart and her navigator probably crashed into the ocean and died.
33. E *Sample answer:* During World War II, some people claimed that Earhart had been a spy. There were reports of Japanese captives resembling Earhart and her navigator.
34. E *Sample answer:* There was no convincing evidence supporting these claims.
35. C *Sample answer:* Many people have become obsessed with the unsolved mystery of Earhart's fate.
36. A from
37. E Besides
38. A farther
39. C into
40. A that
41. C They're, too
42. E quite
43. E ever
44. A except
45. C effects
46. C A
47. A H
48. E A
49. A J
50. C B

**Chapter 22: Using Verbs (p. 138)**

1. C went—past
2. A have asked—past participle
3. A is telling—present participle
4. E are—present
5. E attend—present
6. A are working—present participle
7. E learned—past
8. E study—present
9. C have known—past participle
10. C has depended—past participle
11. E taught
12. A begun
13. A drew
14. C saw, done
15. A taken
16. A cost
17. C tore, threw
18. C written, come
19. E brought
20. A put
21. E dreamed—past
22. A was working—past progressive
23. A had wanted—past perfect
24. C had been hoping—past perfect progressive
25. E use—present
26. A has grown—present perfect
27. E are logging—present progressive
28. A will change—future
29. C have been wondering—present perfect progressive
30. C will have linked—future perfect
31. A have liked
32. E made
33. C had hoped
34. A was dreaming
35. E am working
36. C have been working
37. C will have completed
38. A will demonstrate
39. E enjoys
40. A will win
41. A *Sample answer:* Amanda was doing her math homework.
42. C *Sample answer:* By eight o'clock, she had completed her homework.
43. A *Sample answer:* Tomorrow, Brad will write a report.
44. A *Sample answer:* He will finish the report on time.
45. E *Sample answer:* His teacher appreciates his hard work.
46. A Last night I saw a movie about the Revolutionary War.
47. E The movie taught me a lot about the winter of 1776.
48. A The defeated Americans retreated across New Jersey and dragged their cannons behind them.
49. C Many people thought George Washington should have gone up to the British and surrendered.
50. A correct
51. E correct
52. A Then, Washington did something totally unexpected.
53. C He spoke to his troops and said that he wasn't ready to surrender.

54. E Overnight, Washington's army crossed the river again and attacked Trenton before the sun rose in the sky.
55. C The victory in Trenton raised the hopes of the Americans, even though many difficult times lay ahead.
56. A A
57. A L
58. E A
59. C M
60. A B

**Chapter 23: Using Pronouns (p. 142)**

1. E possessive
2. C nominative
3. E possessive
4. A objective
5. C nominative
6. E I
7. A him and me
8. A him
9. C he and she
10. C she
11. E them
12. E us
13. A her
14. C he
15. A them
16. A yours
17. C It's
18. A theirs
19. E his
20. C its
21. A Whom
22. C who
23. E Who
24. A whom
25. A whom
26. E who
27. E Who
28. C who
29. C whom
30. A whom
31. E Dad is teaching Amanda and me to play chess.
32. C It's a hard game to learn.
33. A correct
34. A We need to find some friends with whom we can practice.
35. E Amanda and I play chess together once a week.
36. C correct
37. A Whose turn is it now, mine or yours?
38. A correct
39. A correct
40. C The best chess players in our class are Danielle and he.
41. A A
42. E H
43. A D
44. E H
45. C D
46. C F
47. A B
48. C F
49. A C
50. C G

**Chapter 24: Making Words Agree (p. 145)**

1. A were
2. E were
3. E were
4. A was
5. C was
6. A Here are
7. C faces
8. E were
9. C were
10. C are
11. A is
12. C was
13. A were
14. C makes
15. E is
16. E their
17. C she
18. C its
19. A their
20. A his or her
21. E their
22. A its
23. E their
24. A he or she
25. C their
26. C her
27. E their
28. C she
29. E their
30. A it
31. E Both Ryan and Brady are planning careers in journalism.
32. A Ryan wants to report on technology, because he thinks he can get more work in that field.
33. C Brady likes medical reporting and business, because they are (or they're) so interesting.
34. A correct
35. A At Career Night, students can meet college representatives and learn what they need to study.
36. E correct
37. A One of the college representatives is setting up his (or her) display table now.
38. A correct
39. C Here are some catalogs Ryan needs if he wants to find out more information.
40. E If Brady wants some catalogs, there are many available.
41. E B
42. C H
43. A A
44. C J
45. A B
46. A H
47. E B
48. C H
49. A D
50. E H

**Chapter 25: Using Modifiers (p. 149)**

1. A sharper, sharpest
2. E deep, deepest
3. E low, lower
4. E talkative, most talkative
5. C icier, iciest
6. E happily, more happily

7. A better, best
8. A worse, worst
9. E afraid, more afraid
10. C clumsier, clumsiest
11. A more stoically, most stoically
12. A few, fewest
13. A evasive, more evasive
14. E long, longer
15. C more, most
16. C far, furthest
17. A more fascinating, most fascinating
18. C lovely, loveliest
19. C better, best
20. A fast, fastest
21. C Of those two skaters, Heather is better.
22. C She is stronger and moves more gracefully.
23. E The best skater in our class is Ashley.
24. A correct
25. A However, my jumps are better than hers.
26. A My worst jump is my double axel.
27. A correct
28. C correct
29. E This jump is harder than that one.
30. E The youngest skater in our class is Melissa.
31. E *Sample answer:* Heather's spins are better than Katie's. (*or* Katie's spins.)
32. A *Sample answer:* Heather can spin faster than anyone else.
33. C *Sample answer:* She has better balance than any other girl in the class.
34. C *Sample answer:* This year's practice times are later than last year's. (*or* last year's times.)
35. A *Sample answer:* I arrive earlier than anyone else.
36. C We all felt bad about losing the figure-skating competition.
37. A Heather and Ashley were the only ones on our team who received high scores.
38. A We did fewer jumps than the other team did.
39. E correct
40. A Heather skated as well as she could.
41. A correct
42. C We have just two weeks to prepare for the next competition.
43. E correct
44. E We have less confidence than we did before the competition.
45. C Our coach says we need to practice just a little harder.
46. E A
47. A H
48. A D
49. C H
50. A B

**Chapter 26: Punctuation (p. 153)**

1. A Days in the desert can be very hot, so many animals sleep in burrows or under rocks.
2. A Do desert bats sleep during the day, or do they just hide in caves?
3. E Wow! Those amazing bats can find tiny insects in the dark! (*or* dark.)
4. E Look at this picture of an owl hunting at night.
5. C Small owls hunt for insects and spiders, and large owls capture mice and snakes.
6. E Scorpions hunt for insects, spiders, and other small creatures.
7. C correct
8. A The mountain lion, the largest wild cat in the United States, weighs 150 pounds or more.
9. A Prowling the desert for rodents, foxes may also catch birds or even eat plants.
10. E The kit fox is a light-colored, big-eared member of the fox family.
11. E Using sound, bats find their prey in the dark.
12. A When the bat's squeaks hit an object, they echo back to the bat's ears.
13. C correct
14. A The sandfish is actually a lizard, however, not a fish.
15. C Moving its long, smooth body from side to side, the sandfish appears to be swimming through the sand.
16. C The sandfish has a long, chisel-shaped nose, which helps it push its way through the sand.
17. E correct
18. A The green toad, you know, can lay its eggs only after a rainstorm.
19. C "On March 15, 2001," Brady said, "this green toad laid more than 10,000 eggs."
20. C To find out about endangered animals, Nick, you can write to the World Wildlife Fund, 1250 Twenty-Fourth Street N.W., Washington, D.C. 20077.
21. E Virginia; it
22. A freely; however
23. E Virginia: Williamsburg
24. C cities: Gettysburg, Pennsylvania; Morristown, New Jersey; and
25. A Notice: The, 12:30, 2:30
26. E "Many important leaders of the American Revolution were Virginians," said Jessica.
27. A correct
28. A Jessica said, "Didn't you know that George Washington, Patrick Henry, and Thomas Jefferson were Virginians?"
29. C Which famous Virginian said, "Give me liberty or give me death"?
30. C "I think," said Jessica, "that James Madison and James Monroe were Virginians."
31. E correct
32. A correct
33. C "Let's go to Jamestown Landing Day next May," said Brandon. "It's a super celebration!"
34. A "Wouldn't you rather go to Norfolk's Harborfest in June?" asked Sarah.
35. E correct
36. C "Gold Fever"<br>The Great American Gold Rush
37. E "To Build a Fire"
38. E Oregon Spectator
39. A "The Gold Digger's Waltz" and "Oh, Susannah"
40. A California
41. A Thirty-three, two-thirds
42. A correct

43. A ex-president, self-confidence
44. C all-American
45. E great-grandfather, much-admired
46. A family's
47. C women's, hadn't
48. C Let's, everyone's, they're
49. E students'
50. A boys', men's
51. E C
52. C F
53. C D
54. A G
55. A A

**Chapter 27: Capitalization (p. 158)**

1. E Last year I went to England.
2. A Wow! What a great trip that was!
3. E At the Tower of London, we took a tour.
4. A "This is the Roman wall," the guide told us. "Here is where the Crown Jewels are stored."
5. C "Long ago," the guide continued, "political prisoners were held here."
6. E Art Institute, Chicago, Italy
7. A Italian Renaissance
8. E Rome, Florence
9. A Michelangelo, Bernini
10. E August, September
11. C Florence, Tuscany, Hotel Berchielli, Arno River
12. C Monday, Duomo, Giotto's Tower, Ghiberti
13. A Pitti Palace, Boboli Gardens
14. E Florence, Rome
15. A Rome, Vatican City
16. C Vatican City, Michelangelo's, Sistine Chapel
17. A God, Adam's
18. A St. Peter's Cathedral, San Pietro, Italian
19. A Rome, Via Veneto
20. C Rome, Romulus, Remus, Roman, Mars
21. A Mother, <u>National Geographic</u>
22. A <u>Out of the Silent Planet</u>, <u>Perelandra</u>, <u>That Hideous Strength</u>
23. A "Scotland the Brave"
24. E Queen, Prince
25. C Mom, Queen, President, United States
26. E Captain, Sir
27. C <u>All Cloudless Glory</u>, President
28. E Miss
29. A Aunt, Mister
30. C <u>The Lord of the Rings</u>, <u>The Lion, the Witch, and the Wardrobe</u>, General
31. E The largest city in Africa is Cairo, the capital of Egypt.
32. A The Mediterranean Sea lies to the north of Egypt, and the Red Sea borders the nation on the east.
33. A Most of the Egyptian population follows the religion of Islam and its holy book, the Koran.
34. E The official language of the nation is Arabic.
35. E In 1981, President Mohammed Hosni Mubarek took office.
36. A The people of Egypt have always depended on the Nile River, which flows through the city of Cairo.
37. C In the desert near Cairo, you can see two famous monuments called the Great Sphinx and the Great Pyramid at Giza.
38. C Egypt's legislature is called the People's Assembly, and its highest court is called the Supreme Constitutional Court.
39. A The nation's largest political party is called the National Democratic Party.
40. A Two thirds of Egypt is covered by a dry, sandy plateau called the Western Desert, which is part of the huge Sahara Desert that stretches across Africa.
41. C My father studied about Egypt with Professor Samuel D. Jones at Smithtown University.
42. E "To me, it is the most fascinating country in the world," Dad said.
43. C "My favorite historical period is called the Old Kingdom," he continued. "That's when the Great Pyramid at Giza was built for King Khufu."
44. C "I can still remember learning about the mythical goddess named Isis and her brother, Osiris," my father said.
45. E Dad bought me a great book called <u>Ancient Egyptian Gods and Goddesses</u>.
46. E C
47. A J
48. A B
49. E F
50. C C

**Cumulative Mastery Test: Grammar, Usage, Mechanics (p. 162)**

The numbers in brackets indicate the chapter and section of the skills being tested.

1. E verb [15.1]
2. A pronoun [14.2]
3. E adjective [16.1]
4. A adverb [16.2]
5. C preposition [17]
6. C conjunction [18.1]
7. C adjective [16.1]
8. E noun [14.1]
9. A interjection [18.2]
10. A adverb [16.2]
11. E subject—domestication [19.1]<br>verb—occurred [19.1]
12. C subject—breeds [19.4]<br>verb—are [19.1]
13. A subject—you (understood) [19.4]<br>verb—Think [19.1]
14. A subject—dogs [19.4]<br>verb—were used [19.1]
15. C subjects—greyhounds, Afghans [19.4]<br>verb—were [19.1]
16. E popular—predicate adjective [19.5]
17. E reputation—direct object [19.5]
18. A direct object—work [19.5]<br>indirect object—border collie [19.5]
19. A beagle—predicate noun [19.5]
20. C direct objects—companionship, service [19.5]<br>indirect object—us [19.5]
21. A America's first pencil-maker—appositive phrase; in 1812—adverb phrase [20.1]

22. C Improving the pencil considerably—participial phrase; to add an eraser—infinitive phrase; at the top—adverb phrase; at the pencil—adjective phrase [20.1]
23. C After he was granted a patent—adverb clause; to a businessman—adverb phrase; named Joseph Rechendorfer—participial phrase [20.1, 20.2]
24. A Doing math homework—gerund phrase; before pencils became available—adverb clause [20.1, 20.2]
25. C Even since typewriters and computers have been invented—adverb clause; that no home or business can do without—adjective clause [20.2]
26. A *Sample answer:* Using my new tools, I made the bookcase in a few hours. [21.4]
27. E *Sample answer:* I made one tall bookcase instead of two smaller ones because that's what my mother wanted. [21.4]
28. A *Sample answer:* My father helped me buy the wood. Then, we took it home and measured it carefully before I started sawing. [21.4]
29. E *Sample answer:* I'm thinking of starting a small carpentry business of my own. [21.4]
30. C *Sample answer:* My dad might give me a small loan because I need some money to get started. [21.4]
31. A There [21.4]
32. C that [21.4]
33. E quite [21.4]
34. A Besides, too [21.4]
35. E anybody [21.4]
36. A effect [21.4]
37. C from [21.4]
38. C further [21.4]
39. A except [21.4]
40. E ever [21.4]
41. A taken [22.1]
42. A saw [22.1, 22.3]
43. E cost [22.1]
44. E hit [22.1]
45. E spoke [22.1]
46. C should have, known [22.1, 22.3]
47. A went, sat [22.3]
48. A said, did [22.3]
49. C taught [22.3]
50. C lies [22.3]
51. E I, her [23]
52. E Who [23]
53. A it's [23]
54. C Whom [23]
55. A she [23]
56. A whom [23]
57. E ours, theirs [23]
58. C me [23]
59. A its [23]
60. C she, him [23]
61. E is [24.1]
62. E There are [24.1]
63. A are, their [24.1]
64. A is, her [24.1, 24.2]
65. E she [24.2]
66. C are [24.1]
67. C come [24.1]
68. A take, their [24.1, 24.2]
69. C has, his [24.1, 24.2]
70. A needs, his or her [24.1, 24.2]
71. E worst [25.1]
72. E colder [25.1]
73. C warmer [25.1]
74. E more comfortable [25.1]
75. A good [25.1, 25.2]
76. A any other [25.2]
77. C anyone else [25.2]
78. C for only [25.2]
79. A badly [25.2]
80. A fewer [25.2]
81. A <u>The Golden Apples of the Sun</u>, a book of short stories by Ray Bradbury, is a well-loved classic. [26.2, 26.4]
82. E Among the many reasons for the success of Bradbury's stories are the following elements: vivid settings, strange conflicts, and ironic climaxes. [26.2, 26.3, 26.5]
83. C Of the twenty-two stories in this book, the one called "The Flying Machine" is many people's favorite. [26.2, 26.4, 26.5]
84. E When a Chinese inventor creates a flying machine, the Emperor Yuan orders the invention and its creator to be destroyed. [26.2]
85. E The emperor admires the beauty of the flying machine, but he fears the consequences of such an invention. [26.2]
86. A The emperor is afraid that such a machine could be used to attack his country; he can foresee the use of flying machines as weapons of war. [26.3]
87. C "I love that story," said Alex, "because it really made me think about different views of creativity, progress, and fear." [26.2, 26.4]
88. A "I like the imagery in his stories," said Dan. "He is one of my favorite writers." [26.2, 26.4]
89. A "What is your favorite Ray Bradbury story?" asked Jamie. [26.4]
90. C "Wow!" said Sarah. "Bradbury sounds great." She added, "I can't wait to read one of his books." [26.1, 26.2, 26.4]
91. E Norway, Sweden, and Denmark make up the European region known as Scandinavia. [27]
92. E Finland is not considered a Scandinavian country because its people originally migrated from Asia, not Europe. [27]
93. E The Finnish language is actually more similar to Hungarian than to Swedish. [27]
94. A The islands of Greenland and Iceland were also colonized by Scandinavians. [27]
95. A The Scandinavian explorer Leif Ericson crossed the Atlantic Ocean and reached the continent of North America many centuries ago. [27]
96. C One famous person from Denmark was Hans Christian Andersen, the writer of stories such as "The Emperor's New Clothes." [27]

97. A The city of Copenhagen is known for a famous amusement park called Tivoli Gardens and for the Christianborg Palace. [27]

98. C Many people of Scandinavian ancestry are Protestants who belong to a Lutheran denomination [27]

99. C My grandfather, Dr. Thomas Nansen, immigrated to the United States from Norway. [27]

100. A "Sometimes," Grandfather says, "I still miss the North Sea and the city of Oslo." [27]

**Chapter 28: Speaking, Listening, Viewing, and Representing (p. 173)**

1. E b. You should speak politely.
2. A Students should choose two of the following answers:
   Think through the directions before speaking.
   Speak slowly so your friend can follow.
   Be specific and give only one step at a time.
   Do not confuse your listener by including unnecessary information.
3. E a. entertaining
   b. persuasive
   c. explanatory
4. C Students' answers will vary.
   *Samples:*
   a. Students appealing to school administrators will use relatively formal language.
   b. Students may want to include air-quality statistics, cite similar programs at other schools that have been successful, and estimate the cost of bike racks. They might research on the Internet, in newspapers, and through interviews.
   c. Students should create a clear outline, with main points and supporting details arranged in a logical order.
5. C Students' answers will vary, but may include any three of the following strategies: review note cards before starting; do not read your notes; speak slowly and clearly; make eye contact with audience members; use verbal techniques such as altering tone and loudness of voice; use nonverbal techniques, such as movements, expressions, and gestures.
6. C Students' answers will vary, but their questions should be related to one of the following ideas: Did the speaker achieve his or her purpose, such as explaining, persuading, or entertaining? Did the speaker elaborate on the main ideas with supporting details? Did the speaker introduce and develop the topic clearly? Did the speaker's nonverbal techniques reinforce the message? Did the speaker give complete answers to audience questions?
7. A No. *Sample:* I would jot down in my own words the main ideas and supporting details.
8. C a. to gain information
   b. to enjoy and appreciate
9. E Students' answers will vary. Possible responses may include the following: put any reading material aside; try to block out noises both inside and outside the classroom.
10. A *Samples:*
    a. A speaker needs to support an opinion with facts for it to be accepted as valid.
    b. A speaker may use connotations to give positive or negative meanings to statements.
11. E *Samples:*
    Verbal signals: volume of voice, speed of speech, emphasis of some points over others
    Nonverbal signals: arm waving, head nodding, moving closer to or farther away from the audience
12. A *Samples:* Restate the message to the speaker to see if I understood it. Ask questions if my restatement is inaccurate. Write my interpretation of the speaker's message, then compare and contrast it with another student's interpretation.
13. A b. *Sample:* The other information is not considered historical.
14. E The map shows the weather across the United States.
15. E *Sample:* The symbols in the key tell you how to determine the temperatures, where it is raining or snowing, and where there are cold or warm fronts.
16. C *Sample:* in a daily newspaper
17. A a. shows the relationship of parts to a whole
    b. compares and contrasts amounts
    c. shows changes over time
18. E a. bar graph
    b. to illustrate that the graph is representing money
19. A Yes, because it takes $4,269,000 to run the government and the government has $4,418,000 of income.
20. C *Sample:* the percentage of each national or ethnic group within the whole Asian American population of California
21. E Filipino; Cambodian
22. E *Sample:* The pie graph makes it easy to compare the parts to one another and to the whole.
23. C *Samples:* a. in order to evaluate the credibility of the information
    b. Students might choose two of the following questions: What kind of program is it? What is the program's purpose, and what are its limitations? What are the facts and opinions being presented? What kind of loaded language is used? Is the program biased? Is there any questionable information?
24. C *Samples:* a. a photograph
    b. the mother, surrounded by young children
    c. The mother looks worried and tired, and the children seem to be clinging to her.

25. A *Samples:* to present visually related information when giving a speech or a written report; to organize research for a paper or to study for a test

26. C *Sample:*
title: American Inventions in the Late 1800's
column headings: Inventor, Date, Invention
row 1: Bell, 1876, telephone
row 2: Edison, 1877, phonograph
row 3: Waterman, 1884, fountain pen
row 4: Woods, 1887, air brake
row 5: Duryea, 1893, gasoline-powered automobile

27. E a. Use a numbered list when steps should be followed in sequence. Use a bulleted list for items that can be presented in any order.
b. Boldface or italics can direct the reader's eyes or give special emphasis to key concepts or ideas.

28. A *Sample:* inspirational songs, played on a tape player or CD; slides of photographs, shown on a slide projector; film footage, played on a video player

29. E *Sample:* a. The shooting script contains the characters' dialogue and directions for costumes and props. b. The outline describes the scenes, places, and shots to be used in the video.

30. A Answers will vary, depending on the play that is chosen. *Sample:* The mood should be serious. I would use dim lighting and melancholy music. My voice will vary in pitch to emphasize important points.

**Chapter 29: Vocabulary and Spelling (p. 180)**

1. A *Samples:*
a. By having conversations with teachers, people from different places, and people whose interests are different from yours, you may hear unfamiliar words in context.
b. By listening to recorded books, you may hear unfamiliar words and learn how they are pronounced and used in context.

2. C *Samples:*
a. Context is the group of words that surround the target word, and/or the sentence or paragraph containing the word. These often contain clues to the word's meaning.
b. Two of these: Read the sentence, leaving out the unfamiliar word. Find clues in the sentence to figure out the word's meaning. Read the sentence again, substituting your possible meaning for the unfamiliar word. Check your possible meaning by looking the word up in the dictionary.

3. C *Samples:*
a. diligently: hard; by making an effort;
b. sibling: sister or brother;
c. deceiving: misleading; causing a mistake in thought or judgment;
d. detonated: exploded;
e. fiasco: a complete and terrible failure

4. C Guess at the meaning of "hermeneutic"
Write a sentence using "hermeneutic"
Look up "hermeneutic" in the dictionary
Evaluate your sentence to see if you have used "hermeneutic" correctly
Revise your sentence if necessary

5. A a. Look up "vizier" in the social studies textbook glossary
b. Write the word and its definition in the social studies section of your notebook

6. A *Sample:* Nullify; "annul" means abolish; to take away the value of

7. C *Sample:* We decided to nullify our agreement, making it no longer effective.

8. E *Samples:* making flash cards; using a tape recorder

9. E c. *Sample:* Synonyms can only occasionally be found in a dictionary, but can always be found in a thesaurus.

10. A a word's synonyms (words with similar meanings) and sometimes its antonyms (words with opposite meanings)

11. C *Sample:* Since the root is the base of a word, if you learn the meaning of a certain root, you will be able to figure out the meaning of many words containing that root.

12. A *Samples:*
a. -nym-; to name
b. spec-; to see
c. -dyna-; to be strong

13. E *Samples:*
a. ex-; to send out
b. re-; to view again
c. un-; unable to be determined

14. C *Samples:*
a. comfortable; adjective
b. confidence; noun
c. hesitancy; noun
d. humorless; adjective
e. lovely; adverb or adjective

15. C *Samples:* First row: re-; -spect-; -able; capable of or worth seeing again; worthy of esteem
Second row: post-; -pon-; -ment; the result of placing after, or putting off to a later time
Third row: syn-; -nym; no suffix; to name together

16. A The Norman invasion in 1066.

17. E Greek

18. C *Sample:* psychology; (si<long i> kol; uh<schwa>; je<long e>); science of mental processes; Why is the p silent in psychology?

19. A *Sample:* two of the following: Look at each word and try to see the pattern of letters in your mind. Pronounce each syllable. Write the word and check its spelling in the dictionary. Review your list until you can write each word correctly.

20. A a. niece
b. correct
c. perceive
d. correct

21. E a. trying
b. beautiful
c. gaily
d. annoyance
22. C a. movable
b. correct
c. traceable
d. judgment
23. C a. reference
b. correct
c. submitted
24. E a. dissatisfied
b. unnecessary
c. de-emphasize
25. E a. taxes
b. wishes
c. circuses
d. benches
e. dresses
26. A a. pianos
b. echoes
c. patios
27. E a. cities
b. keys
c. knives
d. leaves
28. A a. children
b. emphases
c. curricula
d. sheep
29. E a. Their
b. through
c. Whose
d. too
30. A arguments; whose; muddy; bookshelves; definitely; sense

**Chapter 30: Reading Skills (p. 185)**

1. E d., b., a., e., c.
2. A a. table of contents
b. index
c. appendix
d. chapter summary
e. glossary
3. C *Samples:* a. They give you an idea of what the chapter is about, and they divide the material into sections which are easier to follow.
b. They help you retain the information you have read.
c. Pictures can make a confusing idea clearer. Captions provide information describing a picture.
4. A a. skimming
b. scanning
c. close reading
5. C c., d., b., a.
6. C Survey: Look at the features of what you are going to read.
Question: Ask Who, What, When, Where, and Why.
Read: Search for the answers to the questions you just asked.
Record: Take notes, listing main ideas and major details.
Recite: Recall the questions and your answers.
Review: Review regularly, using some or all of the steps above.
7. A Time passes in years
Initiating event: Knights of Labor formed 1869—Only skilled workers could be members.
In-between events: 1879—Powderly elected president; opened union to all workers. 1885—Workers' strike forces Missouri Pacific Railroad to restore wage cuts.
Final event: Knights of Labor membership soars to 700,000.
8. C Who: workers and Terence Powderly
What: labor unions and strikes
Why: to gain a shorter workday and equal pay for men and women, and to end child labor
When: 1869–1885
Where: U.S.
9. C a. main point: Factories, mines, and mills were hazardous.
supporting details: *Samples:* dust, cave-ins and gas explosions, hot metal spills
b. Responses will vary. Students should use their own words, relating ideas to one another.
10. A a. to give information
b. Responses will vary. *Sample:* Students may relate this information about working conditions in 1900 to studies about modern-day labor unions.
11. E a. fact; false
b. opinion; invalid
c. fact; true
d. opinion; valid
12. E a. to instruct
b. to offer an opinion
c. to sell
d. to entertain
13. E a. invalid
b. valid
14. E Words used denotatively describe a situation in a neutral tone; words used in a connotative way imply either a positive or negative point of view or tone.
15. E a. Jargon is the use of words with specialized meanings intended for a particular trade or profession.
b. direct language
16. A a. the reason something happens
b. the outcome
c. *Samples:* because, as a result, therefore, consequently
17. A a. to describe similarities and differences between two or more items
b. *Samples:* like, similarly, both, in the same way
c. *Samples:* but, yet, in spite of, on the other hand, although, nevertheless, whereas, unlike
18. E a. to show events in the order in which they occurred
b. *Samples:* next, then, later, soon
19. E b.
20. A a. first-person point of view
b. omniscient third-person point of view
c. limited third-person point of view

21. A *Sample:* Internal conflict is a mental struggle within a character. External conflict is a struggle between a character and an outside force.
22. A *Samples:* two of the following three kinds of words: action words; adverbs, or words that tell how an action is performed; sensory words, or words that tell how things look, feel, taste, smell, and sound
23. C *Sample:* Reading the list of the cast of characters may tell you the various relationships among the characters. It may also give brief descriptions of the characters.
24. A *Sample:* Stage directions contain information about the sets, costumes, lighting, and sound effects. By knowing these you can picture the characters and the action.
25. C *Sample:* Two of the following questions: Why did the character do that? What does it reveal about the character's personality? What does this event mean? How does this event relate to what has already happened?
26. C a. You should pause only at punctuation marks.
b. By putting the poet's ideas in your own words, you will understand the poem's meaning and remember it better, too.
27. A The speaker of a poem is the voice that "says" the words.
28. E a. simile
b. metaphor
c. personification
29. C *Sample:* One of the following: Understanding the culture; recognizing the storyteller's purpose; recognizing elements such as moral messages or magical transformations
30. A *Samples:* a. to keep informed about your community and the world
b. to read a particular type of literature or literature of a certain time period
c. to find material on a wide range of topics

**Chapter 31 Study, Reference, and Test-Taking Skills (p. 191)**

1. E a. A study area should be free of all distractions.
2. E *Sample:* a description of the assignment and the due date
3. A *Sample:* two of the following: Organize your notebook by subject; take notes on what you hear in class and on what you read; take notes only on the most important information; use a modified outline.
4. C Students' modified outlines will vary. *Sample:*
Hamilton and Jefferson differed on economic policy.
1. Hamilton
favored manufacturing and trade
supported the growth of cities and the merchant class
2. Jefferson
believed farmers the most valuable citizens
feared power in the hands of a small group of wealthy people
5. C Students' summaries will vary. *Sample:* Hamilton and Jefferson differed in economic views. Hamilton supported urban growth, manufacturing, and trade. Jefferson favored the farmer and feared that through manufacturing a few wealthy Americans would be very powerful.
6. E d., c., b., a.
7. E Students' answers will vary. Two of the following: card, printed, or electronic catalogs
8. E a., c., d., b.
9. A *Sample:* Look up the subject in the catalog; find the book's call number; and then follow the number-letter order to locate it on the shelves.
10. E in the biography section, under C
11. A *Samples:*
a. printed materials, such as newspapers and magazines, published on a regular basis
b. concise, current information
c. periodical indexes
12. C *Sample:* Look up the subject "earthquakes" in the *Readers' Guide to Periodical Literature.* Find an article and its periodical's publication information. Then, find the actual article in the library on a database, microfilm, or CD-ROM.
13. E *Sample:* in your library's vertical files
14. E c.
15. A *Sample:*
a. ai, ay, eigh
b. rain, ray, weigh
16. A Answers will vary, but should include two of the following three steps. *Sample:* Mentally divide the dictionary into four sections and turn to the second quarter of the dictionary; check the guide words "jurisdiction" would fall between, such as jural and juvenile; follow letter-by-letter alphabetical order.
17. E a. 3
b. second
18. E adjective
19. A Latin
omnisciently; adverb
20. A Students' answers will vary. *Samples:* The volumes and articles are arranged alphabetically. Look in the index to find the volume and page number of an article, as well as related articles.

21. E a. an atlas or electronic map collection
b. almanac
c. biographical reference

22. C Students' answers will vary, but should include any two of the following: Consult *Library Journal* for lists of reliable sites. Identify the organization that set up the site, and decide whether it might have a bias. Identify the source of the information, and determine whether it is backed up by research. Determine whether or not the information is up-to-date.

23. A Students' answers will vary. *Sample:* Proofreading allows you to make sure that you have followed directions correctly, and that you have answered all the questions.

24. C Students' answers may vary. *Sample:* For multiple-choice items, there are often two *possible* answers, but only one *best* answer.

25. C Students' answers will vary, but should include any two of the following strategies: Count each group to see whether or not there will be any items left over. Check the directions to see whether items may be used more than once. Read all of the items before you start matching. Match the items you know first. Then, match the remaining items.

26. A Students' answers will vary, but should include any two of the following tips:If a statement appears to be true, be sure the entire sentence is true. Pay special attention to the word *not*, which can change the whole meaning of a statement. The words *all, always, never, no, none,* and *only* often make a statement false. The words *generally, much, many, most, often, some,* and *usually* often make a statement true.

27. Students' answers will vary. *Samples:*
a. chauffeur: drive
b. page: book
c. veterinarian: heal
d. mongoose: mammal

28. C Students' answers will vary, but should include one of the following strategies: Identify how the first pair of words relate. If more than one choice seems correct, go back to the first pair and redefine its relationship. If you can't find an equal relationship, look for other possible word meanings.

29. C Body part: function; b.

30. C Students' answers will vary, but should include two of the following strategies: Identify key words, such as *discuss, explain,* or *identify*. Look for restrictions, such as a question that asks for three reasons. Check your space and find out whether you may use more paper. Stick to the point, and don't include unrelated information.